Tragic Flaws

Tragic Flaws

a novel by

Scott Evans

To order additional copies of this book, contact:
Xlibris Corporation
1-888-795-4274
www.Xlibris.com
Orders@Xlibris.com
48340

*Dedicated to Cynthia, my wife and
a cancer survivor.*

CHAPTER ONE

Whenever Patricia Miller drove north to visit her family, she thought of Thomas Wolfe's book *You Can't Go Home Again*. Years earlier, she'd argued with her lit professor about the title, explaining that *her* older brother *had* moved home again after college and was now living happily with their parents in Sacramento. The old professor Dr. Thorne, who'd been a thorn in *her* side all right, had said the title was a kind of metaphor; but as a business major, Patricia found little value in figurative language.

"You *can* go home again," she'd insisted. "I do it almost every weekend." To which the class erupted in laughter, causing Patricia's face to burn with embarrassment. Even now, years after that first year in college and a full year after graduating, she still cringed when she remembered the incident.

She glanced at her bloodshot eyes in the rearview mirror as she drove north on Interstate 5. Even with her degree in business, she was still working as a waitress; and after putting in a nine-hour day, she was looking forward to going home.

A light rain, falling from the black midnight sky over California's sprawling Central Valley, misted her windshield as she drove. The intermittent sweep of her windshield wipers prevented her from dozing off though her eyelids were heavy.

Suddenly, the lights of her 1987 Pontiac Grand Am flickered. The engine sputtered. She tensed. This was the second time since she had left the restaurant that the engine had threatened to die.

Should she pull over and call for a tow truck, or should she push on and try to make it to the first gas station south of Sacramento?

Going seventy-five on an almost-deserted interstate at midnight, she had felt confident she could make it to her parents' home before the drizzle became a deluge. This cold Tuesday night before Thanksgiving, Patricia Miller was looking forward to sleeping late in her old bedroom. She wanted to be pampered by her mother, waited on for a change. Mom would bring coffee and orange juice and even french toast if she asked for it.

The car's engine stopped sputtering, and the lights came back to life as if nothing had happened. Once again, her car seemed like the reliable old friend it had been since her father had given it to her more than six years earlier when she had graduated from high school.

From the radio, Chris Isaak's melancholy voice sang "Wicked Game." She sang along and cranked the music up loud, filling the car. She had once met Isaak—the local Stockton boy who had made good—at Murphy's, the restaurant where she worked. She loved this song, its haunting lyrics reminding her of an old boyfriend she now found repulsive. "Strange what desire will make foolish people do," she sang, trying to harmonize with Isaak.

The car lights flickered again, and the engine sputtered if only for a moment.

She turned off the radio, thinking the less drain on the engine, the better. Then she tried her cell phone, but the battery was dead, and she had forgotten to grab the car charger in her rush to pack before leaving.

Three southbound cars rushed by on the other side of the interstate, their spray of rainwater reflecting their red taillights. Patricia checked her rearview mirror again. Faint headlights appeared behind her. Should she stop? Should she try to press on? What would her father tell her to do?

The decision was made for her as the car's lights went dark, and the engine died.

Without headlights, she could no longer see the pavement in front of her. The power steering was gone too. She pursed her lips and forcefully steered to the edge of the road while pushing the brake pedal. With neither power steering nor power brakes, the car felt sluggish and foreign, like a stranger.

The dark freeway was straight, and she knew it well. As she slowed, she felt the right tires roll off the pavement. Gravel kicked up, pelting the underside of her car as she pushed fiercely on the brake, proud of staying calm.

Suddenly, the car hit something, and she screamed.

But the small aluminum sign bent quickly under the weight of her car, and she coasted to a stop.

For a moment, with the car at a dead stop, she sat still, catching her breath, both hands clutching the steering wheel. Her eyes grew accustomed to the darkness, and she realized she was on an elevated section of the freeway about halfway between Stockton and Sacramento. How close had she come to going over the embankment? If she had coasted a foot more to the right, the car would have tipped over the embankment and rolled down to the brush below. When it dawned on her that she might have been killed, she burst into tears.

Bright headlights startled her as a semitruck roared by.

She stared at the truck's red taillights as they disappeared slowly into the rain. A few cars went south in the lanes across the median. Missed opportunities, she realized. Checking her rearview mirror, she saw no new lights in the distance. She clutched the steering wheel again.

"Okay, Daddy," she said aloud. "What should I do?"

"Try the engine, Patty," she said, mimicking her father's deep voice.

She turned the key repeatedly. Nothing. She opened her cell phone again and tried to turn it on. The light appeared for a second but flicked off.

"Damn it! What next, Daddy?"

"Look for an emergency phone, honey."

Patricia unfastened her seat belt, reached back for her raincoat, and opened the door. The rain fell harder as she climbed out of the car. The back of her white blouse drenched; she clumsily tugged on her short raincoat, pulled up its hood, and walked to the front of the car. She wished she had taken the time after work to change out of her short black skirt into warm blue jeans.

She was lucky. Both left tires were still on the edge of the pavement, and both right tires were still a foot from the embankment's edge.

Patricia looked up the road as far as she could, but she didn't see the distinctive pole and oval yellow phone box. She turned and looked behind the car, but she could see nothing.

Now her face was wet with tears and rain, her socks and tennis shoes soaked, and she felt utterly exhausted. But she leaned forward and trudged north along the shoulder of the freeway. After a few minutes of walking, she nearly bumped into the pole that held the emergency phone as if running into a stranger on the sidewalk.

For a second, she imagined laughing about this little adventure in a couple of days at the dining room table of her parents' house when she would be sharing Thanksgiving dinner with the entire family. She could picture her grandmama scowling disapprovingly and her older brother joking about women drivers just to push her buttons. This would become nothing more than a frightening memory, one of those life lessons she could tell her children if she ever got married.

Right now, though, soaking wet and shivering in the cold rain, she wanted this adventure to end.

Patricia opened the small oval box and felt inside. Nothing? She bent down and put her face as close to the box as she could.

No phone! Only cut wires.

"Shit!" she screamed. "Shit! Shit! Shit!"

She shivered as she walked back to her car. What were her options? She could flag down the next passing car. She could wait until daylight, or she could walk to another emergency phone. But what if that phone had been vandalized too? For now, she wanted to dry off.

As she was opening the car door, headlights appeared behind her, and she turned to look at them. The lights grew brighter, and she wondered if flagging down this car would be the right thing to do.

What if it's loaded with gangbangers?

As the car neared, its driver switched on his high beams. Whoever he was, he was getting a better look at her, she realized; so she quickly got into her car and closed the door.

The little sporty car sped by. Then it slowed, the brake lights glaring bright red in the rain, and the driver maneuvered the car into the fast lane and crossed the median. Patricia watched intently. At least the car was too small to hold four gang members.

"Maybe this is Prince Charming," she said aloud.

The car drove south, disappearing from her view.

"Where are you going, shithead?"

Patricia put the key in the ignition and tried to start the car again, but nothing happened. She flipped the switch for the headlights, but they remained dark. Exhaling an exasperated groan, she sank back into her seat and closed her eyes. Waves of exhaustion swept over her. She'd get a ride in the morning when it was light. She could come back with her dad and her brother tomorrow in the daylight to deal with the car.

Patricia Miller put the seat back and imagined how nice it would be in her own bed. She rested her eyes, listening to the steady tapping of the rain on the roof of her car.

Tapping at the driver's window lurched her awake.

She'd been asleep, but for how long? The windows were completely fogged up. And someone was tapping on her window.

"Are you okay, Miss?"

A man's face tried to peer through the foggy glass. His deep voice sounded mature and polite, like her father's. Patricia rolled the window down halfway. Then she noticed she hadn't locked her door, so she quickly locked it.

"Are you all right?" the man asked again.

"I'm . . . My car broke down," she said. Then she thought she should play it safe. "I called for a tow truck. It should be here any minute."

She couldn't see him very well in the darkness.

"Would you like me to wait until the tow truck gets here?" the dark figure asked. Still groggy, for a moment, she believed her own lie.

"Well, maybe for a few minutes if you wouldn't mind."

"Sure. How long ago did you call him?"

"About fifteen minutes ago," Patricia lied.

"He should be here soon," the man said with a reassuring smile. His white teeth shone in the darkness. Then he walked back to his car. She couldn't see the car clearly through her rearview mirror, but his parking lights glowed orange, and his emergency lights flashed.

The rain pelted the roof and windshield. Patricia sat anxiously for the next fifteen minutes. A car passed and then two trucks. She checked her watch: 12:38. Her parents would worry soon. She heard a car door slam. The shadowy figure approached again. She rolled the window down a crack.

"Do you have to go?" she asked.

"No, but your tow truck should be here by now. You should call again."

"I can't. My phone's dead."

"Would you like me to drive you up to the emergency phone so you can call again, anyway?"

While no Prince Charming, the man seemed kind.

"The truth is, I haven't actually called anyone. I was afraid to tell you before."

"Oh," said the man, grinning. "I don't blame you."

"Do *you* have a cell phone I can use?"

"My battery's run down too," he said. "I tried it myself a little while ago."

Patricia stared at the man's shadowy face. He was getting soaked but leaned in smiling. Dark eyes. She caught a whiff of cologne. *Aramis? Obsession?*

"Can you drive me to the next gas station?"

"Sure," he said. "Be happy to."

She rolled up the window and climbed out, locking the door behind her. The rain pelted her back as she ran back and climbed in on the passenger's side, the man jumping in as quickly as she had. As the man started the car and pulled out onto the freeway, Chris Isaak's song "Wicked Game" came on.

"I was listening to this when my car broke down," she said, smiling.

"It's one of my favorite tapes," he said. "Fasten your seat belt."

Patricia found the cold metal end of the seat belt between the door and her seat cushion. The metal buckle clicked securely.

The dashboard lights were dim green, casting an eerie light underneath the man's features.

They drove north for about ten minutes while the heater blew wonderful warm air on Patricia's face. She wiped the water off her cheeks, took a long, deep breath and closed her eyes. She would be home soon. She could hug her mother and endure the gentle teasing by her father and brother. She would enjoy their routine taunts about being a college-educated waitress. She knew they teased to motivate her, but now she could tell them about her plans to open an Irish pub-styled coffee shop. They'd see her old ambition again.

The clicking noise caused Patricia to open her eyes.

"Why are you taking this exit?" she asked.

"There's a gas station just east of here."

"Where? I can't see any lights."

"About a mile. Only the locals know about it."

"I've driven this highway for years," she said, trying to sound calm. "I never knew there was a gas station on this exit."

She noticed black leather gloves clutching the steering wheel. When had he put those on? Her heart raced. She tried to see his face clearly.

"The place we're going to is just up ahead," he said in a deeper voice. He pointed forward with his gloved right hand, and Patricia turned to peer through the windshield in the dark rain.

Patricia Miller had never been hit in the face before, certainly never as hard as this man hit her. She was stunned.

A second sledgehammer blow to her temple caused flashes of bright lights inside her brain. She felt nauseous and struggled to stay conscious. She forced her right hand to reach for the seat belt buckle—she would have to jump from the moving car.

The third punch plunged her into darkness.

She awoke the first time to the sound of duct tape being ripped off a roll. Her mouth was covered, and her wrists bound. Before she had time to fight back, the man's fist cracked across her jaw brutally—she heard the bone break before she passed out from the searing pain.

Patricia came to as the man tugged her out of the seat. Her jaw burned with pain. She felt dizzy. The powerful man dragged her through tall wet grass. Then he stood her up and slung her over his shoulder.

She twisted and struggled, but it was no use. He was too strong.

He carried her up a hill and reached a level spot where he dropped her on her back again. The fall knocked the wind out of her lungs and forced air out of her nostrils, her mouth bound tightly with the tape. The man grabbed her wrists fiercely and dragged her down a wet embankment. She struggled weakly, but in vain. She thought about the can of pepper spray still in her purse. Why hadn't she grabbed it?

He stopped at a grassy clearing. The rain on her face helped her regain consciousness. Blood filled her mouth with a rusty taste. The man smiled as he kneeled on top of her—she could see his perfect white teeth. She felt his weight on her stomach and pelvis. He spread himself over her, putting his mouth next to her ear. Warm, stagnant breath caressed the soft skin of her earlobe and vulnerable neck as he whispered, "Have you ever made love in the rain?"

She closed her eyes, shivering, and began to cry for the last time.

CHAPTER TWO

On the Monday after Thanksgiving, Joe Conrad lay in bed barely awake. He could hear Sara speaking to their four-year-old daughter as she dressed her for day care. He had dreamed about his parents again. Telling Katie about them during Thanksgiving dinner had brought a flood of memories. The tenth anniversary of their death was approaching. His father's thick arching dark eyebrows had made him look like Sean Connery, and his mother's curly red hair and busty figure had compared nicely to Maureen O'Sullivan. Typical Louisianians, they had smoked and drank too much, but some of Joe's fondest memories were of his father pulling a silver lighter from his pants pocket and lighting his mother's KOOL. She would draw in the first drag slowly, look up, exhale, smile at her husband, and silently mouth the words, "Thank you, darling." Joe had seen this ritual a hundred times while growing up. He had never seen another man light his mother's cigarette though he had seen his father light up other women.

The image of his parents' mangled car popped into his head, even though he fought to keep it out. They had been hit head-on by a drunk. Joe hadn't seen their bodies crushed inside the car, but he often imagined it. His recurring dream always ended with the crash, his parents screaming, the truck rolling over them like a tidal wave.

A pang of guilt washed through him. He knew he should get up and help Sara dress Katie, even offer to take his daughter to preschool himself because Sara had to be at her teaching job sooner than he had to be at his. But he dreaded his long drive to the university.

"Tell Daddy goodbye," Sara said, ushering Katie into their small bedroom.

Katie climbed up on the bed and wrapped her arms around Joe's neck.

"Bye-bye, Daddy," she whispered in his ear.

"Bye-bye, honey," he said. Joe hugged her and tickled her sides enough to get a satisfying little giggle.

Removing Katie from her husband's grasp, Sara looked down sternly. "If you get up now, you could grade ten papers before your first class, Joe."

"Thanks for the advice, *Mizz* Conrad," Joe said sarcastically, trying to sound like one of her smart-aleck junior high students.

"I'll see you tonight, Professor," said Sara as she turned to leave with her daughter attached to her hand.

"No hug or kiss for your loving husband?"

"When you show a little more drive."

"Drive? Drive? I have drive!" he yelled as his wife walked down the hall. "I have a two-hour drive every day!"

Sara had taught algebra in a high school in Baton Rouge while Joe finished his master's degree and started a doctoral program at LSU. They had met at a football game in Tiger Stadium. Sitting behind Joe with her parents, she had struck up a conversation in the beginning of the game and was pouring brandy into his coffee by halftime. He had liked her aggressiveness. By the third quarter, she had poured brandy into his coffee cup for a third time.

"I think you're trying to get me drunk," he had joked.

"I am indeed, sir," she said, exaggerating her Southern belle accent. "I plan to take advantage of you in the fourth quarter, should the Tigers achieve victory!"

"Oh, Sara!" her mother had scolded, smiling.

A few months later, they were engaged.

Joe finally threw back the covers and headed for the shower. Forty minutes later, he was dressed; and with a travel mug of coffee in one hand and a worn leather briefcase in the other, he climbed into blue 1968 Mustang and backed out of the driveway of their two-bedroom rental house in Davis, California.

After moving to California and again dropping out of a PhD program, this time at UC-Davis, he had taken a part-time job teaching literature at Central Lutheran University in Stockton, an hour south.

Joe had a love-hate relationship with his commute. On one hand, it provided an escape from his boring little town. He could stop at a Starbucks off Florin Road in South Sacramento before classes, sip steaming coffee, eat a bagel, grade papers, and watch people. After classes, on the way home, he could take a detour and go to a Borders or a bar, depending on his mood.

On the other hand, the drive was monotonous. Long straight stretches of wetlands, vineyards, pastures, and farmland on both sides of the interstate were flat, dull, redundant. Now that he was teaching an evening class, it was even more difficult to stay awake while driving north on Interstate 5 late at night.

But it was Monday, a cold, sunny morning; and he had driven halfway to Stockton when he felt the engine of his old Mustang chugging. The needle of the temperature gauge was in the red. The engine had been running hot before the Thanksgiving break. He should have taken it into a shop, but he'd forgotten.

Ahead was an elevated section of the freeway. He decided to pull over just after the upcoming bridge. As he slowed, he read the sign that identified the marshy waterway that the flat bridge spanned: Lost Slough. The first time he'd seen the sign, with weeds blocking some of the letters, he'd misread it as Lost Souls.

He slowed to a stop just after the bridge and pulled off the road. Joe checked the traffic and, during a break, got out and popped the long hood of the Mustang. One pinhole leak in the radiator hose was spraying steam. He walked to the trunk where he kept a few tools, a blanket, some flares, a few rags, and a roll of duct tape.

He took a rag and the duct tape to the front of the car, dried the hose as much as he could, and then wrapped the radiator hose a few times, attempting to seal the leak temporarily. The hose was still hot and wet, so the tape didn't stick well. Joe gave up, leaving the tape on the battery.

The car needed water. He picked up a soda bottle and shook out a few dead bugs.

A path in the brush down the embankment to the dark water of the slough told Joe he was not the first to make the journey over the side. He half climbed, half slid down the path until he reached the edge of the water. Thick brush grew to his left along the edge of the water, but under the bridge, only damp mud bordered the slough. Empty beer cans and bottles of liquor suggested this was a favorite spot for someone. Maybe teenagers finding a place to make out. Maybe fishermen.

The water in the slough was black. If there was any current, it was undetectable. As if walking a tightrope, Joe followed the narrow path to a spot under the bridge where he could reach over the green pond scum and get close enough to dip the soda bottle without falling in.

A log with a sheet of old paper on it floated close to the edge. He might be able to put one hand on the log and stretch far enough, assuming the log supported his weight, to reach into the water and fill the plastic bottle. The water smelled like a sewer.

Traffic rumbled above him. As he tried to squat down closer to the water, he glanced to the east and to the west. The marsh spread wide and flat in both directions, the black ribbon of water cutting through it. On both sides of the marsh grew reeds and thick brush. To the west, dozens of bare oak trees stood guardian over the scene, moss hanging from a few gnarled boughs.

Joe leaned closer to the water. The dank air made him shiver, and the nearer he drew to the water, the more he noticed the foul smell. Something dead. He reached out and touched the log to see if it could support his weight,

It sunk immediately under his weight and then bobbed back up. As soon as he touched its yielding surface, he knew it was not a log covered by paper.

It was a woman's body, floating facedown.

Joe Conrad lost his balance and slid into the murky water beside the cold, bloated corpse.

Though the frigid water came up only to his chest, the bottom of the stream was as slippery as ice. He could not climb back out. He felt something in the water—a snake?

After struggling in vain until he was completely wet, he gave up, turned around to face the object of his dread.

The woman's hair, covered by dead leaves and water-soaked twigs, fanned out from the head in all directions. Reluctantly, Joe grabbed a handful of hair and gently tugged the body toward him. A sudden memory—helping his daughter Katie learn to swim—flashed into his mind. He had pulled her toward him, rolled her over, and cradled her just like this.

As Joe rolled the body over, hair covered the woman's face. Her blouse was open, and her bra pushed up above her exposed breasts, their bluish color grotesque. The image of a statue came to mind, Venus de Milo's perfect marble breasts. Was that a leech attached at the areola?

He gagged—the odor intense.

Joe gently tugged the flaps of the blouse closed over the young woman's breasts. He tried to clear the hair away from her face, but it was knotted and tangled; and catching a glimpse of her dark blue lips and grotesquely opened mouth full of water, he decided to leave her face alone.

Wading through the cold water, Joe towed her downstream, out from under the overpass. In the late-fall sunlight, he found some roots to grab on to and pulled himself out of the water. He tried to drag the body up too, but it was impossibly heavy, and the muddy bank was much too slippery. When he released her, the woman's body drifted gently to the middle where it rolled facedown again but seemed to stay put.

Dripping wet, covered with mud, and shivering in the chilly air, Joe climbed up the embankment to the freeway. An emergency call box was a few steps away. People honked as they sped by. Joe opened the call box, only to find that the telephone itself was gone. Bare wires dangled limply.

"Damn it!"

Just as Joe was cursing his situation—his poverty, his lack of a reliable car, and his absence of a cell phone—a CHP car drove by in the slow lane and pulled over. The car backed up rapidly toward him, even as a train of big rigs rumbled by, too close for comfort. After apparently writing something down, the highway patrol officer opened his door and, waiting for a break in traffic, climbed out and strode toward Joe. The man behind the sunglasses kept his right hand on the handle of his gun.

"Thank God you stopped!" Joe yelled over the traffic as the officer approached him.

"What seems to be the trouble, sir?"

Joe felt cold and small as the fit-looking cop approached him.

"My car overheated," said Joe. "I pulled over to let the engine cool off, and I went under the bridge to get some water for the radiator. When I was at the water, I saw a woman's body floating facedown, so I jumped in to save her, but she was already dead."

The CHP officer slowed down as if to size up the soaked, muddy stranger standing in front of him. "You found someone's body?" he asked skeptically.

"I'm not crazy," Joe said. "I'll show you."

Joe turned back to his blue Mustang, its hood still raised.

"Just walk slowly, sir," the officer instructed.

The CHP officer fell in behind Joe, staying about an arm's length behind, which made Joe nervous. He sensed the officer's distrust.

They both could see the woman's body from the bridge over Lost Slough. The officer faced Joe.

"Are you certain she's dead?"

"Yeah, I'm sure." He recalled with a shiver the bloated bluish skin, the odor of death, and the cold, stiff feel of the corpse.

"Did you touch or move the body?"

"Yes!" Joe said. "I told you. I jumped in to see if I could save her." He didn't want to try to explain how he stupidly thought the body was a log. "I used to be a lifeguard. It was just instinctive."

The officer eyed Joe suspiciously.

"Have a seat on the passenger side of your car," he instructed. "And turn on your emergency flashers. Let me see your driver's license and registration."

After opening up his door and sitting down, Joe dug out his wet leather wallet and reached in the glove box for the car registration, both of which he handed to the officer. The police officer examined the papers, glanced back down at the body as if to confirm that it was really there, and then looked around at the fast-moving traffic.

"I have to call this in, so wait here."

"Okay," Joe said. But as the officer was walking away, Joe asked, "Is this going to take long? I'm going to be late for work. I teach at CLU in Stockton."

The officer stopped and turned back, dumbfounded.

"You're a professor at CLU?"

"Yes," Joe said, even though he was only a part-time instructor, not a professor. The distinction would be lost on this officer.

"I'm afraid you're going to be here for a couple of hours."

"A couple of hours?" Joe responded. He knew his concern must have seemed out of place, but canceling classes at the last minute—even for an emergency—was frowned on. Especially after a holiday.

"Do you have a cell phone I can use? Can I call the school?" Joe asked.

"Yes. Please wait in your car as I told you to do," the officer said. "I'll be back in a few minutes."

Joe turned on the emergency blinkers and grabbed a dry blanket out of the trunk to wrap around himself. When he and Sara were first dating in Louisiana, they sometimes drove up to Natchez Trace where they had a picnic and made love on that blanket, wrapping themselves in it afterward. Now a mother, Sara disapproved whenever he suggested "doing it" outdoors.

Joe watched as the police officer sat in his car talking on the radio.

CHAPTER THREE

The officer finally walked back and handed Joe a cell phone.

"Well, Professor Conrad," the secretary answered. "So good of you to check in today."

"Let me speak to Dr. Thorne, Molly," Joe said. "It's an emergency."

"We've had a few of your students here asking for you. Did you decide to extend your Thanksgiving vacation?"

"No, Molly. This is a police emergency, so let me speak to Charles."

The chairman of the English department, Dr. Charles Thorne, listened patiently while Joe explained what had happened.

"Terrible," Dr. Thorne said. "Just terrible. Take all the time you need, Joseph. I'll have Molly put up notices canceling your next two classes."

"Thanks, Charles," Joe said, relieved to hear a friendly voice.

"Let us know if you can't make it to teach your evening class tomorrow."

"Oh, I'm sure they'll be finished with me soon. The CHP officer said a couple of hours."

"Well, just let us know. And, Joe?"

"Yes, Charles?"

"Let me know if there's anything I can do for you."

Several other CHP cars arrived, a Caltrans truck came and blocked the slow lane of the freeway, and traffic backed up and drove slowly by the scene. People in the passing cars stared at Joe as he squirmed in his damp clothes.

A coroner's station wagon arrived, and Joe watched as police and evidence technicians disappeared down the embankment. Thirty minutes later, they hauled up a heavy black body bag and strapped it to a stretcher.

Joe visualized the stiff, cold body again and shuddered. A few minutes later, he was questioned by a different officer. Joe told his sad story again.

This time, the officer took notes.

"When can I go?" asked Joe.

This officer, older than the first, looked at him sternly.

"Are you anxious to leave?"

"Well, yeah. I'm cold and wet, and I have work to do," Joe responded. "Look, I feel awful for the dead girl, but what more can I do?"

The policeman stared at Joe for a moment.

"I'm afraid we have to take you in to be questioned," the officer stated bluntly.

"Why? I've told you all I know!"

"It won't take long, Mr. Conrad, but this is a murder case."

"Murder?" Joe gasped.

"There's evidence of foul play, yes, sir," said the fit Hispanic officer. "Did you see the news about the missing woman?"

Joe thought back over the last few days. "I'm afraid I didn't watch much television during the holiday," he confessed.

"A young lady went missing a day or two before Thanksgiving. Her car was found about five miles from here."

"I'm sorry," Joe said. "I didn't know."

The officer looked at him suspiciously. "It got about as much publicity as the Laci Peterson case. You *do* recall that case, don't you, Mr. Conrad?"

"Of course," Joe said, his face turning red. "Is this the body of that missing woman?"

"Not sure," said the officer. He closed his notebook and walked away.

The Laci Peterson case was hard to forget. She had been eight months' pregnant and disappeared on a Christmas Eve day. Months after her disappearance, Laci's body was found near the Berkeley Marina where her husband, Scott, claimed to have been fishing. The body of the couple's baby had been found nearby just a few days before. Eventually, Scott Peterson was found guilty though his defense attorney had tried to point the blame elsewhere.

That case seemed like ancient history now, but Joe wondered whether this woman's murder might somehow be connected. Was it possible that Scott Peterson *was* innocent after all?

Joe was placed in the backseat of a Sacramento County sheriff's car and driven to the sheriff's office. His car would be towed to the building, an officer explained.

Twenty minutes later, at noon, Joe found himself sitting in a small room that was about the size of his office at CLU. He thought about the papers he could be grading while he waited.

A tall man in his midforties entered the room. "I'm Detective Dunn," he said matter-of-factly, shaking hands with Joe, who half stood as he reached across the small table.

In his pleated dark gray slacks and well-pressed blue dress shirt with an expensive-looking red tie, Detective Dunn looked more like a lawyer.

Joe smiled. *A power tie,* he thought.

"Would you like a sandwich and some coffee?" Detective Dunn asked.

"That would be great," Joe admitted.

The detective stepped out of the room for a few minutes, keeping his foot on the self-closing door to prop it open. For a moment, Joe imagined trying to run out of the office, but the detective came back in and sat down.

"One of the other officers will bring you food in a minute," the detective said. Then he pulled a small tape recorder out of his pants pocket. "Now, Mr. Conrad, I want you to tell me exactly what happened in as much detail as you can remember. Try not to leave anything out, no matter how trivial it seems to you."

Joe chuckled a little. "You sound like me giving instructions to my students. I always tell them to use specific details in their writing."

"Well, good. Then you know just what I'm asking for. Do you mind if I record our conversation?"

"Of course not," Joe said. "I mean, why should I? I'm just a witness, right?"

"Exactly," the detective responded.

"Was the body—was it that missing woman?" Joe asked.

"We're not sure yet," said the detective.

A female officer opened the door and stepped in, handing a vending machine sandwich and coffee in a Styrofoam cup to the detective, who passed them over to Joe.

"Thanks," Joe said to the woman. He took a sip of the lukewarm coffee. It was bitter and stale. He peeled the plastic away from the face of the container and pulled out one of the sandwich halves, which he inspected for a minute. Bologna and American cheese on white bread with a thin leaf of limp lettuce. He took a bite and chewed while the detective watched impassively.

"Well, let's get started," the officer said. Gesturing toward the small tape recorder on the table, he asked, "Can I turn this on?"

Joe nodded, chewing.

The detective turned on the recorder and held it up to his face. "This is Detective Ryan Dunn interviewing Mr. Joseph Lawrence Conrad about the body of a woman he discovered along Interstate 5 in the Lost Slough area. The woman has yet to be identified."

The detective gave the date and time and then stopped the recorder for a moment.

"Mr. Conrad, I'm going to ask you to identify yourself in a minute, and then I'm going to tell you your Miranda rights."

"What?" His heart quickened, and his face flushed red with fear. "But I can't possibly be suspected of anything! All I did was find a body, and I called the police—or I tried to call the police—as soon as I found her!"

"This is just a formality. It doesn't mean we suspect you of anything. It's just something the lawyers require when we interview a witness formally."

Joe tried to calm himself down, but his heart was pounding.

"Should I get a lawyer?"

"Do you need one?" the detective asked.

"No, not at all!"

"Then calm down, and let's get this over with. The sooner we do this, the sooner you can go." The detective looked at him impatiently. "I don't know about you, Mr. Conrad, but I'd like to get out of here before five o'clock."

"Five o'clock! Am I going to be here all damn day?"

"Not if we can get started right now and finish this up. I'm as anxious as you are to get out of here. I've got a lot of work to do on this case."

Joe studied the detective. He seemed honest, articulate, and well educated. If Joe explained himself clearly, the detective would see there was no reason to keep him.

"Christ," Joe said. "I thought the police would be thanking me, not interrogating me. I mean, I found a woman floating lifeless in a river, and I jumped in to try to save her."

"In that case, let's get your story on tape, Mr. Conrad."

Joe exhaled and said, "Okay."

The officer repeated the same Miranda rights Joe had heard on a hundred television shows. When asked if he understood his rights, Joe said he did. Then he began telling his story for the third time that day, only he admitted he hadn't recognized the body as a person at first but thought it was a log. He described how leaves and debris covered the woman's back, how he had reached over to support himself to fill the soda bottle, and how he had clumsily lost his footing and slid into the water. He described everything: rolling the woman over, trying to close her blouse, towing her out from under the shadow of the bridge, struggling back up the embankment, trying to call from the call box—all of it in as much detail as possible.

Detective Ryan Dunn listened intently and gave Joe reassuring nods from time to time. He even smiled a little when Joe admitted he had slipped into the water by accident. When Joe was finished, he said, "So that's about it. I'm not quite the hero I made myself out to be, but I tried to do what I thought was right every step of the way."

"Very good," the detective responded. He continued to make a few notes on a yellow legal pad. "Now you told Officer Harris that you're a professor at Central Lutheran University. Is that correct?"

"Well, yes. He asked me if I was a professor, and rather than explain the difference between a professor and an instructor, I just said yes."

"But just to be clear, your job title at the university is part-time instructor, correct?"

Joe blushed a little. Suddenly, he felt the same inferiority he often felt in English department meetings surrounded by PhD's.

"Yes. That's correct."

"I see," Detective Dunn said. He turned off the tape recorder and stared at Joe for a few seconds. "I'm going to have to check out a few things, but you should be ready to go soon."

Joe sighed as Detective Dunn gathered the tape recorder and his notes and left the room. Joe stared at himself in the mirror and tried to comb his hair with his fingertips. His clothes were still damp and muddy, but he had warmed up. The little room was much warmer than his car had been. He sank back into the chair and closed his eyes. He couldn't wait to get home, take a hot shower, and change into clean clothes.

With his head slumped down, chin on his chest, Joe saw the woman's wet face covered by wet hair like the snakes of Medusa, its opened mouth begging seductively, "Kiss me, Joe," as black water gushed from its mouth.

He jerked awake and looked around, forgetting where he was.

Detective Dunn walked back into the claustrophobic interrogation room. The look on his face was different, cold and mean. "I'm afraid there are a few inconsistencies with your story, Mr. Conrad," he said, grinning tightly. "You'll have to answer a few more questions."

CHAPTER FOUR

Joe started to stand, but the detective stepped toward him, so he sat back down.

"This has gone on long enough. I've tried to be as cooperative as I know how to be. I've done everything you've asked. But now I'm tired and hungry and fed up." Hungry *and* fed up? A mixed metaphor like those he had corrected in a hundred student papers. He'd edit himself later. This was getting ridiculous. "I don't even know that woman!" Joe exclaimed.

"Are you sure?" the detective asked. "You claimed you didn't get a good look at her face."

"Well, let me put it this way. I saw enough." *Did I know her?* "Who is she, anyway?"

The detective looked at him suspiciously and sat down.

"I find it curious that this is really the first time you've asked about her identity since police began questioning you three hours ago."

"No, I asked if it was the missing woman."

"But you didn't ask her name."

"I guess I'm still in shock," Joe admitted. "This is the first time it occurred to me to ask who she was."

"Maybe you didn't have to ask because you already knew her identity."

"Well, who was she?" Joe asked, exasperated.

"Haven't you watched the news lately?"

"Not very much. I don't watch a lot of television."

"A former CLU student has been missing since before Thanksgiving. And you, a teacher at that college, knew nothing about it? That in itself makes me suspicious," explained the detective. "Her name is Patricia Miller. But then, you already knew that, didn't you?"

Joe felt a sense of panic. *Patricia Miller?* He vaguely recognized that name. He *had* seen something about the missing woman. This area had become notorious because of missing women. First, the three women who had been kidnapped at Yosemite and brutally murdered. Next was Chandra Levy, the intern who had worked for Gary Condit though she was murdered in Washington DC. Then there was the Laci Peterson case. Yosemite, Modesto, now Stockton. The Central Valley had become the Bermuda Triangle of murder! Still, if this body was one of his former students, he knew that made him look very guilty.

"When did you say she went missing?" Joe asked. He felt his face burn red, and his heart pounded harder.

"Late Tuesday night," the detective said.

"Tuesday night. The same night I teach an evening class."

"The same night you teach a class that gets out at 9:30 p.m.," Dunn said. "I've had someone check your schedule, so I know you were down in Stockton that night. Patricia Miller left her job about ninety minutes after the time you normally end your night class. So my question for you, Professor, is this: what time did you get home Tuesday night, and can someone verify it?"

Joe's heart sank. On that Tuesday night after class, he had stopped at a bar before going home—a topless bar. Sara had been furious, waiting in bed when he returned. They'd argued bitterly, Joe resentful. Their sex life had been nearly nonexistent.

"Running out of answers, Professor?"

"No," Joe said. "I'm trying to remember whether or not I had a student named Patricia Miller."

"What time did you get home Tuesday night?"

Joe blushed again. "It was pretty late. Since it was my last class before the holiday, I went to a bar to celebrate a little."

"What bar?"

"I'm embarrassed to admit this, but it's a place called Highbeams."

"Highbeams? That's a topless bar, isn't it?"

"Yes," Joe admitted.

"Did you see anyone you know there?"

"The people I know don't go to places like that. At least, they don't admit it."

Detective Dunn looked at him suspiciously.

"Will anybody at the bar recognize you?"

"Maybe. The waitress should be able to. And one girl who dances there might remember me."

"Why? Did something happen with one of the dancers?"

"No," Joe said, blushing again. "But I did have a girl dance for me."

"A lap dance?"

Joe nodded. Images of the dancer's breasts and the dead woman's breasts flashed into his memory. Why the hell had he gone to the topless bar *that* night?

Joe imagined the cops showing his photograph to some of the women who had danced in front of him. Stories in the newspaper and on television would link him to the dead girl and describe his alibi. The administration at the university wouldn't be pleased. CLU was, after all, a religious college of sorts. Could he lose his teaching job?

"Well, Joe," Detective Dunn said. "We have a lot to go over now. With these new admissions—"

"Admissions! I haven't 'admitted' anything! Except a few lapses in judgment."

"These 'lapses' make you look like a viable suspect," the detective said.

"You can't be serious. Me?"

The detective softened his voice.

"We found you with the body, Joe. You have a connection to the dead girl—Central Lutheran University. And we've caught you in two or three lies."

"Lies that mean nothing!"

"And then there's the duct tape," smiled the detective.

"The duct tape?"

"We found a roll of duct tape with your car."

"So?"

"Duct tape was used on the victim," Ryan Dunn told his suspect.

"I didn't see any tape on the woman."

"Marks on her wrists are a telltale sign. The skin looks bleached because most of the hair is removed when the tape gets ripped off."

Joe sat still, silently imagining the wrists of the dead woman he had handled in the cold water.

"Lots of people have duct tape, Detective," he said sarcastically. "C'mon, you must have something else."

The detective leaned nose to nose with Joe. "You want to know what else?"

"Hell yeah," replied Joe, trying not to feel intimidated. Joe could feel the other man's breath on his face.

Dunn drew back and gave Joe a wry smile, saying, "You just look guilty, Professor." Then the cop winked at Joe.

"I *look* guilty? What the hell does *that* mean?"

"I've got a hinky feeling about you."

Joe closed his eyes and rubbed his forehead. *How do I get out of this?* His head started to throb as he imagined explaining all of this to Sara. *How the hell do I get out of this?*

He opened his eyes and looked straight into Dunn's eager, clean-shaven face.

"I want a lawyer!"

Joe drew in a deep breath and knitted his eyebrows, shooting a tough glare back at the policeman. "I'm a college instructor for God's sakes! Not a killer. I'm not going to fall for that *Law and Order* bullshit."

"What do you mean?" Detective Dunn asked, feigning innocence.

Joe laughed a little and shook his head. *Trying to string me along and get new "inconsistencies."*

"Look, Detective. I've answered all your questions. I've tried to be a good law-abiding citizen. If you think I'm guilty, then arrest me. But I'm not saying another word until I have my lawyer."

Detective Dunn stared at Joe coldly.

"Would you like my lawyer's number? She happens to work for one of the most prestigious law firms in Sacramento, and she's my sister-in-law."

"Asking for a lawyer only makes you look guilty," Dunn said.

"Asking for a lawyer only makes me look smart," Joe replied.

The detective stared at him.

"What's your lawyer's name, and what firm does she work for?"

"Her name is Susan Taylor. And she works for Spencer, Glenn, and Raimes."

The detective recognized the firm's name. It specialized in corporate law, not criminal, but the detective knew this firm had clout.

"I've got her card in my wallet if you'd like her telephone number."

Dunn stared at him, considering his options.

"Will you agree to one more thing that could help you?"

"What?" Joe asked.

"Would you allow us to fingerprint you? That way, we can rule you out as a suspect."

Joe thought for a second, but then remembered he had handled the dead woman's body. His fingerprints *would* be on her corpse. He needed to get the hell out of this police station.

"I'm not agreeing to anything without my lawyer right by my side."

"Once you take a tough stance like that with the investigation, Mr. Conrad, then we have to take a tough stance toward you."

"Tough," Joe quipped. "I want a lawyer."

The detective stood up, pushing his chair back loudly.

"I'll be back in a few minutes," he said.

Joe stood too after the detective left and went to the mirror. His hair and shirt were fairly dry, but his blue shirt was wrinkled and dingy. He had loosened his tie when he first got into the interrogation room and taken off his muddy sweater.

The detective came back five minutes later with papers in his hand.
"Are you arresting me?"
"No, Mr. Conrad. These are witness-account forms. We'd like you to write down exactly what happened when you found the body. I also want you to write down your whereabouts on last Tuesday night."
Joe inspected the forms carefully. The heading was Witness Account, and the page was filled with blank lines. *Serves me right for all the writing assignments I've given students.* At the bottom of the form was the phrase "under penalty of perjury" and a place for him to sign and date the paper.
"No," said Joe. "I told you. I'm not saying another word without an attorney."
Dunn glared at him.
"Not one more damn thing without a lawyer," Joe repeated.
The detective grabbed the forms and left. Joe sat there for a few seconds, and then it occurred to him that if he wasn't under arrest, there was no reason he couldn't walk out. He stood up and grabbed his damp sweater. Joe had his hand on the doorknob when Detective Dunn pushed it open. The two men stood face-to-face—Joe saw the detective's jaw muscles clench.
"All right, Mr. Conrad. You're free to go. But you better have that lawyer ready because we will speak to you again."
The detective stepped aside. Joe started out the door but turned around.
"Where's my car?"
"Your car we can keep until we're done with it."
"What?"
"Since your car was essentially abandoned on the freeway, we have the right to search it."
"I didn't abandon my car!"
"Technically, you did when you allowed us to tow it."
Joe's anger rose again.
"This is Orwellian, a police state!"
The detective grinned. "You're not the first to say that."
"How the hell do I get home?"
"You could walk."
"All the way to Davis! It's twenty miles!"

"Take a bus. Call a friend. Call your wife. There's a pay phone in the lobby," the detective said. "Or call your lawyer friends," Dunn said sarcastically.

Joe glared at him.

Using the pay phone in the lobby, Joe phoned Sara at her school. She had to be called out of her classroom. Joe gave a sanitized account of what had happened. Sara was shocked.

"I really need you, honey."

"I'll have to find someone to cover for me. I'll be there in twenty minutes or so."

"Thanks, Sara."

"This is bad, Joe. Really bad."

While he waited in the lobby, Joe remembered his briefcase. It held all his students' papers, his grade book, and his calendar book. He stepped back into the sheriff's office and asked for his case.

"The car's contents have been seized with your car," said Dunn. "You'll be allowed to pick up your car and its contents in a few days when the evidence technicians are done."

"Evidence technicians?"

"Yeah," Dunn said. "You've seen the TV show *CSI*, haven't you?"

Joe shook his head. "I don't watch much TV."

"Crime scene investigators. We call them evidence technicians."

"You think my car is a crime scene?"

"We have to rule it out," Dunn said.

"How do I do my work without my papers?"

Dunn shook his head, adding, "Be patient, Mr. Conrad."

"I need that briefcase."

Dunn's face was stone. The injustice of it infuriated Joe, but all he wanted to do was go home to a hot shower.

As he was leaving, he turned back and said, "I really didn't have anything to do with that girl's death, Detective."

"We'll see."

Joe could feel the detective's eyes boring into his back after he turned and walked away. He felt guilty. But guilty of what?

CHAPTER FIVE

Sometimes, utter loneliness hit Joseph Lawrence Conrad hard, a fist to his chest. It had hit him at his parents' funeral when he stood over their coffins after everyone else had left. It had even hit him hard at his wedding when hardly anyone, only a few friends and his mentor from graduate school, sat on his side of the church. Standing alone, in front of the police station on that gray winter afternoon, Joe felt it again.

At two o'clock, Joe saw Sara's little white Ford Escort turn the corner and drive toward him. The sun struggled to burn through the overcast. Joe had been waiting outside, trying to dry out even though the air was still chilly. He climbed in awkwardly in his damp clothes. They leaned toward each other and kissed.

"Where's your briefcase?" Sara asked.

"I left it in the car, and the police won't give it to me."

"Why not?"

Joe looked at his wife's face as she drove to see her reaction.

"They said they need to rule me out as a suspect in the woman's murder."

Sara blinked once, but her expression didn't change, and she continued to stare straight ahead.

"Why would they need to do that?"

"I guess the dead woman used to be a student at CLU. The detective thinks I might know her."

"Do you?"

"I don't think so," Joe said.

"Who was she?"

"Her name was Patricia Miller. That name doesn't sound familiar, and I didn't recognize her face when I tried to pull her out of the water," explained Joe. "But honestly, I didn't really get a very good look at her. Maybe I *did* have her in one of my classes."

Sara was merging onto the freeway, so she concentrated on her driving. After a few minutes of silence, Sara faced Joe.

"You weren't screwing this girl, were you?"

Joe's mouth fell open.

"Hell no, Sara! How can you even ask?"

She did not answer but stared straight ahead. They drove on in silence.

Near home, they stopped to pick up Katie at the day care center. The preschoolers were in one room watching *Barney* and eating a snack. Like the others, Katie stared at the oversized colorful animals that were singing and dancing while pretending to clean their playroom. Sara had to reach down and lift Katie away from the television set before Katie realized her mother was holding her.

"Here. Take her, Joe," Sara said, handing Katie over. "I have to get her things."

Joe took Katie and hugged her tightly as he walked outside. She smelled of graham crackers and Play-Doh.

"How's Daddy's girl today?"

"Fine," Katie said. "You're wet, Daddy."

"I know, Katie."

"Did you get rained on?"

"No. Daddy fell in a river today."

"Oh," Katie said nonchalantly. "Can we have pizza tonight?"

"We'll ask Mommy."

God bless a child's innocence, Joe thought. To her, falling in a river seemed perfectly routine. Dads fall into rivers sometimes while they're at work. It happens all the time. No big deal.

Before he buckled Katie into her car seat, he hugged her again, saying, "I love you, Katie."

"I love you too, Daddy," she said.

At home, Joe showered and changed while Sara cooked dinner. At six o'clock, Joe got up from the table and said, "I'm going to watch the news, Sara. Why don't you let Katie help you with the dishes?"

They exchanged glances. Normally, if Sara cooked the meal, Joe did the cleanup. They'd agreed Katie should see them doing tasks that contradicted the usual stereotypes. Sara wanted Katie to grow up without the *Leave It to Beaver* image of June Cleaver in her head. But tonight was different, and Sara understood.

The top story in the news was the discovery of Patricia Miller's body. Each station had a reporter at the scene. With the volume low, Joe quickly switched back and forth between channels.

On one station, the male newscaster said, "The body of missing waitress Patricia Miller was discovered by a teacher today when he stopped on the side of the highway." On the other channel, a young Asian woman gave the most thorough account: "The Sacramento County sheriff's office confirmed the identity of the body as Patricia Miller, missing since before Thanksgiving. Her body was discovered midmorning by a college instructor who stopped on his way to work."

In two minutes, it was over. Each station moved on to other stories. Joe sank back and muted the television. He stared out the window across the street at the new two-story house that had been built the year before. Most of the houses on their street were forty years old. Many had been remodeled, but not as thoroughly as this home. It had been demolished down to the foundation and rebuilt while Joe and Sara had looked on enviously. Joe wondered if he and Sara would ever make enough to own a house. The more they worked, the harder life became, it seemed, and the more they grew apart. Would Katie be enough to keep them together?

Sara stepped into the small living room.

"Where's Katie?" Joe asked.

"In her room, coloring."

"Good," Joe sighed.

"Well?" Sara inquired.

"Two channels reported that the woman's body had been found."

"Did they say who found it?"

"Not by name, thank God."

Sara pulled her hair back into a bun, saying, "It's only a matter of time, Joe, before it gets out that it was you."

"What do you mean 'gets out'? I didn't do anything wrong! I found the body of a missing woman. Shouldn't I be called a hero? I mean, if Katie were missing, wouldn't you want someone to find her, dead or alive?"

Katie appeared from the hallway. "Am I going to be dead, Daddy?"

Sara swung around and picked her up. "Oh my god, Joe! How could you say something like that!"

Joe jumped out of the chair and walked toward Katie to reassure her, but Sara was carrying her back to her bedroom.

"No, Katie, honey," Joe said. "We were just talking about something we saw on the news."

Joe stopped and leaned against a wall in the hallway, his eyes closed. "I hate my life," he whispered.

By seven-thirty, Katie was bathed, and Sara was getting her ready for bed. Joe sat at his small desk, in the corner of the small master bedroom next to their bed. He liked this room. The window was right on the corner of the house, so he had a view in two directions—north and east. On sunny mornings, with the blinds open, sunlight poured in.

The telephone rang, and Joe went into the kitchen to answer it.

"Is this Joseph Lawrence Conrad?" a woman's voice asked.

"Yes."

Joe expected a sales pitch. No one called him by his hyperliterary full name, a curse from his mother who was an avid reader.

"This is Jan Lykert. I'm a reporter with the *Sacramento Examiner*, and I have a few questions about the woman whose body you found today."

Joe's chest tightened.

"How'd you get my name?"

"The police just handed out an updated press release naming you as the person who found Patricia Miller's body."

"Oh," Joe answered.

"As a writing instructor at Central Lutheran University, you understand the job journalists have to do."

Joe considered how he should proceed.

"Are you still there, Professor Conrad?"

"First of all, I'm not a full professor. The title is full-time instructor."

"So how should I refer to you? As 'Dr. Conrad'?"

"No. I haven't finished my doctorate yet," Joe answered, feeling himself blush. "It's a long story," he said. "I started teaching before I finished a PhD. We needed the money."

"You're married?" the reporter asked.

"Yes. With a little girl."

"You have a daughter?"

"Yes. A lovely little girl named Katie."

The reporter was quiet for a minute. Joe could almost picture her smiling.

"I'll just refer to you as Joseph Conrad, then."

"You mean in the newspaper?" He suddenly realized whatever he told her would be published in the paper.

"I take it that you were named after the English writer?"

"Yeah. My mother was a fan. But he was Polish born, you know. I can tell you everything you'd ever what to know about him. Born Józef Teodor Konrad near Kiev. Landed in England when he was twenty, unable to speak a word of English."

"You *are* an English teacher, aren't you?"

"Sorry," said Joe.

"How exactly did you find the body?"

"Well, my car was overheating, so I pulled over to let the engine cool down. I went to get some water for the radiator. While I was under the bridge filling up a container with water, I literally stumbled upon the poor girl's body."

"That must have been pretty surprising? What time was that?"

"Must have been about nine-thirty. My first class isn't until eleven."

"I see," the woman's voice said. "And what did you do once you realized you had found Patricia Miller's body?"

"I didn't know it was her. I'd seen something about her disappearance on the news, but I really didn't make the connection at first."

"Okay. What did you do once you realized you had found a body?"

"Well, I sort of slipped into the water and tried to drag her to the bank. I didn't know how long she'd been dead, so I thought I might be able to save her. I used to be a lifeguard."

"Oh, really? Can I mention that in my story?"

Joe smiled. She saw things from his perspective. Maybe after reading her story, Sara would too. He wondered what Jan Lykert looked like.

"Sure," Joe answered. "Anyway, I tried to get her up on shore, but she was too heavy, and the bank was muddy. So I rolled her over, thinking I could give her mouth-to-mouth resuscitation in the water."

"You rolled her over?"

"Yes. When you can't get the body on shore, you administer mouth to mouth in the water."

"Did you give her mouth to mouth?"

"No. It was too late—I could tell from the way she looked."

"Can you describe how she looked, Joe?"

Her face covered by hair and the gaping mouth appeared in Joe's mind.

"I couldn't see her face very well, but I could tell by that point that she had been dead too long to revive."

Joe could hear the soft tapping of the reporter typing on a computer keyboard. She was writing the story exactly as he was telling it. Joe smiled again.

"How could you tell?" she asked.

"It was apparent. Her body was very stiff and cold to the touch."

"Stiff and cold to the touch," the reporter repeated. "That's a good description. How was she clothed?"

Joe blushed again. "She had on a white blouse. I couldn't see her legs, so I don't know if she was wearing pants or a skirt."

"What did you do next?"

"I managed to climb out of the water. By that point, I was shivering from the cold. I ran up the embankment. There was an emergency phone box by the side of the road, so I tried to use it."

"Did you call the police?"

"No," Joe said. "Somebody had cut the phone cord, so there was no phone. But fortunately, a CHP officer had spotted me by that point. I had propped up the hood of my car to let the engine cool, so I guess he knew I was in trouble."

Sara appeared then in the kitchen and gave Joe a quizzical look. He covered the mouthpiece of the phone and said, "It's a newspaper reporter interviewing me about finding the missing girl."

Sara knitted her eyebrows and whispered, "Is that a good idea?"

Joe nodded, annoyed. He turned his attention back to the phone call.

"I'm sorry," Joe said. "My wife was just wondering who was on the phone."

"What happened next, Joe?" Jan Lykert asked.

"Let's see. I told the highway patrolman about the body. We went back to the bridge, and I pointed it out to him."

"You mean, you could see her body from the bridge?"

"Yes. I had pulled it out far enough that it could be seen."

"Okay. And then what happened?"

"The cop—I mean, the CHP officer—took over. He called for other police, and they examined the scene and recovered the body while I waited in my car. I was shivering my—I . . . I was very cold. I got a blanket out of my trunk and wrapped up."

There was a pause. *She's writing this down, trying to catch up*, Joe thought.

"Now I understand the police took you in for questioning. Is that correct?"

"Well, yes. I agreed to go with the police as a witness to give a statement. I wanted to help in any way I could," he tried to explain. "It's not every day that you find a dead person."

"In the latest press release, the police state that you were questioned for several hours in order to clear up some inconsistencies with the statement that you gave. Is that an accurate account?"

Joe's heart pounded again.

"The so-called inconsistencies were about trivial matters totally unrelated to the missing woman or her death," Joe said firmly. It was a pretty good statement, he thought, except for the use of "totally," which made him sound like a Valley girl.

"What kind of inconsistencies?"

"Just like with us," he answered. "About my teaching position at the university. They jumped to the conclusion that I was a professor, and I corrected them."

"I see," the reporter said, sounding skeptical. "The press release states that there are, and I quote, 'possible links' between Patricia Miller's disappearance and your activities. Were there links between you and Patricia?"

"Links? What do you mean?"

"Were you seeing her?"

"What? No, of course not."

"The press release implies that you knew Patricia Miller. What's your response to that, Mr. Conrad?"

Joe closed his eyes and spun around, leaning against the wall. He shook his head. *No no no!*

"My response is this, Ms. Lykert—absurd! Ridiculous! There are no links between me and Patricia Miller. Other than the fact that I happen to be the good law-abiding citizen who found her body and tried to do the right thing by reporting it."

He realized he was yelling into the phone.

"And you may print *that* statement verbatim!"

"No reason to get upset, Joe. I'm just trying to tell your side."

"Well, write this down too. My advice to anybody who finds a body, based on the way I've been treated, run the other way! And don't tell anyone! Especially not the police!"

He was tempted to slam the phone down but stopped himself.

"Joe," the reporter said softly. "Calm down. Are you sure there are no connections between you and Patricia Miller?"

"I'm sure."

"Could she have been one of your students at CLU?"

"I don't think so. I've only been there for two and half years. Didn't she graduate before then?"

"Patricia Miller was a waitress at Murphy's Bar and Grill. Did you ever eat there?"

Joe thought for a minute.

"Yes. I've eaten there a couple of times. But not very often."

"Is it possible that she waited on you?"

Joe tried to think before answering. He'd eaten there no more than three times in two and a half years. He didn't know anyone by name. But he'd probably paid his bill with a credit card. If Patricia Miller had been his waitress, there was probably a record of it.

"Yeah. I suppose it's possible that she waited on me once."

"So it's fair to say that it's possible you knew her," the reporter stated bluntly.

"No. That's not accurate. I didn't 'know' her for God's sake. I mean, how many waitresses do *you* know?"

"Actually, quite a few."

"Maybe *you* knew Patricia Miller, then," Joe said sarcastically.

"No. I work in downtown Sacramento, not in Stockton like you."

"This conversation is about to end, Ms. Lykert."

"I have to ask again. Were you romantically involved with Patricia?"

"God no!" Joe screamed.

"For the record," the reporter asked, "did you kill her?"

Joe looked at the phone for a few seconds in disbelief before slamming it down. He closed his eyes and, leaning against the wall, said aloud to no one, "I'm screwed!"

It was then that he heard the doorbell ring. He rolled around the corner to see Sara open the front door. Her face was suddenly bathed in bright light, and Joe could see through the large living room window that a television news crew was standing on his front porch.

Sara looked stunned. A female reporter held a microphone, asking her questions while a cameraman pointed a camera like a bazooka at her. Joe rushed over and reached for the door to slam it shut, but Sara was blocking him without realizing it.

"Are you Joseph Conrad?" the reporter asked.

"No comment," Joe said.

"Do you have something to hide, Professor Conrad?" the reporter yelled.

Joe finally managed to push Sara aside and slam the door closed, but the woman with the microphone knocked on the door loudly.

"Don't you want to make a statement about the accusations the police are making?" the woman yelled through the door.

Sara turned to Joe, her face bright red.

"What in the hell have you gotten us into, Joe?"

"I don't know how this got turned into such a mess!"

"Well, it's your mess, Joe. You'd better clean it up."

Sara stared at him coldly for a few hard seconds. Joe thought she might slap him, but she turned and stomped off toward the hall. The reporter still knocking on the door, Joe pulled the cord that drew the curtain closed on the picture window that looked out on Tenth Street. *What are the neighbors thinking?* he wondered.

The telephone rang incessantly. Joe rushed in, only to find Sara standing at the telephone.

"Don't answer it!" he yelled.

He reached over and took the entire telephone off the wall, disconnecting it.

"This is like something out of Kafka!" he said to Sara.

"No," Sara replied. "It's more like a bad episode of *Murder, She Wrote!* Fix the problem, Joe."

"How?"

"I don't know. Maybe we need to call my sister."

This was not the first time Sara had suggested her own family help them.

"I'll take care of it," he said firmly. He spun around and walked back into the living room. The knocks on the front door grew louder.

He took a few deep breaths and tried to compose himself. He put his hand on the doorknob and waited for a few seconds before opening the door.

Shielding his eyes from the glare of the lights, he tried to look at the reporter's face. He recognized her as the woman from the evening news, but he couldn't recall her name.

"Turn off your equipment, and let me talk to you. If we can set some ground rules, then I'll be happy to give you an interview."

The woman motioned to the cameraman, and he cut the lights.

"What ground rules do you have in mind?"

Joe considered for a few seconds.

"You can come inside and sit down so we can talk to each other like normal people. I don't want to be seen as some nut trying to duck questions on my front porch. And we'll speak civilly to each other. I just got off the phone with one of your colleagues, and she was rude. She tried to trap me."

"Oh," the woman said, her face brightening. "Whom were you speaking to?"

"A woman from the *Examiner.* She was rude and accusatory, and I didn't like that. If you can be polite and if you'll let me tell exactly what happened instead of trying to twist things around, then we can talk."

"All right."

"I mean, this is getting out of hand."

"I understand," the woman said, smiling. "Let me introduce myself. I'm Joan Ngo," she said, pronouncing her last name as "no." "This is my assistant, Andy."

Joe shook her hand, and she held his hand longer than he thought appropriate. While holding his hand, she said, "I want you to feel comfortable with me, Professor Conrad. I went to Central Lutheran, and I have deep feelings for that school."

Joe nodded and tried to free his hand.

"I want you to tell your story so that we can report the truth," she said, still gripping his hand.

Joe looked into her face. She seemed as sincere as anyone could be. She was about the same age as he was, Joe guessed, and very beautiful. Her hair was shoulder length and professionally cut, curving inward to frame her face. Though mostly black, her hair had streaks of brown and red. She wore a cream-colored blouse under a dark green business jacket. A wide gold necklace hung just above the top of her blouse, its curve following the same line as the blouse. Below her suit jacket, she wore tight blue jeans and shiny black high-heeled boots.

The cameraman, Andy, in a Raiders sweatshirt and faded blue jeans, wore a battery pack around his waist. He lowered the camera as he followed Joan Ngo into the living room. Sara reappeared from the kitchen.

"You let them inside?" she gasped.

"Yes, Sara. I'm just going to tell what really happened."

"Are you Mrs. Conrad?" the reporter asked.

Sara shot her a suspicious look.

"Leave me out of this. This is Joe's mess."

Joe walked over to Sara and escorted her back into the living room.

"If I don't tell them what happened, they're going to make me look guilty."

Joe held Sara's shoulders and looked deeply into her watery eyes. She was trembling. For a moment, her eyes softened, and she looked like the woman Joe had fallen in love with.

"I need your support now, Sara," he pleaded. "This is one of those 'for better or worse' moments."

Sara looked up at him—half laughing, half crying.

"All right."

She wiped her eyes and took a deep breath. They sat down together on the sofa. Joan Ngo had pulled a chair up so that it was facing them.

"Are you ready to tell us what happened now, Joe?" the reporter asked.

Joe and Sara sat down on the sofa, and Andy turned the camera's bright light on again.

"Just start at the beginning, and tell exactly what happened," Joan instructed.

Joe took a deep breath and stared into the camera.

"It's better if you look at me instead of at the camera, Joe," the reporter said. She had a soft, encouraging voice. "You'll come off as nervous and cross-eyed if you look directly into the camera."

"Okay," Joe said, looking into the woman's face.

She smiled reassuringly.

"Look, Joe. I went to CLU. I loved my years there. I had a great relationship with all of my professors. That's why I want to do this story. I'm on your side."

Sara laughed a little, saying, "I thought journalists were supposed to be objective."

"Yes. We are. And I'll deny saying what I just said. And Andy often has trouble hearing things, don't you, Andy?"

"I'm sorry," he said. "Were you talking to me? I was adjusting the focus."

Joe and Sara laughed.

"Start at the beginning," Joan Ngo repeated.

"Well," Joe began, "I was headed to work this morning—was it just this morning? It seems like it was days ago. Anyway . . ."

Joe told the tale again for the fifth time that day. He spoke clearly, looking at the reporter's face. She nodded and grinned reassuringly. At Joe's description of falling in the water and grabbing the body, she grimaced appropriately. When Joe described the body being loaded into the coroner's station wagon, both Joan and Sara dabbed their eyes.

Then Joe described the grilling by the police, the tension he felt in the little room. He explained how he had tried to be as helpful as possible. "I was just trying to do right by this poor woman," he said. He went on to describe his feeling of betrayal when he realized Detective Dunn was trying to implicate him in the woman's murder.

When he was finished, Sara squeezed his hand, and Joan said, "Good job."

Andy turned the camera off but left the lights on while Joan looked back over notes she had taken while Joe had recounted the events of the day.

"Okay, Joe," she said. "I just have a few follow-up questions." For the first time, Joe detected a slight Vietnamese accent.

Joe tensed up. *Here it comes.*

"I have to ask a few tough questions. You can answer or not."

Joe and Sara looked at each other.

"Maybe we should stop here," Sara said.

"That's a good idea," Joe replied.

The reporter stared at Joe's eyes.

"The entire segment won't seem credible if you don't respond to some tough questions. I won't seem like a credible journalist if I don't ask some tough questions. Understand?"

Joe glanced at Sara, then back at the reporter.

"You'll make me look guilty. I don't want this to seem like a segment on *60 Minutes*. I don't want to come off as someone who's squirming, you know, the way people look when Mike Wallace grills them."

The female reporter looked back at her cameraman. He turned around and reached into his camera bag as if looking for something.

"I'm not trying to make you seem guilty if you're not, Joe," the reporter said softly. "But I have a job to do. Look, let me give you some pointers. This might be a breech of ethics, but let me suggest a few things."

"Okay," Joe said.

"If you choose not to answer, just say so. Don't say something like 'No comment' or 'I take the Fifth.' Say, 'I'd better not answer that right now' or 'I'd better wait until later to answer that.' Understand?"

"Yes," Joe said.

"When people say 'No comment,' it makes them sound guilty."

"Okay."

Joan motioned to Andy, and the little red light of the camera came on again.

"Did you know the victim, Patricia Miller?"

"Not that I'm aware of, although I've learned that she was a waitress at a restaurant where I ate two or three times. So I may have been acquainted with her in passing."

"Patricia Miller was not one of your students at CLU?"

"Not to my knowledge. I haven't checked my old roll books yet, but I believe she graduated from CLU before I started teaching there."

"You worked late on the night of Patricia Miller's disappearance, correct?"

"Yes," Joe admitted. "I teach a night class on Tuesday nights from six-thirty to nine-thirty."

"So you drove the same route as Patricia Miller on the night of her disappearance, correct?"

"Yes. But probably earlier in the evening."

"Did you stop to assist Patricia Miller on the night she disappeared?"

"No," Joe said calmly. "I drove back to Sacramento on I-5 right after class at about nine-thirty, so I must have passed the spot where her car was found by ten o'clock. From what I've been told, she was still working in Stockton at that time. I didn't see anyone stopped on the side of the road when I was driving home."

"Did you come right home that evening?"

Joe blushed visibly and looked down at the floor. Sara gently pulled her hand away.

"No. I stopped at a cocktail lounge for a drink. It was my last night of teaching for a few days, and I wanted to celebrate a little."

"Where did you stop?"

Joe looked back up at the reporter.

"I'd rather not say."

"Sources at the sheriff's office say that you stopped at a place called Highbeams," the reporter said. "Isn't that a topless bar?"

Joe stared at the reporter.

"I'd better wait and talk about this at a later time," he said.

"All right. What time did Joe get home, Mrs. Conrad?" Joan asked, shifting her steady gaze toward Sara.

Sara tensed. "I'd rather—I mean—I'm not exactly sure. About midnight, I guess."

"Please don't involve my wife," Joe said firmly.

"All right. I apologize. Now I have to ask, did you have anything to do with the disappearance or death of Patricia Miller?"

Joe leaned forward and turned his face directly toward the camera.

"Absolutely not!" he said fiercely. "I tried to help a woman whose body I found in the water. That's all I've tried to do all day."

"What have you tried to do all day, Joe?" the reporter asked.

Joe looked back at her.

"I've tried to help! Like the lifeguard I used to be, I tried to help a drowning victim. Like the good citizen I am, I tried to help the police. That's what teachers do. We try to help people."

Joan looked at him and smiled. She nodded in agreement then turned back to Andy, who released his finger on the trigger of the camera and turned off the intense lights.

"That should do it," she said. "Great way to end your story."

Joe slumped back and collapsed against the sofa cushion, utterly exhausted, wishing he could turn off his life as easily as Andy had turned off the camera.

CHAPTER SIX

After the TV reporter left, Joe and Sara locked up and got ready for bed. They left the phone unplugged and kept their front porch light off. Together, they looked in on Katie, who slept soundly in her world of innocence. At ten, Joe turned on the small television in their bedroom. The news show began with the "exclusive interview" by Joan Ngo.

A picture of Patricia Miller appeared on the television screen behind the reporter, with another smaller picture of the university campus inserted in the background. Looking directly into the camera, Joan said, "Tonight, I had an opportunity to interview Mr. Joseph Conrad, an English instructor at Central Lutheran University, about his role in recovering the body of missing waitress and former CLU coed Patricia Miller who has been missing since before Thanksgiving."

The scene then cut to Sara and Joe sitting together on their sofa, the curtains of the picture window drawn behind them. Both of them looked serious and nervous. The interview had been edited considerably. What had taken half an hour to do earlier that night was now presented in less than two minutes. Sometimes, the camera showed Joe talking, with quick flashes of Joan nodding her head spliced between different portions of the story. As brief as it was, the story was accurate, but it ended with the few embarrassing final questions:

"Where did you stop?"

"I'd rather not say."

"A topless bar?"

"I'd better wait," the television version of Joe said.

From off camera, Joan's voice asked, "Did you have anything to do with the disappearance or death of Patricia Miller?"

The camera showed Joe leaning forward. Andy had zoomed in for a close-up. Joan was right. Television Joe did look nervous and cross-eyed, staring into the camera as he had.

"Absolutely not!"

"Oh god, Joe!" Sara said. "You look like Bill Clinton saying, 'I did not have sexual relations with that woman!'"

Watching himself from bed, Joe was glad he had not wagged his finger at the camera.

"I tried to help," television Joe said to the camera. "That's all I've tried to do all day."

"What have you tried to do?" Joan's disembodied voice asked.

"I've tried to help! Like the lifeguard I used to be, I tried to help a drowning victim. Like the good citizen I am, I tried to help the police. That's what teachers do. We try to help people."

"Good, Joe," Sara said. "She left that in exactly as you said it. You were great."

Joe smiled but then strained to listen to the rest of the story. It was back to a live shot of Joan, who was speaking directly into the camera.

"A spokesman for Patricia Miller's parents said they are grateful that their daughter's body has been found."

Joan turned to the coanchor sitting next to her.

"Are police saying whether or not this English professor who found the body is a suspect in Patricia's murder?"

"No, Tom," Joan responded. "Officially, the sheriff's office says they haven't ruled anyone in or out as a suspect at this time."

Tom, the young dark-haired anchor who looked like a Tom Cruise wannabe, raised an eyebrow and said, "Is this teacher now eligible for the reward money?"

"Yes, he is, Tom. As you know, Patricia Miller's family offered fifty thousand dollars for information leading to the recovery of their daughter."

"Fifty grand is a lot of money. Motive enough for anybody—even the killer—to tell what they know."

The implication was clear, and Joe grew furious.

"Remember, Tom," Joan said. "So far, there's no evidence linking anyone to Patricia Miller's death."

The next story was about a fiery crash on Highway 99 involving a tanker truck and a minivan. The truck driver escaped injury, but a family of four in the van was killed.

"Why in the hell do people leap to the illogical conclusion that I am somehow involved with this dead girl!" he yelled.

Sara merely sat still in bed, shaking her head. "I don't know, Joe," she said finally.

Once the lights were off, Sara slipped into sleep. Joe listened to her heavy breathing. But he could not sleep. Whenever he started to drift off, an image or a statement flashed into his brain, and he was jolted awake again. Finally, about three in the morning, he drifted to sleep, only to be awakened by Sara and Katie four hours later.

"You can take the Escort today," Sara was saying. "I'm getting a ride with Eleanor."

Eleanor worked at Sara's school and lived in Davis. She and Sara sometimes commuted together; but Eleanor, whose children were grown, liked to stay late and finish her work before coming home while Sara liked to get home earlier to have more time with Katie.

Katie, standing by the bed at eye level with Joe, leaned forward and kissed him on the cheek.

"Bye-bye, Daddy," she whispered.

"Bye-bye, Minnie Mouse," Joe whispered.

"You're a sleepyhead, Daddy."

"You're Raggedy Ann," Joe whispered.

Katie's laughter helped Joe wake up.

"Good luck today, Joe," Sara said. For the first time in days, she bent down and kissed him on the temple. "Come straight home after your night class tonight. Don't make any stops."

Joe's heart sank as he remembered everything that had happened in the past twenty-four hours. He dreaded his long day of work. Normally, he would sit in his office on Tuesdays grading papers, preparing for classes, and meeting with the occasional student who came by for a conference. His evening class began at six-thirty and was scheduled to end at nine-thirty, but he rarely kept his students the full three hours, preferring to let them go at nine-fifteen in case a few had questions afterward.

The course he was teaching this semester was designed to appeal to older students. Over sixty students had begun the program the year before, and Joe had had many of them in a preparatory writing course the previous year. Now only about forty students were left, and about half were taking Joe's evening class.

Joe reflected on the tenuous nature of his position at Central Lutheran as he got ready for work. He had no briefcase, no papers to grade; but he felt compelled to get to campus early in order to deal with some of the concerns that others, including the department chair and his nosy secretary, might have.

Joe backed his wife's Ford Escort out of the driveway at 333 Tenth Street, made a left onto B Street, and headed for the freeway. From Interstate 80, he took the ramp from the bridge over the Sacramento River and headed south again on I-5, just as he had done the day before in his old Mustang.

After twenty minutes of driving, he was coming up to Lost Slough where everything had happened less than twenty-four hours before.

On this slate gray morning, a high damp fog covered the sky. These were the kinds of days in the Central Valley when Joe just wanted to stay in bed, reading and dozing. The low bare trees and tangled bushes of the slough came into view, and as Joe approached the bridge that spanned the water of the slough, he saw a highway patrol car pulled over in the same spot where he had parked the Mustang yesterday. He merged over to the slow lane and reduced his speed as he neared the CHP car. An officer was sitting inside, looking down, apparently writing something as Joe passed. Joe couldn't tell if it was the same officer who had stopped for him yesterday. Beyond the police car rose the bare branches of wild valley oaks shrouded in fog. The scene sent a chill down Joe's back.

Central Lutheran University was a small private college founded in 1891. The cathedral and the four-story library were the two massive redbrick buildings that stood at the center of the campus, designed to imitate Ivy League colleges of the east. Newer buildings surrounded the campus core, connected by paved walkways that linked the outer buildings to the inner buildings like the spokes of a wagon wheel. The university served three thousand students and seemed hemmed in by the old neighborhoods.

CLU was only a few miles northeast of its main rival, the University of the Pacific in Stockton, a town known for one of the first schoolyard shootings in America's recent history. Half a dozen Southeast Asian elementary school students and a teacher had been gunned down by a racist with an automatic weapon. Stockton had worked hard to change its image of death and violence, but each year, it was a city plagued by one of the highest murder rates in California. Joe spent as little time as possible there and rarely ventured off campus.

His office, on the third floor of Anderson Hall, was one of five small offices designated for part-time and untenured faculty. The four part-time visiting lecturers shared two offices while Joe and two other instructors had small offices to themselves. It was a meaningful distinction in academia. Also on the third floor of Anderson Hall were three medium-sized classrooms with tall windows and old slate blackboards. The wooden desks that filled these classrooms were covered with carvings and graffiti that dated back to the Vietnam War. Though dilapidated, the classrooms had charm and character, their high ceilings inspiring lofty thoughts.

As Joe unlocked his office, he read three Post-it notes stuck on his door, each apparently written by a different student panicked about the research paper assignment due in one week. One note said,

Prof. C.
Help!
Computer crashed!
Lost my hole paper!
Can I get a extinction?
                    James

The errors were typical of this student's work, and it didn't surprise Joe that James had "lost" his paper. Not the dog, but the computer ate it. Another note said,

Dear Professor Conrad,
May I please meet with you
to discuss my research paper.
I can't find any recent sources
from the last 2 years but I know
that's required.
                    Cathy

The third note was different. It said,

Professor Conrad,
Please call Det. Marino at the
County Sheriff's Office asap.
I need to speak with you about
a case. Very important. The number
is 959-9999, ext. 12.

In the familiar setting of his office, Joe had almost forgotten the events of the last twenty-four hours, but the note from Detective Marino produced a flood of images and emotions in him. He put the notes on his desk and turned on the large old lamp that threw warm orange light against the wall his desk faced, spotlighting posters of Paris and London. Under the dormer window to his left stood his computer table; and behind him rose a wall of shelves covered by books, photos, and odd artifacts, which he sometimes used as props in the classroom. A chair for students sat on his right between his desk and door to the office. Joe disdained the overhead florescent lights, so he depended instead on the light from a small lamp.

Sitting at his desk, Joe stared at the note from this other detective. Was he obligated to call? The feeling of dread returned, and he crumpled the note into a ball and tossed it into the trash can next to his computer desk. Next, he checked his voice mail messages. The first three were from students who had questions about assignments due this week. One call was from the same Cathy Jenkins who had left the Post-it on his door, a good student, but irritatingly persistent—the kind who forces teachers to follow their own course requirements.

The next five messages were from reporters—two different reporters from Stockton's newspaper the *Record* and the rest from local television stations. He deleted each one without listening to the complete message. The last message was from the department chair, who asked Joe to meet with him sometime Tuesday to "discuss the recent events that had placed the school under a microscope." CLU did not like bad publicity.

Joe turned on his computer and pulled up his e-mails, several from students. Several more were from reporters. After opening the first few and reading requests for interviews, Joe began deleting the rest without reading them.

When he was finished, he looked around his office. Without the stacks of papers to grade, he had nothing to do. He checked his watch and realized it was only nine-thirty. He had stopped at Lost Slough almost exactly twenty-four hours ago.

There was no putting it off. He needed to face the chairman of the English department. The chairman's suite was on the first floor of Anderson Hall and took up as much space as three of the smaller offices on the third floor. Molly, the chair's administrative assistant, was working at her computer when Joe walked into the offices. When she looked up, her face became ashen.

"Hello, Molly," Joe said.

"I'll tell him you're here. He wants to see you right away."

Charles Thorne, by contrast, stood and reached out his hand to greet Joe as he entered the spacious office. He gripped Joe's hand firmly, shaking his arm heartily. Thorne was a good-sized man who wore his age well. He stayed fit by working out at the gym on campus. His short graying hair looked almost military, and his rugged jawline belied his age. With his wire-rimmed glasses, Thorne reminded Joe of Teddy Roosevelt.

"Joe," Dr. Thorne said sympathetically, "how are you holding up?"

"I'm okay. This has been quite an ordeal."

"Yes, I'm sure it has. Take a seat."

Joe sat in one of the three red leather chairs that faced Dr. Thorne's massive walnut desk. These offices had been refurbished and remodeled within the last ten years, unlike the rest of the building.

"I had a call from the president earlier this morning. He's concerned about the negative press this is getting. He's also concerned about you as well, of course. You are, after all, a member of the CLU community now. He and I agree that we want to be absolutely fair in all respects."

Joe did not like the direction this conversation was taking, but he struggled not to show his displeasure or nervousness.

"Well," Joe said. "I appreciate the support that you and President Hansen are offering. And of course, as someone who teaches ethics in my courses, I believe that it *is* important to be fair and wait for all the facts to come out."

Dr. Thorne grimaced. "Unfortunately," he said, looking down at his desk, "some of the facts that have already come out paint you in a rather bad light."

"What facts are you referring to, Dr. Thorne?"

"Have you read this morning's *Examiner?*"

"No," Joe admitted. He blushed. "I can only imagine the way that reporter twisted things, though. I tried to explain what really happened, but she seemed more interested in sensationalizing the story."

Dr. Thorne tapped his fingers on his desk, and Joe saw that he was tapping a folded page from a newspaper.

"Is *that* the story?"

"Yes," Thorne answered. "Why don't you read it."

Joe took the folded paper and read the headline: PATRICIA MILLER'S BODY FOUND BY COLLEGE PROF. BY JAN LYKERT.

> The body of missing waitress Patricia Miller was discovered twenty miles south of Sacramento on I-5 Monday morning at approximately 10:00 a.m. by a CLU professor who was driving to Ms. Miller's alma mater. The twenty-four year old, who was on her way to her parents' home for Thanksgiving, was apparently beaten and strangled sometime late Tuesday night or early Wednesday morning, according to police.
>
> Ms. Miller's body was discovered when Professor Joseph Conrad, an English instructor at Central Lutheran University in Stockton for the past three years, pulled off the freeway with engine trouble. Professor Conrad claims to have spotted the body from the bridge at Lost Slough while attempting to repair his car. In an odd coincidence, Ms. Miller had been a co-ed at CLU, graduating around the same time Professor Conrad was hired.
>
> Detective Dunn, of the Sacramento County Sheriff's office, stated 'There are some discrepancies in the Professor's story, but nothing concrete points to him as a suspect in the victim's death. One such discrepancy is that the CLU teacher has no alibi for the time of the murder, though he claimed to be drinking at a local bar, where young women only slightly older than college students work as exotic dancers.

When asked to comment on his relationship with Patricia Miller, Professor Conrad admitted being acquainted with the victim, who is survived by her parents and an older brother. Professor Conrad, who teaches at the well-regarded and expensive private school, is eligible to receive the $50,000 reward posted by the Miller family. Anyone with information is urged to call the Sheriff's office.

Joe shook his head as he read the story. "She practically accuses me of murdering this poor girl!"

"Is that how you read it too?" Thorne asked.

Joe looked Dr. Thorne in the eyes.

"You *know* me, Charles. I had nothing to do with this girl's death!"

"Is it true that you knew her, Joe?"

"I told this reporter that I might've had her as a waitress. Maybe once or twice. I've been to that restaurant where she worked a few times, but I don't remember Patricia Miller, even if she had been my waitress." Joe massaged the back of his neck. "That's one of the lies in this story. I mean, it's not a very accurate account," Joe said. He scanned the story and pointed to a line in it. "I didn't spot the body 'from the bridge' as she described it. I told her I went down to get some water to cool off my car engine, and that's when I saw the body. This story is filled with inaccurate statements like that, Charles," Joe pleaded.

"Calm down. What about the other points of the story, Joe?"

"Like what?"

"Well, it's distressing to us to learn that you went to one of *those* bars where women dance in the nude for money." As Dr. Thorne spoke, he grimaced when he said "nude." "You have to remember, Joe, that this is a *religious* university. Admittedly, the ties between the college and the Lutheran Church aren't as strong today as they used to be, but they are there nonetheless."

Joe blushed. "Yes," he said. "I understand. "I . . . I don't make a habit of it."

"And remember, Joe, there's a morals clause in your employment contract."

Joe's heart pounded, and his mouth became dry.

"Are you firing me, Charles?"

"No no! We just want you to understand how bad this is for the school. You have to understand that many of the families who send their sons and daughters to CLU are religious people themselves, and their hope is that their children won't be exposed to the rubbish out there."

Rubbish? Joe thought. *Now I'm being lumped in with society's rubbish!*

"Well, as I said, Charles, I don't make a habit of that sort of thing. It's been a stressful semester, you know. I'm teaching in the outreach program, and that's an overload course, and all of my classes are full."

"I'm sure you're as busy as the rest of us are."

The comment was condescending.

"Looking at nudes isn't exactly a crime, Charles. Nobody complains about the nude models, many of whom are older students, who pose for the figure drawing classes in the art department."

"Joe," Thorne scolded, "that's entirely different. You're comparing apples to oranges."

More like cantaloupes and grapefruits, Joe thought. He'd walked by the art building a few times in the late spring when the doors were propped open and passersby could look in to see the attractive young women and men posing nude for a roomful of salivating students. One art teacher had left some years before because of a scandal involving a few of his student models, and people around campus were still talking about it. He had moved to Colorado. Joe suddenly recalled a more recent scandal.

"What about the controversy surrounding last year's production of that play?" Joe countered. "Weren't seven students, male and female, naked on stage?"

"Not that it's any of your business, but Professor Wallace was censured for that," Dr. Thorne said, leaning back in his chair. A slight grin almost surfaced on his lips, but he regained his composure immediately. "Now listen, Joe. Here's what President Hansen and I have discussed. You will, of course, complete this semester and turn in grades. If there is no more bad publicity connected with this matter during the Christmas holidays, then you'll be allowed to come back and teach next semester as planned. That will complete your three-year contract."

"I'm supposed to be reviewed next semester. I was hoping to be given another three-year contract."

Dr. Thorne rocked back and forth in his plush office chair a few times, a serious and concerned expression on his strong but aging face.

"That's not entirely out of the question at this point. After all, your students give you excellent evaluations, and you've been a good colleague. You don't publish much, but then we have put more emphasis on your teaching."

"I . . . I was hoping to get a permanent instructorship."

"Well, Joe," Dr. Thorne said, "it would help if you and your wife would move to Stockton so you could be closer to campus and participate in more activities."

Joe sat silently. Davis, with its low crime rate and excellent schools, was a better place to raise Katie.

"That's something Sara and I have discussed. I suppose we're waiting to see whether or not I land a permanent position here first."

"Well, we have a Joseph Heller dilemma here, don't we, Joe?"

Joe thought for a moment.

"Yes, I guess we do. It is a catch-22."

"But you're no Yossarian, are you, Joe?" stated the older English professor.

Joe laughed aloud. "I've sure felt his sense of frustration these past twenty-four hours!"

"And true irony as well if what you say is true."

"What do you mean?"

"Try to calculate the odds of you, a teacher at this school, stumbling upon the body of a murder victim who was a former student of this school. You were trying to help, but all of your actions have only made matters worse for you. That's situational irony."

Joe considered his situation for a moment. Since it had actually happened to him, it was not merely academic.

"Finish the semester, Joe. Be professional and discrete, and be sure to turn in your grades on time." Dr. Thorne stood and reached out his hand. Joe was dismissed. "We'll let the rest sort itself out."

Dr. Thorne's grip was like a vise as he pumped Joe's arm. He was impressive for a man his age.

Before going back upstairs to his office, Joe went to the restroom. Craig Richmond was standing at the urinal and looked over at Joe.

"You're in a bit of hot water, Conrad," Richmond said.

"Actually, the water's a bit chilly," Joe replied, glancing down. "Or doesn't yours reach that far?"

Richmond looked away after a curt chuckle then shook a few times, zipped, and went to the sink.

"I don't engage in toilet humor, Conrad. It's beneath me."

"Toilets usually are," Joe countered. Even though he and Joe were the same age, Craig Richmond's snobbish prepschool voice and PhD from Rutgers and recently published book on T. S. Eliot assured him tenure at CLU.

"Be careful, Conrad," Craig said. "You may want some friends in this department . . . if you hope to stay long." With that, he turned and left while Joe washed his hands.

In the hallway outside the restroom, Joe found Craig at the drinking fountain.

"Seriously, Richmond, why do you dislike me?"

Craig Richmond wiped some water from his lower lip.

"What makes you think I dislike you?"

"Well, maybe because you always treat me like a second-class citizen. What is it with you, anyway?"

"It's nothing against you personally, Joe. I just feel that everyone who teaches at a university should have a doctorate."

There it was, out in the open. Craig Richmond had voiced what Joe had suspected.

"That's why I wear a tie," Joe replied. "To compensate for not having a PhD."

Craig Richmond stepped closer. "You're the kind of workhorse third-rate colleges exploit, *Mr.* Conrad. You attract fourth-rate students and keep this place a bastion of mediocrity."

"A 'bastion of mediocrity'? I wonder how the dean would like hearing that."

"Teach at a junior college where you belong!" Richmond said. He spun around and took the stairs two at a time. Joe might have decked him if he hadn't believed what he'd said was true—at least partially.

As Joe ascended the stairs, he saw that his overly zealous student, Cathy Jenkins, was waiting outside his office.

"Hello, Cathy."

"Hello, Professor Conrad," she replied eagerly. "I need to talk to you about my research paper."

They went inside Joe's office together and sat down. Cathy Jenkins was a beautiful eighteen-year-old girl with long curly brown hair, large dark eyes, a cheerleader's figure, and a sense of style out of *Vogue*. Joe tried to ignore her tight-fitting pink V-neck sweater. The light brown suede skirt ended just above her knees. Joe couldn't place the perfume, but he guessed that it was expensive.

"Did you get my note?"

"Yes. Did you bring the articles with you?" Joe asked her.

"Yes," she said, pulling two photocopied articles out of her binder.

Joe took them and began reading the abstracts.

"These are good, Cathy," he said, still reading. "Even though they aren't that current, they're both written by experts and published in credible scholarly journals."

"Can I use them, then?"

Joe thumbed through both of them, turning to their bibliographies.

"Let me show you something, Cathy," he said. She drew closer as he pointed to the last page. "See these names? In this list of twenty or thirty sources, five of the articles were written by the same authors."

"Is that good or bad?" the student asked, turning to look at him. As she turned, her hair brushed Joe's face.

"It's good," he said, moving away. "It means these particular authors have written extensively on the topic. That means they're probably well-respected authorities. Otherwise, these other peer-reviewed journals wouldn't have published their articles."

Cathy sat back in the seat next to the desk, crossed her legs, and smiled. "Then it's okay to use them?"

"Sure," he said, handing the pages back.

She held his gaze for a few uncomfortable seconds, and he tried to read her expression. Had she seen the news stories last night?

"Anything else, Cathy?"

She shook her head as if coming out of a trance. "That's such a load off." She exhaled loudly while putting the articles back in her binder. "I've got your paper due on Friday, a lab final in bio next Monday, and a final in chem next Friday."

"A final next week?" Joe asked.

"Yes."

"But finals aren't for two weeks."

"I know, but our professor is going on a trip to give a paper or something in Italy during finals' week, so he's giving his final early."

"He's not supposed to do that," Joe said.

"Well, there's not much we students can do about it," Cathy sighed, ready to leave. "We pretty much have to do what you professors tell us to do, don't we?"

She shot him another knowing glance, and he squirmed in his seat.

"You students have more power than you know," he said, trying to make the sudden tension disappear.

Joe worked in his office preparing notes for the final weeks of classes. At noon, he ate his lunch and checked headlines on the Internet, reading backstories about Patricia Miller's disappearance from the previous week, about her parents being too distraught to speak to reporters, and about the second mortgage they had drawn on for the fifty thousand-dollar reward. A good photograph of Patricia Miller appeared with one of the stories, and Joe studied it carefully. Did he know her?

In the afternoon, a few students dropped by with questions; and between conferences with students, Joe read and prepared notes for his night class. At a few minutes after four, when he was just thinking of leaving campus for a while to get dinner, he was startled by the sudden appearance of a large middle-aged man with short neatly combed black hair. The lumbering man, who looked like a former football player, was dressed in a dark suit.

"Professor Conrad?"

"Yes," Joe said, pushing his chair back.

"I'm Detective Marino." He handed Joe a business card and then moved the chair out from the corner next to the desk, blocking the doorway as he sat down. "I have a few questions about Patricia Miller. Is this a good time?"

"Actually, it isn't. I have to teach a night class tonight, so I was just about to leave for dinner."

The detective didn't budge.

"Dinner will have to wait, Mr. Conrad. This won't take long."

Joe frowned at the detective. "My attorney has advised me not to discuss anything with the police," he lied, wishing he had called Sara's sister after all.

"Look," Detective Marino said, leaning forward. "I'm going to be honest with you. I know you didn't have anything to do with Patricia Miller's murder or kidnapping. You just ain't the type. And you come off as, well, too dumb about criminology to have done it."

Joe laughed. "What I know about criminology I learned by reading Sir Arthur Conan Doyle. You know, Sherlock Holmes mysteries."

"That's what I figured."

"Actually, I guess I've read Raymond Chandler and Dashiell Hammett too. *The Big Sleep? The Maltese Falcon?*"

"Yeah," Marino said. "I've seen those flicks."

"You know, of course, that those films are based on novels."

"Never read the books," the large man said as he shifted his weight in the small chair. Detective Marino withdrew a notepad from the breast pocket of his suit jacket and took out a small gold pen. "I have about a dozen questions, Mr. Conrad, and then you can get your dinner."

"I told you. I'm not talking without my attorney present."

"That's your choice, of course. But between you and I, it ain't helping you any."

"Between you and *me*," Joe corrected.

"Sure," the detective said.

The two men stared stubbornly at each other for a few seconds.

"You got to understand, we got to rule you out as a suspect first before we can proceed with the investigation. Now like I said, I don't think you had anything to do with it. But I gotta tell you, this case is important, and I plan to solve it."

"As I said," Joe repeated, "I'm not talking without my lawyer. Arrest me if you wish."

"No," the detective said, raising his voice. "I don't *wish* to arrest you, damn it! But I do *wish* to get some information from you that might solve this case. I want to find who killed this woman before he kills again."

The force of the detective's words caused Joe to remember the young woman whose dead body he had held.

As if to make his case more convincing, Detective Marino added, "We've had too many cases like this in the Central Valley. Remember Laci Peterson?"

"Look, Detective," Joe said, leaning forward. "I understand your feelings. And believe me when I say this, I also want you to catch this young woman's killer. I have a daughter of my own. But the last time I tried to be a good citizen and talked to the police, a Detective Dunn up in Sacramento made me out to be guilty."

"I know Detective Dunn. He's a good detective. Clears a lot of cases. He was doing it by the book. Grilling you is one way of getting at the truth. And you gotta remember, Mr. Conrad, we're working in the dark here. We got few leads, and we gotta question everybody who's got any connection to the victim."

Joe inspected the detective's face. His large clean-shaven face made him appear earnest. He looked like someone who had worked his way up through the ranks.

"Tell me what *you* know first," Joe said. "Then I'll feel like you're being honest when you say that you don't think I'm guilty."

"It doesn't work that way."

"Then call my attorney, and we'll set up an appointment. I have Thursday off."

The detective's face reddened. "All right. I'll tell you a couple things to show you why I don't like you for this. There's a former acquaintance who used to slap Patricia around a little. There's also been one or two other cases of missing girls in this area. You just don't look like a serial rapist to me. It ain't your style."

Joe smiled. "What is my 'style,' Detective?"

Marino grinned. "*You* read poetry to women. You don't strangle 'em. They might gag on your bullshit, but you don't kill 'em," he said.

Joe laughed. "Okay, Detective, ask me a few questions. I'll answer until I think you're trying to trip me up."

"Fair enough," Marino said, grinning. He opened his notepad again and got ready to write. "I already have details on where you found Patricia. In the creek under the freeway. How did you find the body? I mean, what position was she in, and how did she look?"

"She was facedown. In fact, I couldn't even tell it was a body. It was dark under the overpass, and her shirt was muddy and wet, and her hair looked like moss or something. It didn't look like a person at first."

"Okay. Facedown. What did you do next?"

"When I realized it was a person's body, I panicked and fell into the water. It was frightening. Except for my parents, I've never touched a dead body before."

Detective Marino looked up at Joe. "What happened to your parents?" he asked softly.

"Died when I was in high school. Hit head-on by a drunk driver."

"Sorry to hear that," the detective said. He looked down at his notepad again. "What happened next? Describe the condition of the body."

"I rolled her over to see if she was still alive, I guess. I used to be a lifeguard, so I was thinking about giving her mouth to mouth."

"How did she appear when you rolled her over?"

"Cold and dead and stiff. Her blouse was open. Her bra had been pushed up, I guess by the killer, and hair covered her face."

"Did you notice any bruising on her neck or face?"

"No. I mean, the condition of the skin was kind of bluish anyway. And I was too scared to look very closely at anything."

"What about her blouse? Did you notice whether or not any of the buttons were missing?"

Joe thought for a minute. "No," he said, sighing. "I didn't look very closely at anything. Wait a minute," Joe said. "Don't you guys have her clothes? Can't you inspect her blouse yourself?"

"Yes, of course. But sometimes clothing gets torn or damaged during the removal of the body. It helps if witnesses can establish that the clothing was torn prior to the body being moved."

"I see," Joe said.

"You said her blouse was open when you rolled her over?"

"Right."

"Were her breasts exposed?"

Joe blushed. "Why does *that* matter?"

"If the killer pulled her blouse open wide enough to expose her breasts and push up her bra, then that's a pretty good indication that he also sexually assaulted her. On the other hand, the blouse and bra might have torn open when the body was moved if the killer dragged her by her feet, for example."

"Oh," Joe said. "Yes. Her blouse was about as wide open as it could have been and still be on her body. I actually tried to pull her blouse closed to cover her up a little."

"Why did you do that?"

Joe shook his head. "I don't know exactly. I was embarrassed for her, I guess. I don't think it mattered, though, because she rolled over again when I let go of her."

"I see. What did you do next?"

"Well, as I told Detective Dunn, I pulled her out from under the bridge to see her in better light. And I tried to drag her body out, but I couldn't. I managed to climb up the bank, and I was going to the telephone when the CHP officer arrived."

"Did you go back down to the body after that?"

"No. I showed the officer the body from the bridge. Then I waited in my car until they brought the body up in the black bag."

Detective Marino finished writing, turned a page, and wrote some more.

"Did you know Patricia Miller at all?"

"No!" Joe said firmly. "The only way I might have come into contact with her is a few times when I ate at the restaurant where she worked. I looked at her picture this morning, but I didn't recognize her."

"How did you get her picture?"

Joe motioned toward the computer screen. "I went online and looked up articles about her. There was a pretty good photo of her there."

"Did you know that that picture was taken when she graduated from CLU?"

Joe frowned. "No, I didn't. I've only been teaching here for two and a half years, and I think she graduated the year before I arrived."

"Yes. That's the information I have," the detective admitted.

"Are we almost finished, sir? I've got to get a little dinner before my night class."

"Yes," Detective Marino said. "Just one or two more questions."

"Shoot," Joe said, smiling.

"Do you know a young lady named Autumn Smith?"

Joe's smile faded. "Yes," he admitted. "She's a former student of mine. Why do you ask?"

"Have you ever visited Autumn Smith at her apartment off campus?"

Joe tried to act calm.

"Yes, Detective. Earlier this semester, she asked me to help her with an application for a scholarship. I agreed to help her, but we couldn't find a convenient time to meet on campus. So she invited me over for dinner as a way of thanking me. I met with her for approximately one hour during which time I edited her letter, gave her some advice, and ate the spaghetti she had cooked for us."

"You were inside her apartment for an hour?"

"Yes. I think so. Maybe less than an hour. It was before my night class, so I couldn't stay very long. Even if I had wanted to," Joe added. "What does this have to do with Patricia Miller's death, anyway?"

Detective Marino looked up slowly from his notepad and stared stone-faced at Joe.

"Did you know that Autumn Smith had a roommate?"

"Yes," Joe said. "Her roommate was in the bedroom watching television the entire time I was there. Sort of like a chaperone."

Joe still hadn't guessed.

"Autumn Smith's roommate was Patricia Miller."

CHAPTER SEVEN

Joe collapsed against the back of his chair and closed his eyes. "Oh my god!" he blurted. "Could this get any worse!"

"Mr. Conrad," Detective Marino asked fiercely, "did you know Patricia Miller?"

"No! I never met Autumn's roommate! I had no idea who Autumn's roommate was!"

"Are you sure you didn't start seeing Patricia Miller on the side? Just like you were seeing Autumn Smith?"

Joe stood up. "I wasn't 'seeing' Autumn on the side, damn it! I met with her once to help her. Ask her yourself for God's sakes!"

"I have questioned her. Earlier today, in fact. She was the one who admitted that you two had dinner together."

"Then she also told you that nothing happened. I mean, it wasn't a romantic dinner between a student and a teacher, the way *you're* trying to make it sound."

"Well, Professor. When a college instructor meets a student for a candlelight dinner and drinks wine with an underage girl, that sounds pretty damn romantic."

Joe remembered the dinner. After he helped her with the scholarship letter, she had set the little table, lit a candle, and poured some red wine before he could protest. It was a charming scene. Autumn was one of his favorite students. Had he flirted with her? Had she flirted with him? Yes, she had turned off the lights. Yes, they did sit in the dark and eat and drink together in the candlelight. Yes, he had to admit, it was romantic. It had made him remember his earlier times with Sara, and it had made him long for romantic evenings again.

"Did you tell your wife about this little dinner, Professor?"

Joe decided he was finished talking to the police.

"Call my attorney," Joe said, his voice cracking. He clumsily withdrew his wallet and found one of his sister-in-law's business cards. He handed it over to the detective, his hand trembling. "You and I are finished."

Detective Marino put his notepad away, stood up slowly, pushed the chair back into the corner, and slowly ambled out the door and into the hallway. The hallway was dark. The large man's silhouette looked imposing. Joe sat in the lamplight of his office, stunned, and watched as the big man disappeared down the staircase.

Suddenly, the phone rang, and Joe jerked. He calmed himself for a few seconds and then picked up his phone.

"Joe?" Sara's voice asked weakly.

"Yeah?"

"It's me. How are you doing? Did you call Suzy?"

"No," Joe admitted. "I . . . I've just been grilled by another detective!"

"Did you say anything damaging?"

Joe's heart sank. He pictured Sara's reaction when he confessed having had dinner with a student. Was there any way to keep it from her?

"What's the matter, Joe?"

"It's not good, Sara. They're making me look guilty as hell."

Sara was silent for a few seconds. "Is there something you need to tell me, Joe?"

"Oh god, Sara. I think I'm going to be sick."

"Why? What's going on?"

"I'll have to talk to you about it tonight."

Sara stayed silent.

"I'll try to let the students go early tonight so we can talk when I get home."

"All right, Joe. See you tonight," she said. Then she hung up.

Night had fallen, and Joe sat in the dim light of his office, staring at picture of Sara and Katie on his desk.

Someone turned the hall lights on, and blinding fluorescent light flooded the hallway, causing Joe to wipe the tears away from his eyes and take a deep breath. He went to the restroom, splashed cold water on his face, and then stared at himself in the mirror.

An hour later, after a quick sandwich in the campus coffee shop, Joe was in the classroom, watching it fill up with the adults who were his students. All of them held full-time jobs during the day and came to these classes three nights a week to improve their lives. "To get ahead," they were fond of saying. The diversity of the population helped the university meet goals set by an accreditation committee that had been on campus three years before.

Joe stood at the podium and surveyed his class. This was the best part of his life, right now. Except for Katie.

Facing his students, Joe decided to deal with the news reports right away in order to dispense with it and move on to the course work. Realizing that the teacher was about to speak, the class quieted and faced forward.

"Some of you may have seen the news last night, but in case you haven't, I wanted to tell you what happened before we get to work."

A few students turned to one another, perplexed. Evidently, most of them had not seen the news.

"Yesterday, while I was driving to work, my car overheated. And when I stopped to let the engine cool off, I happened to discover the body of the young lady who's been missing since Thanksgiving. It's been in the news, so I'm sure some of you are familiar with it. The woman's name was Patricia Miller, and it turns out that she used to be a student here."

A few women put their hands up to their mouths.

"Needless to say, it was a very traumatic experience for me. I've never touched a dead body before," Joe said.

"You touched her?" a woman in the front asked.

"I wasn't sure she was dead at first. I tried to do CPR."

"She was in water?" another asked.

"Yes," Joe said. "She was floating facedown in the slough along Interstate 5. Anyway, since yesterday, I've been interviewed about this case by several policemen and a few reporters. And I've been trying to cooperate in order to find whoever killed this woman."

"Then the police think she was definitely murdered?" Nicholas asked. Tall, thin, and good looking, the dark-haired young man appeared to be fascinated.

"Yes. At least that's what the police have indicated."

A few of the women hung their heads. One got some tissue from her purse and wiped her eyes. A few began whispering.

"Look," Joe said. "I know this is very sad news, and I'm sure you can appreciate how shaken up I am, especially since this woman used to be a student here. But we only have tonight and next week to prepare for the final exam, so I think we need to focus on our schoolwork. As hard as that might be."

A few students nodded, but a few others lowered their heads.

"Maybe we should cancel class," Nicholas said, his deep voice softening.

"I did consider doing that," Joe said. "But we have to get some work done."

Some of the students seemed unconvinced.

"I'll let you out early, though," Joe said. "We can do our peer editing of the research paper drafts in the first hour and spend the second hour prepping for the final. How does that sound?"

Many of the students nodded in agreement, and Joe felt relieved. If they had chosen to walk out, what could he do?

"Okay, then, class," Joe instructed. "As difficult as it might be, please forget about Patricia Miller for a couple of hours, and take out the drafts of your research papers."

The students knew the drill. They clumped into groups of three, moved their desks close together, exchanged papers, and began reading and marking on the drafts. Joe went from group to small group to answer their questions and offer advice.

After forty-five minutes, Joe called for a break, and a few students left the classroom. Nicholas approached Joe during the break and started to ask something, but another student raised her hand, so Joe went over to her. He noticed Nicholas leave the classroom with his books and coat.

By 7:40 p.m., everyone except Nicholas had returned and had moved their desks back into straight rows facing Joe. He began his lecture on Plato's dialogue *Crito*, which the students would have to compare to Martin Luther King's "Letter from Birmingham Jail" in the final exam.

He walked the students through the logical arguments that Socrates had made to his friend Crito while in jail. Socrates had been sentenced to death for "corrupting the youth of Athens" by encouraging them to question authority. His friend Crito had come to the jail to beg Socrates to escape the punishment of drinking hemlock, but Socrates argued that he had to face his punishment because a good citizen had to obey the laws of the state.

Summing up as the students wrote furiously, Joe said, "Socrates argues, then, that when we live in a place, especially all our lives, we enter into a pact—an agreement or covenant—with the state to obey its laws. We enjoy the benefits of the laws that the state has provided—the marriage of our parents, their requirement to educate us, the protection from enemies and invaders—and these benefits oblige us to follow the laws of the state."

He paused for a few minutes to let the students catch up.

"If we don't wish to live by the rules of a place, Socrates argues, then we are free to move elsewhere. Socrates raises a thought-provoking question in this dialogue. Why would we want to raise children, Socrates asks, in a place whose laws we do not like?"

As Joe finished, he stared down at his notes. "Why indeed," he said aloud. Though he had taught this dialogue several times, its meaning had never seemed quite as relevant to him. Joe looked up at his students, who were staring at him.

"Well, that's all for tonight," he said. "Revise your research paper carefully—it really is due next week. And please think about the arguments in *Crito* as you read King's 'Letter.' By the way, do you see any similarities between the *Crito* and Martin Luther King's 'Letter from Birmingham Jail'?"

Several students looked down at their books.

"Both were set in a jail cell?" one bright student said.

"Yes." Joe smiled. "Now look for other more significant comparisons. See you next week."

Joe closed his book and erased the outlines he had written on the blackboard at the front of the classroom. The students stuffed books and notebooks into backpacks, put on their coats, and started to file out of the classroom one by one, saying "Good night, Professor Conrad" and "Good lecture, Professor."

"Thank you," he said, erasing the board, his back toward the students.

"Professor Conrad," a deep voice said. "I need to talk to you."

Joe recognized the voice immediately. It belonged to Gary Grimes. Joe had dropped him from the course, which had put the student in danger of being dropped from the special program altogether. Joe did not want to turn around.

"What can I do for you, Mr. Grimes?" Joe asked, still cleaning the board.

"Can we speak in private?"

Joe finally turned around. Grimes hadn't changed. An ex-marine, dishonorably discharged for some reason he hadn't shared with the class, he always appeared to be angry. Although his dark hair was short, it looked greasy. His face was broad and clean shaven, but crude. He wore a black T-shirt under a black sweatshirt and faded black jeans. The classroom was empty, except for Grimes.

"We can talk here, Gary. Class is over."

Grimes stepped closer to the lectern, putting both hands on it.

"I want you to reinstate me in the course."

Joe smelled liquor on his breath.

"Gary, the semester's almost over. You've missed six weeks of classes. Even if I wanted to let you back in, there's no way you could make up the work you've missed." Joe watched the man's face tighten.

"Kicking me out wasn't fair."

"You ridiculed other students every time they spoke!"

"I was defending my position!"

"But your attacks were personal—against the students, not their arguments, Gary," Joe said, lowering his voice.

"They were attacking me!"

"Not you personally," Joe tried to explain. "They defended their positions on issues by offering counterarguments, not by resorting to personal attacks and insults."

"When you care about an issue, it becomes part of you." Grimes banged his fist on the desk. "Ergo, any attack of your stance *is* an attack on you!"

Joe had forgotten the way Grimes used "ergo" to punctuate his statements, an irritating affectation.

"Look, Mr. Grimes. I can't reinstate you. Try again next semester. Maybe you'll have a better experience."

Grimes pulled his hands away from the podium and strolled around the desk closer to Joe.

"You *are* going to reinstate me, Professor. I'm not taking no for an answer."

Joe backed away and kept the desk between them.

"Stop advancing on me, Gary, or I'll call campus security."

"You're involved with that murder that's been on TV. I saw your interview last night, and I seen the newspaper stories too." Grimes still circled the desk as did Joe.

"What in the hell does *that* have to do with reinstating?" Joe yelled. He hoped his loud voice would attract someone.

"Well, Mr. Conrad, by dropping me, you caused me to go on academic probation. I'm not going to be forced out of another fucking college!" Grimes yelled.

Joe was close enough to the classroom door to make a run for it.

"Maybe we could work out an incomplete, Gary," Joe said calmly. "Come by my office in the morning, and we can fill out the paperwork."

Grimes grinned.

"You think I'm stupid? You really think you can fool me with that condescending punk-ass voice of yours?"

"Gary," Joe said firmly. "If you go much further with this, I'll have you expelled."

Grimes threw up his hands in mock terror.

"Oooh! You're scarin' me, Professor!"

Joe stepped closer to the door.

"You're going to reinstate me, and you're going to give me a B in the course. I ain't greedy. I deserve an A, but I'll settle for a B."

Joe took a deep breath and stood up straight. He'd had enough macho crap in the past twenty-four hours to last a lifetime.

"What the hell makes you think I'd do that?"

"'Cause if you don't, I'll tell the police I seen you with Patricia Miller. That you and her was meeting secretly. I'll say I seen you with her on the night she disappeared!"

Joe stopped.

"Got you thinkin' now, don't I, bitch?" Grimes hissed.

Joe stood there.

"Do what you want, asshole," Joe said, turning toward the door. "I'm leaving."

Blinding pain exploded in Joe's head. He staggered sideways, and then another punch caught his other temple.

Joe managed to turn around, trying to raise his fists when a third punch slammed against his lips and teeth. Instantly, blood filled his mouth. He saw Grimes throw another fist, so he ducked just in time, punching Grimes in the gut with all his might.

Grimes stumbled back a few steps then screamed, "I'm going to kill you, bitch!"

As Grimes rushed toward him, Joe stepped aside and used his hands to push Grimes away. Off balance, Grimes stumbled and fell. Joe pushed the heavy wooden lectern over onto Grimes' body, then he ran to his office and slammed the door closed, locking it. He picked up the phone and started to dial 911, but he hesitated. *Do I really want police again?* With the phone to his ear, he turned and looked out the window of his door. The hallway outside was clear, but he couldn't see the door to the classroom.

Grimes suddenly appeared at the window, rage in his eyes.

He rattled the door then drew his arm back as if to smash the glass. Joe turned away, covering his eyes, and waited for the sound.

After a few seconds in darkness, Joe opened his eyes and turned around. Grimes was gone. The telephone receiver began beeping in Joe's ear, startling him, so he hung it up.

He stood still for several minutes, waiting for Grimes to reappear. Then he sat down and stared at the door.

Is it safe? he wondered. He thought of Dustin Hoffman in *Marathon Man*.

"Is it safe?" he said aloud. "Yes, it's very, very safe," Joe said, impersonating Hoffman's voice. He laughed aloud, almost hysterically. "Is it safe?" he repeated, mocking the cruel Nazi dentist. "No. It's not safe," he said in Hoffman's voice.

Joe looked up the number of campus police and called.

"This is Professor Conrad," he said. "I'm on the third floor of Anderson Hall. I need an escort to my car. I'm being harassed by an angry student."

Fifteen minutes later, a young security guard showed up outside Joe's office. The guard was no more than twenty-two, skinny and frightened. Joe grinned when he opened the door.

"Are you alone?"

"Yes, sir."

"Well, the student who attacked me is dressed in black. He's got short hair and looks like a marine."

"How did he attack you, sir? We'll need to fill out a report."

Joe pictured going to the campus police station and spending hours telling another story.

"Look," Joe told the kid. "I've got a long drive home, and I don't want to waste my time filling out forms. Let's just say he verbally assaulted me."

"I can see the blood on your lip and chin, sir," the kid said. "And you've got a goose egg on your right temple."

"Well, I'm going home. You can either walk me to my car, or you can leave me alone. But I'm not filling out any paperwork tonight. You can't imagine the hell I've been through the past few days!"

"Okay, sir," the young guard said. "Take it easy. I'll get you to your car."

As they walked toward the staircase, the young guard reached over and patted Joe's back. Joe looked over at the young man and smiled.

"Take out your pepper spray, Officer," Joe said, still smiling. "You might need it."

As Joe drove home, he touched his lips and felt the bump on his temple. The freeway wasn't very crowded, and north of Stockton, fog was beginning to rise from the wet fields. Before Joe realized it, he was passing Lost Slough again. The fog hung over the slough eerily, and Joe shuddered. One week ago, Patricia Miller had been murdered near this spot.

CHAPTER EIGHT

The Safeway on Kettleman Lane in Lodi was busy Tuesday night until ten-thirty. By eleven, the store was empty, so Lilly Nguyen clocked out to walk home after working a six-hour shift bagging groceries. She put on her secondhand goose-down ski jacket and said goodbye to her manager as she walked toward one of the front doors of the large store.

"Go home and get some sleep, Lilly," her manager called. He was a kind but strict supervisor who reminded Lilly of her father though he was Caucasian.

"Two hours of calculus waiting for me," she replied, thinking how much she hated this final year of high school.

"Oh, Lilly!" he said, sounding concerned.

An older woman, one of the checkers, smiled and called "Good night!" as Lilly went out the door.

"Good night, Dotty," Lilly replied, trying to smile. Tired, she wanted to go home, finish her schoolwork, and climb into bed. As she stepped into the chilly air, she noticed the layers of fog in the parking lot.

The fog was cold and damp; and Lilly, a short slender girl with long black hair, zipped her jacket and squinted as she marched across the almost-empty parking lot. Home was in a small neighborhood twelve blocks from the store. Her parents did not allow her to drive, so she usually either walked or got rides with friends from school when she went to work. She felt her hair. She hated it going limp in the damp fog, so she walked quickly.

A car engine startled her. Lilly glanced back across the parking lot in time to see the car's headlights come on. She grew frightened. Sometimes, when she walked home, men pulled over and offered her a ride; but she never accepted. The men leered at her as if she were a prostitute. At least, that's the way they made her feel. The car behind her slowly headed toward the parking lot exit. Soon, it pulled out, heading west on Kettleman, its red taillights disappearing in the fog.

Lilly breathed a sigh of relief. She had to walk along Kettleman Road for five blocks before she could turn onto the street to her house. As she walked along Kettleman, she lit a cigarette. Her parents demanded that she become a doctor or a pharmacist. She had other ideas.

She wanted to go to LA. She wanted to change her hair, wear wild clothes, and be anonymous. She wanted to get lost in large crowds, party, and go crazy.

As Lilly turned off of Kettleman, she danced a little as she walked, pretending she was at some wild Hollywood party.

A car pulled over beside her, and she caught herself, embarrassed. The driver of the car leaned over, rolling the window down on the passenger side.

"Hello, Lilly," the driver called out.

The voice sounded familiar, so she stopped and leaned in to look at the driver. She didn't recognize him at first, but he could have been a customer.

"I'm headed toward your house if you want a lift," the man said. He sounded friendly enough, but Lilly still didn't recognize him.

"No, thanks," she said politely. "I enjoy the walk."

"Sure," agreed the man. "Got to let off steam after a hard day at work. Say hello to your parents for me."

The man rolled up the window and drove away. Lilly watched as the car turned a corner. The car looked familiar, and Lilly was trying to remember where she had seen the man. He must be a regular customer.

As she walked farther down the street, she noticed a house with Christmas lights strung along the eaves. "Not even December!" she said aloud. "Too early!"

The cheerful Christmas lights suddenly went off, leaving the street a little darker and somehow sadder. A single streetlight held off the darkness.

She reached into her jacket pocket and extracted another cigarette from the pack. She stopped momentarily to get the cigarette lit when a gloved hand knocked it from her mouth.

"I don't like women to smoke," a man's voice said.

Those were the last words Lilly heard. The blow to the back of her head stunned her, and she collapsed to the ground.

She watched as her unlit cigarette roll off the curb into the gutter in front of her as she struggled to stand. Another blow slammed into her head, and she was plunged into blackness.

She came to fighting for breath. Duct tape covered her mouth. In a car. Seat belt across her and her hands bound with duct tape, she squirmed as the man wrapped tape around her ankles. She kicked but only banged her shins on the dashboard.

A fist hit her jaw. Again, she blacked out.

Lilly opened her eyes while being pulled out of the car by her wrists. The man dragged her from the car through wet grass then down an embankment. Pitch black, but Lilly could see fog being blown across the sky above. She struggled, weak and nauseated.

He stopped dragging her, and she arched her neck to see his head silhouetted in the darkness. He dropped her and walked around by her feet. He sat on her, his weight crushing the breath out of her body, and unzipped her jacket. She squirmed, but he was too heavy. He tore open her shirt and unhooked her bra, running his hands over her small breasts. No one had ever touched her there. She tried to scream, but it was no use.

This is how I lose my virginity?

Streams of tears fell from her eyes as she convulsed spasmodically.

"Stop!" he hissed.

But she could not. "Mama, Papa," she tried to say under the tape.

The man slapped her, but she only cried harder. Then she felt his hands on her neck, squeezing until blackness overwhelmed her.

As she came to, her body tingled and stung as when an arm loses circulation. She gradually became conscious again, but she was shivering.

Her pants were off, she realized; and he was on top of her, her legs spread and his penis inside. She smelled his sour breath as he groaned on top of her. She sobbed again, quietly, as she felt him finish and go limp. His weight squeezed the breath out of her.

How dare he!

She tried to fight him, but he was much larger. *What if I get pregnant? What if he has AIDS?*

He rolled off and lay beside her. She looked down at him. Weird. No pubic hair. He must shave it off. At least he was wearing a condom. For a moment, Lilly felt relief. She wouldn't get a disease.

It didn't matter. She knew he would kill her.

She looked at his face as he lay beside her. His eyes were closed, and he was smiling. *Smiling!*

Rolling over and kneeling quickly, she made a fist with her taped hands and struck the man's face as hard as she could. From her knees, she landed three good blows to his temple before he rolled away.

He was trying to stand, but his pants dropped around his ankles, and he fell backward.

She rocked back and sprang to her feet.

The tape had been removed from her ankles, so she was able to run. She ran fast through the wet grass, hoping to disappear into the heavy fog.

Maybe I can *get away.*

She pushed through a thicket of tall reeds. *Good cover*, she thought.

Suddenly, she dropped into waist-deep water and lost her balance. Her head went under, and her nose filled with water. She managed to get her feet back under herself. As she pushed up out of the water, she coughed and gagged, tearing at the tape on her mouth. She waded back to shore, but the embankment was steep and slippery. She fell again, going under before regaining her balance.

Something slimy, a snake, crawled over the bare skin of her neck as she stood. She shook it off and tried to climb out of the freezing water.

A loud splash, and as she turned around, she saw the monstrous silhouette wading toward her. She took two steps in the opposite direction before he caught her.

Lilly reached out for the black snake she'd just thrown off. She grabbed it and swung it back at the man. The snake's head slapped the man across the face. He leaned backward but then lunged after her. She whipped him with the snake, but it slipped free.

The rapist was too strong. Lilly Nguyen folded under his weight. He held her head under the dark water until she went limp. Even with her eyes open, she could see nothing in the cold, cold water. She pretended to be dead, staying limp and perfectly still, hoping he would let go and leave; but he held her down firmly for as long as it took to be sure.

Unable to hold her breath any longer, Lilly closed her eyes as, finally, the cold darkness filled her.

CHAPTER NINE

When Joe arrived home that night, Sara was sitting in the living room, watching the local news and smoking a cigarette. Sara had smoked in Louisiana before they got married, but she had quit when she realized she was pregnant, and she hadn't taken it up again. Until now.

"You know I don't like it when you smoke, Sara," Joe told her.

She blew a stream of smoke toward him, crushing out the cigarette in the ashtray on the table next to her chair.

"They said on the news tonight that Patricia Miller was sexually assaulted before she was strangled."

"Horrible," Joe said, taking off his coat. "Is Katie asleep?"

"It's almost eleven, Joe. Of course she's asleep."

Sara looked more closely at Joe's face.

"God, Joe, what happened?"

He started to sit on the edge of the coffee table facing her, but she took his hand and led him into the bathroom, turning on the light and drawing him over to the sink.

"Remember that obnoxious student I had to drop?"

"Yeah." Sara ran water over a washcloth and then dabbed Joe's lower lip with it. "The white supremacist?"

"Yeah. Gary Grimes. He showed up after class tonight and demanded I reinstate him."

Sara looked at him quizzically, still cleaning his face. Dried blood caked his chin.

"I take it you turned him down."

"He wanted me to give him a B in the course!"

Sara laughed. "Huh, a B?" she said. "Don't students usually demand an A?"

"He threatened me."

"Threatened you how?"

"He said he would tell the cops that he had seen me last Tuesday night with Patricia Miller."

Sara stopped cleaning Joe's face.

"Did he, Joe? Did he see you with Patricia Miller?"

"Of course not!"

Sara stared at him and then noticed his temple.

"Jesus. You've got a goose egg on the side of your head!"

Sara finished cleaning the blood from his face and led him into the kitchen. She sat him down at the table and went to the freezer where she pulled an icetray out and began placing ice in a dishtowel.

Joe held the ice against his temple, and Sara sat down facing him.

"Did you report this?"

"No," Joe said. "I've had enough police for a while."

Then Joe recalled the visit from Detective Marino, and he looked at the floor.

"What's wrong? I'm going to find out sooner or later."

Joe drew a deep breath. He took Sara's hand, which she gave reluctantly.

"A detective from the Stockton Police paid me a visit today. He dropped a bombshell on me. You won't believe this, Sara," Joe said, shaking his head. "Last fall, one of my students asked me to help her with some application essays she was writing for a scholarship."

Joe looked at Sara's face. His mouth was going dry.

"Go on," she said.

"Well, our schedules didn't match very well, so we decided to meet around dinnertime before my night class. She invited me to dinner as a way of thanking me."

"Let me guess," Sara said, pulling her hand away. "This student who had to have *your special* help was Patricia Miller!'

"No no! It was a girl named Autumn Smith."

"Okay," Sara said, trying to understand. "So you went out to dinner with one of your students."

"No. I went to her apartment to help her, and we had a quick dinner before I went to class."

"You went to a student's apartment?"

"Yes, Sara. I was there only as long as it took to edit her application letter and eat dinner. I went to class right after we finished eating."

"Did you screw her, Joe?"

"No!"

Sara stood up and walked away, wiping her face.

"How could you?"

"She wanted my help. She made me feel needed. Lord knows, I haven't been treated like that around here lately."

Still wiping her eyes, Sara turned around. "I don't understand," she said. "What does this little tryst have to do with Patricia Miller?"

Joe shook his head in disbelief again. "There was no tryst! The girl I helped had a roommate. I never saw the roommate, but she was in the apartment while I was helping Autumn."

"Patricia Miller was this girl's roommate?"

"Yes," Joe said. "Can you believe it?"

Sara simply stared at Joe.

"No, Joe," she finally said. "No, I can't believe it. I can't believe any of it!" Sara stomped into the living room. "Goddamn you, Joe!"

"Quiet, Sara. You'll wake up Katie."

"Good! She *should* wake up," Sara screamed. "I'm finally waking up. Why shouldn't your daughter wake up and find out what kind of sorry son of a bitch her father is?"

"Sara," Joe pleaded, "nothing happened."

"You sound like Bill fucking Clinton!"

"There's a big difference, Sara. I didn't actually have sex with *my* intern!"

"Neither did *he*, according to him!"

Joe grabbed Sara's shoulders and pulled her toward him. "I love *you*! And I need *you*, Sara."

Tears filling her eyes, Sara shook her head. "I don't think I can. I don't think I trust you anymore."

The words stunned Joe.

"You've got to, Sara."

"I don't think I even love you anymore."

Her body went limp. Saying the words out loud made them real. He dropped his arms and stepped back, staring at her in disbelief. Sara wiped her eyes with the palms of her hands.

Joe shook his head and tried to speak. "I . . . I'm going to sleep out here tonight. On the sofa."

"Good."

"Maybe you'll feel different in the morning."

Sara turned and walked slowly toward the hallway. "By the way," she said, stopping. "The police called this afternoon. We can pick up the Mustang in the morning. They're finished with it."

Joe nodded. "Did they find anything?"

"They didn't say," Sara told him. "Did you expect them to find something?"

"Of course not."

Sara stared at his face for a few seconds.

"Good night, Joe."

Joe said nothing. He watched her walk into the darkness of the little hallway that led past their sleeping daughter's bedroom. Then Joe went to the hall closet and pulled a comforter off the top shelf. He made a bed for himself on the couch then went to the kitchen to turn off the light. The dishes were washed and stacked neatly on the wooden rack to dry. Three of Katie's crayon drawings were stuck to the refrigerator door with magnets. The images lingered in his mind even after he switched off the light.

Then he went to the bathroom and inspected his swollen lip and bruised face. "You're losing your family, Joe," he told himself.

Joe lay in the darkness of the living room, his mind swirling.

In the morning, Joe had to rush in order to leave with Sara and Katie. For Katie's sake, Sara and Joe acted as if nothing was wrong. They loaded Katie into the car and drove her to the preschool. Joe signed her in, hugging her fiercely before leaving her there. Walking back out to the car on a cold gray morning, he fought back tears. It was bad enough to leave Katie there for the day. How hard would it be to leave Katie for weeks or months if Sara left him? He was sure Sara would move back to Louisiana if they divorced. Maybe he would too. After all, it looked as if he'd have no job at CLU after the spring semester.

As Sara drove the Escort to Sacramento, Joe tried not to watch as she occasionally wiped tears from her cheeks. She remained silent. Traffic on the freeway was heavy as it was on the streets of Sacramento. Before Joe climbed out of the car at the police station, he leaned over and tried to kiss Sara goodbye, but she turned away.

"I'll see you tonight," she said coldly.

Joe stood on the sidewalk and watched her drive off. The air was cold and damp, so Joe held his tweed sports jacket closed as he walked up the steps to the office. It took him half an hour to learn that he had to walk eight blocks to get his car.

At first, the officer at the impound lot expected Joe to pay $120 to have the car released; but Joe protested, telling the overweight man to call Detective Dunn. The officer walked to his desk, made the call, and then came back with Joe's keys. When Joe found his car among dozens of others in the lot, he opened the door and saw various swirls of powder covering the surfaces, including the driver's seat. He checked the backseat, but his briefcase was missing. He opened the trunk but found no briefcase there either. For a moment, he contemplated leaving without it, but he walked back to the office.

"There was a briefcase in my car when you guys confiscated it. Where is it?"

The officer looked annoyed. He had just filed Joe's paperwork, so he had to dig it out of drawer again.

"Oh yeah," he said. "It's back in the property room."

The officer meandered back behind the tall shelves on the other side of the counter. Joe could follow his casual progress in a concave mirror up in one corner of the office. Soon, the officer came back with Joe's briefcase, which also had swirls of powder on the handle and latches. Resting the briefcase flat on the countertop, Joe opened it. Everything was there, even the stacks of student papers.

Joe sighed, saying, "Oh well."

"Anything missin'?" the heavy officer asked.

"I was hoping you guys graded these essays for me."

The officer stared at Joe without expression.

During the drive down I-5 that morning, Joe once again slowed as he came to Lost Slough. No cars parked there today. Joe examined the stark black trees. A hawk roosted on a bare branch close to the roadside. It cocked its head sharply as Joe passed, as if to inspect him, but then it reached a talon up to its mouth, and Joe saw a field mouse still struggling in its beak.

Joe inspected the flat landscape and stark trees just south of Lost Slough. It was an unfarmed parcel of land, a tangle of brush. The next freeway bridge spanned Middle Slough, which seemed somehow less threatening. He had a sudden urge to stop and explore the boggy forest. He used to explore similar wooded areas in Louisiana as a young boy. But duty called.

Fifteen minutes later, the needle of the temperature gauge climbed slowly into the red, and Joe remembered that he had not yet fixed the Mustang. *How stupid*, he thought. He was almost to the Hammer Lane exit, so he risked overheating the engine and drove the car straight to West Lane Automotive, a repair shop he had used before, within walking distance of campus. After dropping off the Mustang, he walked through the damp air to Central Lutheran University.

Campus bustled with students hurrying to their eight-thirty classes. Several waved and said hello. In his office, after making coffee, Joe began grading the stack of essays. At ten o'clock, his office door creaked open; and Joe's head jerked up, startled by the noise. He thought it might be Gary Grimes back for round two.

"You startled me."

"Oh, I'm sorry, Joe. Can I steal some coffee?" Cassandra Johnson asked.

A visiting poet hired to fill in for the creative writing instructor who was on sabbatical, Cass was a statuesque African American woman with long black hair and striking features. In her hand was an unusual coffee mug, one she'd made in a pottery class, Joe suspected.

"It's not fresh."

"That's okay. Just need some caffeine to get through my next class."

After Joe poured the coffee, Cass took the seat next to his desk.

"I'm going through a stagnant period with my writing, and it's beginning to worry me," the poet said. She had a way of frowning as she spoke. Even minor concerns seemed serious. "I can't write during the holidays. Too much normalcy."

Joe put his pen down and removed his glasses. "Normalcy? I wish my life could get back to normal."

"What do you mean?"

"You haven't seen the news?"

"No. What's going on?"

"Nothing much," Joe laughed. "I'm just under suspicion for the rape and murder of a former student."

Cass's mouth literally dropped open.

"You're not serious!"

"I wish I weren't," Joe said. He recapped the events of the last two days, even the incident with Gary Grimes, leaving out a few incriminating details. Cassandra sipped the stale coffee as she listened.

"What was the murdered woman's name?" Cassandra asked.

"Patricia Miller. There's been a lot of news about her disappearance. And her parents posted a reward to find her. You haven't seen the news?"

"I don't watch the news," Cass said, frowning. "Too depressing. Especially after September 11."

"Don't you read the paper?"

"Sometimes, but mostly the *LA Times*."

Cassandra was on leave from UC-Santa Barbara where she had been teaching creative writing after finishing her MFA at Iowa State University. She had arrived last fall, lean and dark, a true southern California beauty who might have been a fashion model. Few in the CLU English department had taken her seriously until she gave a reading of her poetry at the Fall Convocation. Some had compared her poetry to Maya Angelou's; others to Nikki Giovanni's. Joe recognized Plath and Sexton. Joe had liked her from the start and was glad her office was next to his.

"Patricia Miller," Cass repeated. "That name sounds familiar. Maybe she was one of my students."

"Not likely. She graduated three years ago."

Cassandra turned toward the window, thinking.

"You must have heard it on the news, then."

Cass glanced at the time. A man's watch dangled loosely around her wrist like a heavy bracelet.

"Got to get ready," she said, standing. Before pulling the door closed as Joe put his glasses back on, Cass leaned back into the office. "You didn't kill her, did you?"

"Of course I did!" Joe said, smiling. "Didn't you know? I'm Jack the Ripper, reincarnated! No, better yet, I'm the Boston Strangler."

"You mean the Stockton Strangler, don't you?"

In class that morning, Joe's young students listened eagerly as he explained finding the body and described being questioned by police. Several had seen the TV interview and had read the newspaper stories. Joe had never seen so many eighteen-year-olds in such rapt attention. After talking about his own predicament, Joe tried to focus the class on their assigned reading.

"Now we have to do some preparation for the final exam, especially since we've lost a day. Please open your books to page 718 so we can continue *Hamlet*."

The students dutifully, if reluctantly, opened the massive textbooks to the thin pages of the great tragedy. Joe sat on the desk in front of the class.

"One question on the final will ask you to compare and contrast the soliloquies in the play. Most people focus on the 'To be or not to be' soliloquy in which Hamlet clearly contemplates suicide but resolves to face his 'sea of troubles' and the 'thousand natural shocks that flesh is heir to.' But what soliloquy provides more insight into the plot and Hamlet's motivation?"

Most of the students stared blankly. A few rifled through the pages of the book.

Marco raised his hand. "Maybe the first one?"

"You mean the one that begins, 'O that this too too solid flesh would melt, / Thaw, and resolve itself into a dew?'"

"Yeah," Marco said. "The melting flesh one."

"Perhaps. Make your case. How does it reveal plot and motive?"

"Well, Hamlet is rippin' on his mom for not staying loyal to the old man."

Several students laughed, but Marco's translation was exciting to Joe. "Go on," he instructed.

Marco had returned to college after six years in the army, and his determination had impressed Joe, even if he didn't always know how to phrase his ideas properly. He seemed uncomfortable around the younger students, but also determined.

"Well, Hamlet says that his mother used to hang all over his father, Hamlet senior. But yet now that Dad's dead, she seems to be hanging all over the king's bro."

"Exactly. And how does that make young Hamlet feel?"

"He's pissed! I can relate too, man. When my pops was killed, my mom hooked up with this other dude about six months later. I was pissed too. Just like Hamlet."

The class laughed.

Joe quieted them. "How do you know he's angry?"

A blonde named Laurie spoke up, "Hamlet compares his mother to an animal, a mute animal."

"Good." Joe smiled at her.

Another student thumbed through the pages to find the soliloquy. "Where does he do *that*?"

Laurie answered defensively, "In that line that goes 'O God, a beast that wants discourse of reason / Would have mourned longer!'"

"Very good," Joe responded. "But why does it upset Hamlet so much that his mother married his uncle?"

The room fell silent as students read through the words again.

"Consider how Hamlet felt about his father in contrast to the way he regards his uncle," Joe instructed.

Marco's hand went up, and Joe nodded. The handsome Latino student began reading. "'So excellent a king, that was to this / Hyperion to a satyr.' That sounds like a slam against the uncle, Professor, but what's it mean? What's a Hyperion?"

"Good question, Marco."

"For that matter, what's a satyr?" Laurie asked.

"That I know," said Marco. "I looked it up. It's a creature that's half goat and half human. And the dictionary said it was 'lascivious.' What's that mean, Professor?"

"It means sex crazed, Marco," said Laurie. "Like you!"

The other students laughed. Laurie smiled at Marco, but he blushed.

"Why don't you look up 'Hyperion' and share the meanings with the class on Friday. But you're right, Marco. To call someone Hyperion is high praise."

Marco read aloud, "'My father's brother, but no more like my father / Than I to Hercules.' He calls his old man Hercules. He thought pretty high of the old man, Professor Conrad."

"Indeed," said Joe. "Hamlet loved and respected his father dearly, much more than he loved his uncle. These feelings, combined with his contempt for his mother—who, he believes, has shown terrible disrespect for her husband—drives Hamlet to both suicidal and homicidal thoughts."

"Wow," Marco said. "Hatred and revenge. Maybe that's what caused somebody to kill that waitress you found, Professor."

Joe stared at Marco's intense face. A chill traveled down his back.

"Remember Hamlet's words, Marco? At the end of his first soliloquy?" The student shook his head. "It is not, nor it cannot come to good."

CHAPTER TEN

After his eleven o'clock class, Joe returned to his office and ate lunch while grading papers for his afternoon class. At about one o'clock, he made a fresh pot of coffee and offered Cassandra another cup. She was in her office next door, her glasses on, reading typed poems under lamplight.

"Have you figured out why that name sounded familiar?" Joe asked while pouring coffee into her cup.

She let her glasses drop to her breasts, held by a gold chain at their stems, and looked at him squarely.

"As a matter of fact, I have. One of my students dedicated a poem to a Patricia Miller."

"I wonder if it's the same person."

"It might just be," Cass replied seriously. "I was going to ask my student this morning, but she wasn't in class."

"Who's the student?"

"A girl named Autumn," said Cassandra.

"Autumn Smith?"

"Do you know her, Joe?"

"Yes," Joe replied. "She's a former student of mine. She was Patricia Miller's roommate."

It was Cass's turn to look surprised now. She rocked back in her desk chair, an antique oak chair with a rounded back whose rusty metal springs creaked loudly when pushed too far.

"What kind of poem was it? Do you still have a copy?"

"No, I returned it to Autumn. But it's listed in the table of contents of the portfolio she's going to submit next week. That's how I confirmed the name. The dedication to Patricia Miller is listed under the title."

"What's the title?" Joe asked.

Cassandra reached around to the bookshelves beside her desk and pulled a colorful folder off a stack. Autumn's folder was covered with a print of fall-colored leaves—reds, golds, yellows, browns. Cass opened the folder and showed Joe the title as she read it to him.

"'Fantasy Lover.' It was, if I remember it correctly, a very sensual description of imagined lovemaking between two women. It was one of my assignments, to imagine yourself as another kind of person. I encourage white students to write from the perspectives of blacks, Asians, and Latinos. Women to write as men, men to write as women. They write three poems from three different ethnic or gender roles, and then we select one for the portfolio . . ."

Joe was barely listening. Was this poem good news or bad news for him?

"What are you thinking, Joe?"

"I'm not sure what this means," he replied. "Maybe Autumn is somehow connected to Patricia Miller's murder."

"How?"

"Well, suppose Autumn's poem was not fantasy, but reality. Maybe they had experimented with each other, but Patricia wasn't into it and threatened to move out. Maybe Autumn killed her."

"Autumn?" Cass laughed. "She's tiny! Besides, she's the sweetest thing. She couldn't bring herself to slap somebody, let alone dump somebody into a river."

"Maybe she had a boyfriend do it," Joe said, trying to puzzle through the scenarios. "Or better yet, maybe one of Patricia's old boyfriends learned about the girls' affair and got jealous. Maybe an old boyfriend killed Patricia Miller because she dumped him for a girl. *That* would upset a lot of guys!"

Joe watched as Cassandra sat with the lamplight on her face, apparently thinking through the scenarios he'd suggested. She cupped her hands around her coffee cup, blew steam from the coffee, and sipped it. Then she looked up resignedly.

"Or the poem is exactly what it is purported to be—a fantasy. And it has nothing to do with Patricia Miller's death."

"True," Joe had to admit. "Still, I'd like to see that poem. And I can name two police detectives who might be interested too."

"Well, if Autumn comes to class Friday, I'll ask her to bring me a copy. Of course, when she finds out her roommate's been murdered, she's going to be upset."

"She already knows," Joe offered. "When that detective questioned me yesterday, he said he'd already spoken to Autumn."

"That explains why she wasn't in class today."

Cass needed to get back to work, so Joe returned to his office and tried to focus on grading his own students' papers. The coffee helped. Forty minutes later, his telephone rang. Hoping it was Sara, Joe answered.

Jan Lykert's voice didn't please him. "I'm doing a follow-up about Patricia Miller, and I have a few questions."

"No comment," Joe replied sharply.

"But, Mr. Conrad, we've all but cleared you as a suspect. So it's in your best interest to provide a few comments."

"What do you mean?"

"Well, I can't go into detail. But based on what police have told me, you just don't look like a good suspect for this."

"Are you going to write that?"

"I'd like to, but I need a few statements from you first."

Joe sat quietly weighing whether he should trust this woman who had already implicated him once. *I'm smarter than she is*, he told himself.

"What's your first question?"

"It's an easy one. I just want to know if you taught your Tuesday night class last night."

Joe smiled, wondering. "Why do you ask?"

"You know. 'Professor Conrad returns to a normal life after being cleared of suspicion.' That kind of thing."

"Yes, I taught last night."

"What time did you leave campus?"

"Why?"

"Well, you have to drive back and forth almost every day past the spot where you found the dead body of Patricia Miller. That must be unnerving for you. I just thought it would be colorful to describe that in a story."

It suddenly dawned on Joe that, for the rest of the time he would teach at CLU and live in Davis, he would have to pass that spot. It gave him a creepy sensation.

"I left campus about nine o'clock, I guess," Joe said.

"What's your route home?"

"What do you mean?"

"Do you always take I-5? Do you ever take Highway 99?"

"I always go up Interstate 5."

"Do you ever get off the freeway, maybe to buy gas at the truck stop on Highway 12?"

"Sometimes."

"Did you happen to stop for gas there last night, Professor Conrad?"

Where is she going with this? Joe recalled Sara's admonition: "No stops on the way home, Joe."

"Why are you asking?"

"Just trying to get an idea about your normal commute."

"Sorry, but you don't have a lot of credibility with me at this point."

"Well, tell me what time you arrived home in Davis, then."

"A little after ten," Joe replied before he could stop himself. "Why?"

"Ten? Are you sure it wasn't later than that?"

"It was a little after ten. I'm sure," Joe said, exasperated.

"Maybe it was after twelve midnight?" the reporter asked. "That's after ten."

"No. It was about 10:15 or 10:20."

"Can anyone verify that?"

"My wife can. She was awake when I got home."

"You know, Professor Conrad, I tried calling your wife a few minutes ago to ask her what time you got home. But her school said she wasn't available."

"She's in the classroom all day. Some of us do an honest day's work, you know," Joe scoffed. "We don't sit at our computers making up lies."

"And some of us are serious journalists with a serious job to do, Professor Conrad," the reporter snorted. "I have one more question. Did you pick up a girl last night on your way home?"

"What?"

"Did you pick up a girl in Lodi last night?"

"Of course not," Joe said loudly. "What the hell's going on?"

"Another girl has gone missing," the reporter told him. "A Vietnamese girl named Lilly Nguyen. She lived in Lodi, which is on your way home."

He suddenly understood. Another girl missing on another Tuesday night, and he had driven by the town where it had happened.

"Is she a student at CLU?"

"No, Professor Conrad. She's a young girl, a high school student."

"Oh."

"Her parents reported her missing early this morning. She was last seen leaving the store where she works. She usually walks home."

Joe closed his eyes, remembering the stiff, cold, bloated body of Patricia Miller.

"Maybe she just ran away."

"Maybe," the reporter said. "Or maybe she was picked up by the same person who killed Patricia. Maybe that person has her tied up somewhere. If she's still alive, then the person who took her would be doing himself a favor by releasing her, Professor."

"You can't really believe I had anything to do with this, can you?" Joe asked. "I mean, really. I have a daughter of my own for God's sake!"

"Yes, I know, Professor. Believe me. I hope to God you didn't have anything to do with this for your daughter's sake. But God help her if you did."

This reporter seemed convinced he was guilty.

"For the record, Mr. Conrad, did you pick up a girl last night?"

"For the record, Ms. Lykert, screw you."

Joe slammed the phone down in its cradle. Immediately, he regretted having said it. He had forty minutes before his next class, but try as he might, he could not focus on grading more essays. He decided to go downstairs and walk from the campus to the repair shop to get some air. As Joe descended the stairs, Craig Richmond was climbing them.

"You had some excitement last night, I hear," Craig said.

Joe stopped on the landing. "What do you mean?" he asked, thinking Craig somehow knew about the missing Lodi student.

"I just came from Dr. Thorne's office. Campus police reported your run-in with a student last night."

"Oh, that," Joe said. "Gary Grimes. A hothead. He wanted me to gift him with a B in a course he hasn't attended for over six weeks."

"Bad luck for you, Conrad," Craig said. "The student is filing charges against you for assault and battery."

"What?" Joe yelled. "He attacked me! If anyone should file charges, it should be me."

"Says you attacked him with the lectern."

"Yeah. After he hit me in the face three times," Joe said. "Unbelievable!"

"This just isn't your week, Joseph," Craig said, continuing his ascent.

Joe saw symbolism.

Craig's career was ascending while Joe's was rapidly heading for the toilet. He tried to laugh, but rage swept through him suddenly. He wanted to find Gary Grimes and kick his head in.

"Now could I drink hot blood!" he said.

Joe contemplated going into the department chair's office to explain what had really happened, but instead, he went outside and walked through the campus. The sky was gray, the air still damp. Joe longed for the sun.

A few students stared at Joe as if they could see all the trouble he was in as if, like Hester Prynne, he wore a scarlet letter on his chest. He walked briskly off campus to the auto shop, learned that the radiator had been flushed and two holes sealed, inspected the new hose on the radiator, and wrote a check for $120. The Mustang drove smoothly, and Joe parked in the usual lot near Anderson Hall.

As Joe headed back to the building, he stared up at his tiny office window. Orange light from his little lamp glowed behind the glass like an inviting warm fire in a fireplace. He loved working in the little office. He loved teaching in that magnificent redbrick building. But as he marched back to it, he wondered if he would ever teach there again.

His afternoon class was further along in their discussion of *Hamlet*. Joe had guided their discussion about the soliloquies before the Thanksgiving break, so they had moved on to consider other topics.

"What are Hamlet's possible flaws?" Joe asked the class after writing "Tragic Flaws" on the worn blackboard.

"He thinks too much," one student blurted.

"What do you mean?" Joe asked. "Make your case."

"He thinks he's got to prove his uncle's guilt before he takes him out."

Joe wrote the words "Thinks too much" under the heading. "Go on."

"If it was me, once I found out my uncle had killed my father, I'd do him right away."

"Yeah, but he wasn't sure," Tiffany, an African American girl, offered.

"Why wasn't Hamlet sure of his uncle's guilt?" Joe asked her.

"Well, like you told us before, Professor Conrad, Hamlet couldn't exactly trust the ghost, even though it seemed to be reliable. It could have been some devil trying to trick Hamlet into committing murder in order to lose his soul or something."

"Very good, Ms. Williams."

"But still," the first student responded. "If Hamlet had killed Claudius sooner, then he wouldn't have killed that old dude behind the curtain."

"You mean Polonius behind the tapestry?" Joe corrected.

"Yeah, whatever. Once Hamlet killed the old dude, who was totally innocent, well then, hell—ah, I mean, heck—his fate was sealed. He had to die."

"Sounds like you've read CliffsNotes, Jake," Joe said, smiling.

"Yeah, I mighta found a copy at my mom's house over Thanksgiving break, Professor. But what's up with that? I mean, how come we ain't supposed to read those things if they help us understand this stuff?"

"That's an excellent question, Jake," Joe said smiling. "I wonder if someone else can answer for me."

A girl in the back raised her hand, saying, "Because we're supposed to figure this stuff out for ourselves, right, Professor?"

"Yeah, that's right, Ms. Collins. It's more fun that way. It's like trying to solve a riddle. And it's good training for the mind."

"Using CliffsNotes is like using cheats in video games like *Motor Mayhem* and *Doom*, right, Professor?"

"Well, I don't play video games, but CliffsNotes is like cheating," Joe told the class. "Let's get back to Hamlet's flaws. What's another flaw that's related to his thinking too much?"

"His indecisiveness?"

"Yes, Ms. Collins, go on."

"Hamlet should've decided earlier to expose his uncle's guilt. He should've accused his uncle sooner. I mean, he goes off with Rosencrantz and Guildenstern and has them killed. And then poor Ophelia commits suicide, all because he delayed in doing what he knows he's gotta do."

Joe smiled. Was he, like Hamlet, delaying in doing something to show his innocence? But what could *he* do?

"What would have happened to Hamlet if he had accused his uncle, the king, before he had enough evidence?" Joe asked, looking around to draw other students into the discussion.

"The king would have had him killed for mutiny or something," a quiet student said from the back of the room.

"Yes. Good," Joe said. "But probably, the charge would be treason."

"Yeah," the student replied. "Hamlet shoulda got off his lazy, depressed butt and did somethin'."

"Yes," Joe said. "But remember, Hamlet was young, like you guys. He was a college student, remember? Bright and noble, but young and uncertain nonetheless. Inexperienced in politics, even though his father had been king. He's still learning how the world really works. He's a little naïve. And yes, Mr. Vasquez, he's also depressed. He's just lost his father, whom he loved dearly. Hamlet was reluctant to act without solid evidence."

The students were no longer looking at him. Joe turned to see what had caught their attention. Detective Marino and a uniformed police officer were standing at the door.

"Professor Conrad," Marino said. "Sorry to interrupt, but we need to speak to you again."

Joe blushed and felt his heart pound. "Okay, class," he managed to say. "That's all for today, but keep thinking about character flaws in Hamlet and the other main characters in the play." *Character flaws?* thought Joe. His own flaws were coming back to haunt him, like the ghost of Hamlet's father.

"We start *Death of a Salesman* on Friday," Joe said. "See if there are any similarities to *Hamlet*."

The students closed their books solemnly and put them into their backpacks, filing out of the classroom slowly, pushing by the two police officers. Joe erased the board and closed his own textbook, feeling weak in the knees.

Once the students were gone, Marino and the policeman walked over to Joe. The uniformed officer took out handcuffs.

"Another girl's gone missing," said Marino. "We have to take you in for questioning."

"Do you have to use *those?*"

"Sorry, Professor," Marino said. "It's for your own safety."

As Joe was being led down the hall, Cassandra Johnson and Craig Richmond stood to the side and watched. Cass covered her eyes, dropped her head, saying, "Oh my *god*!" Craig looked solemn as he put an arm around Cass, but Joe detected a smirk.

CHAPTER ELEVEN

For Joe, the next few hours were surreal. The police led him through the damp gray air of campus while students looked on. They drove to the Stockton Police Department. There, Joe was taken into another interrogation room, introduced to a younger police detective, who sat silently in the room while the older Marino asked the questions. They repeatedly asked him to describe his "whereabouts" Tuesday night, and Joe said he refused to talk. He sat silently for half an hour until Marino finally left the room.

"Do you want a cigarette?" the younger detective offered.

"No," Joe said. "I don't smoke."

"I thought all English teachers smoked. All mine did. I had one in high school, Mrs. Ewings—nicest teacher, but dragon breath."

"Reminds me of Mrs. Frye," Joe said. "A delightful English teacher, but like many people in Louisiana, she smoked and drank coffee all day. Still, she was one of the reasons I majored in English."

"How 'bout some coffee?" the detective asked.

"No," said Joe. "Unless you're buying at the Pete's in Davis?"

The detective shook his head and then took out his handcuffs.

"Is that really necessary?"

"It's for our protection. Sorry." He handcuffed one of Joe's wrists to a large O-bolt on the table and went out. A few minutes later, he came back with coffee. Joe took the hot porcelain cup with his free hand and smelled the aroma of the coffee.

"Starbucks?"

"From my own coffeemaker. I don't drink the battery acid they serve around here."

Joe took a sip, blew off the steam, and sipped again. "Thanks," he said. "This is great."

"You know, Professor Conrad," the young detective began. "You don't really look like a good suspect for this disappearance to me. I wish you'd just take us through your footsteps from last night so we can rule you out as a suspect."

Joe grinned over top of the coffee cup. "You guys all read the same playbook, don't you? This is the 'good cop, bad cop' routine, isn't it?"

The young man smiled. "Maybe a little. To tell you the truth, I just made detective in October. I'm really new at this."

"It shows," Joe said. "You're still decent."

They sat together, silently sizing each other up.

"What are you?" Joe asked. "About thirty?"

"Twenty-nine."

"You've got two years on me, then."

"Well, you know, you should respect your elders."

Joe laughed. "I didn't have anything to do with that girl's disappearance," he said. "Nor did I kill Patricia Miller."

"Well, what *did* you do last night? Walk me through it."

Joe put the coffee cup down and straightened up in the chair. "I assume you know already that I taught my class until about eight-thirty. Then one of my former students, a guy named Gary Grimes, attacked me in my classroom. Look at my lip," Joe said, putting his finger up to his mouth. "And look at my temple."

"Yeah. There's swelling on your lip, and your temple looks swollen. But those injuries could have been caused by the girl. Maybe she fought back when you kidnapped her."

"Ridiculous! These injuries were caused by a disgruntled student named Gary Grimes. He attacked me last night."

"Do you often fight with students, Professor?"

"Grimes hit me first. About three times, I think. I managed to hit him once or twice, and I knocked the lectern over on him just to get away. I thought he was going to kill me!"

The detective stared impassively.

"You should check out Gary Grimes," Joe said. "*He's* more likely to be the killer than I am."

"We'll look into him."

"Check with the campus police," Joe said. "I called them right after the attack and got a campus security guard to walk me to my car."

"Yeah. We know about that."

"Then you know I left campus about nine."

"Yes. We have that."

"It's an hour's drive to Davis. I got home just after ten," Joe said, shrugging. "Check with my wife."

"We've tried. She's not available."

Joe checked his watch. "It's after four. If she isn't at home, she should be in her classroom working. You called her school?"

"Yes. Repeatedly."

"And what did they say?"

"The principal told us she left the school during her prep period at two-thirty and went home as far as she knows."

"You've called our house?"

"Yes," the young detective said calmly. "No answer."

"Try the day care center. See if she's picked up Katie, our daughter."

"The principal gave us the number, and we've already called. Your daughter's still there. Is there somewhere else your wife might have gone?"

Joe tried to think. "I guess she could have gone shopping. She often stops at the store on her way home."

"Do you have her cell phone number?"

Joe blushed. "We're both teachers. We can't afford cell phones."

Detective Peterson chuckled, saying, "If the department didn't pay for mine, I couldn't afford one either on my salary."

"Are you married?" Joe asked.

"No," the detective replied, somewhat surprised. "Why do you ask?"

"I don't know," Joe said. "We're about the same age. I thought maybe you could relate to me better than those older detectives."

"No. Not married. Been close a few times."

"Well," Joe cautioned. "Don't do it until you're ready."

"How's your marriage?"

"This has put a strain on it."

"Is it serious?"

"Yeah," Joe snorted. "Being accused of murder? It's getting pretty serious."

The young detective rocked back in his chair, scrutinizing Joe carefully.

"Here's how it looks to me, Professor. It looks like you're a guy whose marriage is on the rocks. Maybe you're not gettin' any at home, so you have to go looking for it elsewhere. Maybe you're very angry at women in general right now. You know, they say rape isn't just about the sex. It's about power, control, anger. Maybe this is your way of controlling women since you can't control your wife."

Joe laughed out loud.

"Let's face it, Professor. You've got a history of abusing your students."

"What?" Joe screamed. "What the hell do you mean?"

"Gary Grimes has filed assault and battery charges against you. Autumn Smith says you had dinner together. *She* says she felt creepy having you over to her place."

Joe shook his head. "How do *you* know about Autumn Smith?"

"Detective Marino and I shared notes earlier today. That's why we picked you up. When this other student, Gary Grimes, came forward, his complaint was passed on to Marino because he's in charge of the investigation for San Joaquin County. He filled me in about Autumn Smith."

Joe looked at the mirror and realized Marino had probably been standing back there the entire time watching the young detective work, grinning and nodding his plump face as Joe opened up to the "good" cop.

"We've also been looking for your wife. We know you couldn't have picked up Lilly Nguyen in your Mustang because it was in impound in Sacramento all night. We suspect your wife is having your other car cleaned this afternoon to get rid of any evidence of Lilly Nguyen."

"Who is Lilly Nguyen?" Joe asked. Then he recalled his earlier interrogation by the reporter Jan Lykert.

"Lilly Nguyen is a high school girl who didn't come home last night, Professor. And if you've got her tied up somewhere—if she's still alive—then it will go a lot easier on you if you tell us where she is. But time's running out, Professor. If she dies because you refused to talk, then you're going on death row."

Joe laughed. "You know, in Louisiana, that would be a real threat. They burn a guy about every month down there. But here in California, death row is a joke. I'd become a cause celeb."

For the first time, Joe saw anger flash in the young detective's eyes. He lurched forward and grabbed Joe's tie under his sweater, jerking Joe toward him.

"You know, Professor," the young man hissed. "Lilly is only seventeen. Child killers have a way of getting themselves shanked in prison. Sometimes, they hang themselves in their jail cells before they even go to trial. You should think about that."

The detective let go, and Joe pulled back.

"I'm telling you, I didn't have anything to do with either girl!" Joe pleaded. "Not Patricia Miller! Not this girl, Lilly! Ask my wife what time I got home last night. I couldn't have stopped. I didn't have time!"

"Wives tend to cover for their husbands. Even if she does give you an alibi, she's not a credible witness because she knows you."

Joe shook his head again in disbelief.

"Call my attorney," Joe said, exasperated. "Her name's Susan Taylor of Spencer, Glenn, and Raimes."

The young cop stared at Joe coldly. "Once you bring in a lawyer, there's no way for us to help you. If you cooperate, if we can find Lilly right away, dead or alive, we can tell the DA that you helped. That you were remorseful."

"Suzy Taylor. Call her," Joe insisted.

"Maybe things started out innocently," the detective said, regaining his composure. "Maybe Lilly was hitchhiking. You gave her a ride. Maybe she started to flirt with you. Hell, Professor, you're a good-looking guy. Maybe she wanted to make it with you. Then you found out she was underage, and you panicked. It was an accident."

"I won't say another word without my lawyer," Joe repeated.

"I can see it happening just that way. Maybe she isn't dead, Professor. Maybe you only thought she was dead, but she's laying out there, injured."

"Lying out there," Joe corrected.

"What?"

"You said 'laying out there.' That's the wrong verb form."

Detective Peterson frowned. "The sooner we find her, the sooner we can get help to her."

The door of the interrogation room opened, and Marino stepped inside.

"I'd cooperate with Detective Peterson if I were you, Professor. His version of events gets you off the hook. You'd probably only be charged with involuntary manslaughter if it went down like he says. Write it up like an accident, Professor. You're an English teacher. I bet you can tell a great story any jury would buy."

Joe looked squarely at the large older detective, fearing for the first time that he might not leave the police station alive. A vision of the Rodney King beating flashed into his mind. He could picture these two detectives stringing him with his own belt. He could imagine the news reporter Joan Ngo, on television, saying, "Professor Joseph Conrad, suspected in the deaths of two women, was found hanged to death in his jail cell, an apparent suicide."

"I want a lawyer now!" Joe screamed.

Marino stared hard at Joe for a few seconds then turned to Peterson. "Let him make his phone call," Marino said.

Joe was taken to an office where he could use the phone. After taking the business card out of his wallet, he dialed the number for his sister-in-law, but a secretary would not put him through at first. After Joe insisted, he finally reached Sara's older sister and explained briefly what had happened.

"I need your help, Suzy."

"Have they arrested you?" she asked. Her voice was deeper than Sara's from years of smoking.

"Well, I'm in handcuffs."

"But have they booked you? Have they taken your picture and fingerprinted you yet?"

"No. But they did read me my Miranda rights on the drive up here."

"Is the arresting officer there or one of the detectives?"

"Yes. The two detectives are both here."

"Put one of them on," Suzy said.

"She wants to talk to you, Detective Marino," Joe said, handing the receiver over.

Marino took the phone and announced who he was. Joe could hear Suzy's voice speaking loudly on the phone though he couldn't make out what she was saying. As she spoke, Marino's face became red. He tried to explain why they were questioning Joe and nodded a few times. Then he listened attentively for several minutes. "Yes, ma'am," Marino said more than once. Then he said something that gave Joe hope: "We aren't obliged to drive him back to the college for his car, but you or his wife can pick him up anytime." Finally, he handed the phone back to Joe.

"She wants to speak to you," Marino said.

"I'm here, Suzy."

"Joe, they haven't formally arrested you yet, and they're not going to. You can leave anytime. I'll have Sara drive to the police station to get you so you can go to campus for your other car."

"But we can't reach Sara. She's not at school, and she's not home," Joe explained.

"I know, Joe," Suzy said. "She's been here with me."

The statement surprised Joe. Sara never visited her sister at work.

"Oh," Joe said. "What's she doing there?"

"We'll talk about it later. She can tell you if she wants to. Joe, listen to me. They can't search the Escort until they have a search warrant. If they try to seize the car when Sara gets there, don't let them. And don't say another goddamn word, Joe. Do you understand? Not another word without me present. You're up to your neck."

"Okay, Suzy," Joe said. "Thank you."

Joe hung up the phone, and Marino removed the handcuffs. "I have a feeling we'll be seeing more of you," Marino told him.

Joe shook his head, saying, "Not without my lawyer." Peterson walked Joe out to the lobby where Joe took a seat and waited.

For the second time in a week, Sara picked Joe up at a police station. They rode in silence back to the freeway toward the college.

"Why were you visiting your sister, Sara?"

Sara wiped a tear from her cheek. "I was discussing divorce with her, Joe."

Joe stared at his wife for several minutes, feeling betrayed and alone. Then he felt angry. The events of the past few days had magnified the problems they had been having, and Joe felt trapped and bound in a way he had never experienced. It seemed that no matter what he did to correct things, the problems became worse.

"How serious are you, Sara?"

"Pretty serious. Suzy advised me to wait until after Christmas for Katie's sake, which is what I was thinking too."

"What will you do after Christmas?"

"Sometime in January, we'll file divorce papers. It's easier in California than it is in Louisiana, Suzy says. No fault divorce."

Joe snickered at the phrase. "But it is our fault, Sara. We haven't been working at this marriage. You've been so damn busy with your job and Katie. My job's been stressful too."

Sara laughed. "Joe, you teach three or four courses a semester! At most, you have 120 students! I teach six classes of math with thirty-five students in each class! I have over two hundred students this year, Joe!"

"Yeah, I know, Sara. That's part of the problem. We're both overworked."

Sara laughed again.

"We've had this discussion before, Sara. You know it takes longer to grade essays than it does math homework. Hell, you use a damn Scantron machine for tests! How hard is that?"

"But, Joe, I have six sets of math homework every other night! You have one or two sets of essays each week. There's a big difference."

"But I have committee meetings, and I'm supposed to be writing articles for publication."

"Yeah, but you don't write articles, Joe. I could respect the amount of free time you have if you used it productively."

"When I find a topic that hasn't been written to death, I'll write about it. I read the articles my so-called peers are publishing. Most of it's crap. I don't feel like adding to the mountain of bullshit out there."

"Well, that 'bullshit' gets people promotions and tenure, Joe. And higher salaries. Maybe you could lower yourself to the level of your fellow scholars a little bit."

"Jesus Christ, Sara! Do we really have to go through this same old argument again!"

"I work as hard as you do, coming home at night and fixing dinner and cleaning the house and doing all the goddamn laundry! Where's the sharing you promised when we got married?"

"I know I haven't been as helpful as I should be."

"You've gotten worse, Joe. I married you because I thought you understood. You used to cook for me all the time. Remember?"

Joe nodded when Sara glanced over. "I remember."

"I'm not your fucking servant, Joe!"

"Christ, Sara. I know you're not my servant."

"Well then, stop acting like I am!"

They sat silently together for a while, nearing the exit for the university. Then Sara spoke up again, "Think about it, Joe. What am I doing right now?"

"You're driving your husband to get his car."

"Yeah. I'm your chauffeur again, Joe," Sara said. "After I drop you off, I've got to drive an hour back up to Davis, pick up Katie, fix dinner, get her bathed and into bed. And then I have two or three hours of homework to correct."

"I've got papers too."

"Yeah, but you've got all day to do them, Joe. You get to stay home. I'll probably come home and find you asleep on the sofa in front of the TV, dirty dishes stacked up in the sink—"

"Okay, Sara. I get the point."

"No, Joe, I don't think you really do get it. All the promise you showed when I first married you—it's all gone. You've squandered it, Joe."

"Well then, help me get it back, Sara."

Sara navigated through the streets to the campus parking lot where Joe always parked the Mustang. When she found his car, she stopped behind it to let Joe out.

"I don't think I know how to help you get it back, Joe," she said. "I've got enough on my hands. One of us has to make sure Katie lives up to her potential. I don't have enough energy to nurture both of you!"

Joe looked at her for a few minutes until a car in the space next to the Mustang honked its horn. Joe got out and watched Sara drive away. He started to get into the car, but then he remembered that his papers and briefcase were still up in his office.

The campus was dark and quiet. It was almost six, so most of the students who lived on campus were either in their dorm rooms or in the dining halls eating dinner. The aroma of fried chicken and mashed potatoes filled the air as Joe walked by one of the dining halls. Anderson Hall was dark and quiet as well. Joe climbed the stairs to third floor, hoping to encounter no one. Cass's office was dark as was Craig's. Joe unlocked his office, gathered the ungraded papers together, put them into his briefcase, and left, feeling like a thief in his own building. As he hurried back to his car, the chimes from the bell tower sounded out the hour. Six o'clock on campus, and all's not well.

CHAPTER TWELVE

As Joe drove out of the parking lot, he spotted the figure of a man who could have been Gary Grimes lurking in bushes behind one of the dorms. *Grimes is a damn Peeping Tom!* He considered calling the police or confronting Grimes, but he dismissed the idea. The last thing he needed was a run-in with another student or the cops. Joe simply drove away, trying to ignore what he'd seen.

Traffic was heavy on the freeway until Joe made it north of Highway 12. Before long, he was approaching Middle Slough. Up ahead, several police cars with their lights flashing were parked on the side of the freeway. People slowed down as they drove by. Joe could see people with flashlights scouring the field below, the beams of light cutting through the growing fog. At Lost Slough, news vans from two different channels were parked by the side of the freeway. Reporters stood by the roadside talking, looking into cameras whose lights glared against the mist. *Have they found another body?* Joe wondered.

By the time he got home, Sara was already cooking dinner, and Katie was in the kitchen helping to set the table.

"Can I help, Katie?" Joe asked.

"Sure, Daddy," Katie said. "You can fold the napkins and get the knives. Mommy won't let me get the knives until I'm older."

Sara and Joe talked little to each other during dinner, but both of them asked Katie to tell about her day. After dinner, Joe helped clear the table and did the dishes while Sara played with Katie in her room. Joe took out the garbage and stared up at the sky. The fog had grown thicker, shrouding the streetlight.

When Joe went back in, he automatically went to the living room and picked up the remote control to the television, but he stopped himself before clicking on the TV. In Katie's room, Joe found his wife and daughter building something unrecognizable out of Lego blocks.

"What are you making, Katie?" Joe asked.

"It's a garden, Daddy. Can't you tell?"

"Sure, honey, I can tell. But is it a vegetable garden or a flower garden?"

The question stumped Katie, who stopped and looked at Sara.

"Is it a vege-table garden, Mommy?"

"Well, I think it has both flowers and vegetables, Katie."

"It's both, Daddy," Katie said with confidence, resuming her work. Sara had made an effort to mix boys' toys in with typical girls' toys, and Katie had taken to building with Lego pieces early on. At first, Joe had worried that Katie might choke on the small plastic pieces; but Katie took her play with the building blocks seriously, especially when Sara helped.

"You might be an architect when you grow up, Katie," Joe said.

"Or maybe an engineer," Sara said.

Holding up a round red piece, Katie asked, "Is this a flower or a vegetable, Mommy?"

"Maybe it's a carrot, honey," Sara said.

Katie seemed unconvinced.

"Or maybe it's a beet," Joe added.

"What's a beet?" Katie asked.

"You know," Sara said. "It's that dark red vegetable we have in salads sometimes."

Katie thought for a moment. "You mean that round thing that looks like a jar lid?" she asked.

"Yes," Sara replied.

"Ooooh, I don't like those!" Katie announced, turning up her nose. "This is a flowa, a bright red flowa."

"Can I smell it, Katie?" Joe asked.

Katie giggled. "It doesn't smell, Daddy."

"Let me see." He leaned over and sniffed at the red plastic that she held up to him. "Smells like poo-poo," Joe said, wrinkling his nose.

Katie giggled. "It doesn't smell like poo-poo, Daddy!"

"I think it's a poo-poo rose, Katie," Joe teased. "Or maybe a poo-poo pansy!"

Katie giggled and threw the piece at Joe's face. It hit him on the nose, sending Katie into almost hysterical laughter.

"That's enough, you two," Sara scolded. "Let's get back to work, Katie."

Joe sat down on Katie's bed and watched the two girls build and play some more. As Katie became absorbed in what she was doing, Sara looked over at Joe. She neither smiled nor frowned. Joe stretched out on the bed, gathering Katie's pillow under his cheek.

After about half an hour, Katie looked up at Sara, saying, "I'm getting bored of this. Let's do something else."

Joe had nearly nodded off.

"You're getting bored *with* this," Joe corrected.

"It's time for your bath, Katie," Sara said.

"Can Daddy give me a bath tonight?"

Sara glanced at Joe, who sat up on the bed.

"Sure, honey," Joe said. "Let Mommy get you undressed while I go in and start the water."

A little while later, as Katie sat in the bubbles and played with two plastic tugboats, Joe washed her back with a washcloth, rinsing it again and again. The image of Patricia Miller's body in the water flashed into his mind. It unnerved him. He could visualize Patricia Miller as a little girl, her father bathing her just as Joe was bathing Katie. Realizing the pain that Patricia Miller's parents must be feeling, Joe's eyes watered. He reached over and took a dry towel to his face.

Katie turned around to look. "Are you crying, Daddy?"

"I just got sad for a minute, honey."

"How come, Daddy?"

"Oh, I was just thinking about someone who died, and that made me sad."

"Was it one of your friends, Daddy?"

"No. But it was someone who used to be a student at Daddy's school."

"Did you love her, Daddy?"

"No, honey," Joe said. "I didn't even know her. But it's sad whenever anyone dies, Katie."

Katie considered this idea for a moment.

"Is Mommy going to die?"

"No, Katie. Not until you're all grown up with children of your own."

"'Cause everybody dies, right, Daddy?"

"Unfortunately."

"I'm not going to die, Daddy," Katie said, looking down at the water. "I don't want to."

The way her little voice sounded when she said that sent a chill down Joe's spine. He reached into the water and hugged his daughter.

"No, honey. You're not going to die. Mommy and Daddy won't let you."

Sara appeared in the doorway.

"C'mon, bug," Sara said. "Get out, and let me dry you off. Time for bed."

Katie stood up in the tub as Joe reached over and opened the drain. Joe turned on the water, adjusted it to a lukewarm temperature then used a pitcher to rinse off Katie's shiny body.

"Bye-bye, bubbles!" said Katie.

In a deep voice, Joe answered, "Bye-bye, Katie-bug. See you tomorrow."

Sara wrapped Katie up tightly in the towel and carried her away.

Joe went to the bedroom and turned on the light at his desk in the corner of the room. The curtains were still open. The street was quiet, shrouded in thick fog. Across the street, houses were bathed in the orange glow of porch lights and streetlights. Reflections of the lights shimmered on the wet pavement. Joe opened his briefcase and took out the stack of essays.

He had thirty left to grade. Joe sat down and picked up his red pen. The title of the first essay was not promising: "To Be or Not to Be: Odeipus's Dilemma." He corrected the misspelling of Oedipus in the title and every place it appeared on the first page then began reading it in earnest.

The next paper, written by one of the brighter young women in the class was more promising: "The Wife as Mother Figure in Oedipus Rex." Joe read the nearly flawless paper with interest, making only a few corrections and comments in the margins. In the conclusion, Samantha, the author, wrote, "Perhaps all men, like Oedipus, want and need a strong mother figure in their lives, to guide and challenge them; however, today's men will be sorely disappointed to learn that modern women prefer to play the role of partner, not parent." Joe laughed out loud at the timely observation, writing the word "perhaps" in the margin before drawing a capital *A* at the bottom of the page. Beside the *A*, Joe then wrote,

Your essay demonstrates not only mastery of literary analysis, but also a level of insight into human nature beyond your years. Excellent work. Keep it up!

After he had finished three more essays, Sara came in. "Katie's already asleep if you want to kiss her good night."

"Why didn't you get me before she fell asleep?"

"I was reading to her. And before I knew it, she was out, Joe."

Joe pushed his chair back and went into Katie's room. Light from the hallway fell across her face. Joe knelt down by the bed, kissing her lightly on the cheek. "Sweet dreams, Katie-did," he whispered.

Joe found Sara at the kitchen table grading her students' math pages. It was her method to underline or draw a box around the portion of the solution that was incorrect so that students could rework the problems from that stage on. It was time-consuming work, but it had proved effective.

"Can we talk a little, Sara?"

"I'd rather not tonight. We've already talked enough for one day. Let's get through the next couple of weeks until Christmas vacation. Then we'll have time to get into things more deeply."

"So you can just put your feelings on hold for three weeks?"

"Yes, Joe. I've been putting my feelings on hold for months. I want us to be civil to each other, especially in front of Katie. Then Katie and I are going back to Louisiana for Christmas break. We'll stay with my parents, and you can come back on Christmas Eve. I don't want you there the whole break, Joe. Just for a few days around Christmas."

"Sara!"

"Christmas Eve, Christmas Day, and the day after. But I want you gone for most of it."

"I'm not going along with this, Sara. You're not going to deny me access to my own daughter during the holidays!"

Sara took off her glasses and stared coldly at Joe. "I'll leave here tonight with Katie if I have to, Joe. Suzy says that I can stay with her. She'll get a restraining order if she has to."

"Jesus Christ, Sara. You're serious?"

"The last thing you need right now, with everything else that's going on, is a hysterical wife telling the police she's afraid you'll hurt her daughter."

Joe rocked back in his chair.

"You don't really mean that, do you?"

"Do I think you'd hurt your daughter? Of course not. Will I make that kind of charge if you force me to? You're damn right."

Joe stared at Sara. The betrayal stabbed him in the chest.

"I don't . . . I don't deserve this, Sara," he said. Instinctively, he reached out for Sara, wanting to bury his head in her hair and shoulder; but she pushed him away.

"I'm sorry, Joe. I've got to be strong for Katie, and I've got to sort this out for myself. It's going to take time."

Joe wiped his eyes.

"Just give me some time," Sara whispered.

Joe nodded, wiping his eyes again. Then he got up and went into the bathroom. He turned on the light and looked at himself in the mirror. His eyes were bloodshot and puffy. He splashed cold water on his face, patted it dry.

Later, Joe fell asleep on the bed, but Sara did not join him. Instead, she slept on the sofa. Joe slept fitfully, waking up and checking the clock each hour. Finally, at four in the morning, he fell into a deep sleep. Dreaming of bathing Katie, washing her back as he had before. Then it was not Katie, but Patricia Miller, whose back he was washing. Her pale bloated body partially covered with algae, her face distorted grotesquely, and Joe was in the water with her. She turned around slowly—her wet, stringy hair down over her eyes, her blue lips cracking into a smile. "Kiss me, Joe," the ghastly mouth said.

In pushing away, Joe found himself alone in the muddy water, which had thickened around him. Now it was as if he was buried in a field. Only his shoulders and head were above the surface of the mud. Everyone was standing around him. Sara and Katie held hands, looking down at him. "Poor Daddy," Katie said. Cass Johnson and Craig Richmond stood over him too. So did Dr. Thorne. The three police detectives were standing behind him.

As he tried to turn, he realized that he was sinking in the mud. It was quicksand, and the cold, wet mud was up to Joe's chin. All of the people shook their heads and turned away. They walked away slowly as he continued to sink. Mud covered his mouth. He could taste it. His chest felt tight. He was suffocating. He couldn't breathe.

Joe awoke with a jolt. Katie was smothering him with a kiss. He jerked back from her face, unsure if he was awake or still dreaming.

"Goodbye, Daddy," Katie said. "Did I scare you?"

"Yes, honey. Daddy was having a bad dream."

"What were you dreaming about, Daddy?"

"Never mind," said Joe, relieved to be awake. "You be good at school today."

"It's preschool, Daddy. Not real school."

Joe sat up in bed, rubbing his eyes as Katie walked away. Sara stood in the doorway.

"Goodbye, Joe," she said.

"I love you, Sara," he told her.

Sara took Katie's hand and turned away without speaking. Joe could hear them walk through the house and out the front door. He listened to the car doors slam, the engine start, and the little Ford Escort drive away. He lay there, staring up at the shadows on the cracked plaster of the ceiling, his eyes burning with anguish.

CHAPTER THIRTEEN

After breakfast, Joe graded papers until noon then turned on the news as he sat down to eat lunch. The screen showed a body bag being loaded into the back of a coroner's van as the newscaster announced, "Two more bodies were found last night in the vicinity of Lost Slough on Interstate 5 where the body of missing waitress Patricia Miller was found earlier in the week. Though badly decomposed, the bodies seem to be those of young women. Acting on a tip, police were searching for Lilly Nguyen, the high school student from Lodi who was reported missing early Wednesday morning. Several suspects in that case were questioned and released, according to police."

Joe watched with interest, surprised that more bodies had been found and equally surprised to hear that other suspects had been questioned. He felt relieved. If the report was true, then the police had other people in mind in connection with Lilly Nguyen's disappearance.

"In a related story," the male newscaster said, "a memorial service for Patricia Miller will be held today at 4:00 p.m. at the United Methodist Church in downtown Sacramento. Although they were not willing to go on camera, the parents of Patricia Miller said that the person who found their daughter's body had not yet inquired about the fifty thousand-dollar reward."

The next story concerned a train derailment in Roseville that resulted in the release of several tons of propane gas. Nearby houses had to be evacuated. Joe wasn't listening. He was thinking about the reward money. Should he ask for it? If he and Sara were going to get divorced, he could use that reward. He might have trouble finding another teaching job for a while. Certainly, today would not be the time to contact Patricia Miller's parents. He should discuss it with Suzy.

Then it occurred to Joe that he should attend the memorial service. After all, he *had* found the body, and she was an alumna of CLU. He could offer his condolences and get to know the Miller family a little. They would want to express their gratitude.

Joe called Suzy's office, but she wasn't available. He left a message for her to call and hung up. The phone rang immediately, but it was another reporter, a Scott Smith from the Stockton *Record*.

As he drove by the River Cats minor-league baseball stadium, Joe questioned whether he should attend the service; but while he was on the Tower Bridge, a little bridge that connected West Sacramento and downtown Sacramento, the sun broke through the clouds for the first time in days. This had to be a good omen.

The church itself was old and impressive, a small cathedral. Outside it, two news crews were setting up. He recognized Joan Ngo, but she didn't see him. Joe took a seat in the back. The church was filling with people. A large photo of Patricia Miller, framed by flowers, stood on a tripod at the front. From where he was sitting, Joe couldn't get a good look at the photo.

Dressed in a low-cut black dress, Autumn Smith stepped through the doors of the church just as Joe happened to look back. Their eyes met instantly. Joe fought an urge to smile at her. He hoped she would sit near him, but she glanced nervously away and walked far down the aisle, taking a seat near the front.

At about a quarter after four, the church was nearly full, and Joe shared his pew with a row of strangers. A minister led the Miller family, dressed in black, in from a side door; and they took their seats in the front row.

This was a memorial service, the minister explained. A private funeral had taken place in the morning, and her coffin had been lowered into the grave at that time. The minister, whose speaking voice was deep and eloquent, said, "Patricia's parents were heartened to see the sun break through the gray clouds today as if God himself had welcomed their daughter into heaven." He spoke of the sadness all people feel, the tragedy that it is whenever a young person is stolen. "Justice awaits Patricia's killer in this lifetime and in the next," the minister said. Then he invited family members to speak.

A tall young man of about twenty-five walked up to the podium. He announced that he was Patricia's brother, speaking on behalf of the family. He spoke of Patricia as a little girl, calling her Patty. He told several humorous stories that made people laugh and then cry. "One time, when I was ten and she was still six, I had to make her lunch every day during the summer when our mom volunteered at our church for a few hours in the middle of the day. We stayed home with my grandmother, who refused to make us lunch. One day, Patty was being especially stubborn—you all know how stubborn she could get—and so I put an earthworm in her bologna sandwich." The crowd provided a collective gasp, and a few chortles followed. "She didn't notice at first, but then she pulled the pieces of bread apart, and there was half a worm squirming in the mayonnaise!"

The crowd erupted with noises of disgust and a little laughter. When the people grew quiet again, they noticed, as did Joe, that the brother's head was bowed. He wiped a tear from his cheek. "I was mean to Patty sometimes," he continued, "but most of the time, I tried to be nice to her. I'd stick up for her at school. She never knew, but more than once, I had a serious talk with the guys who tried to date her." He wiped his face again. "I tried to protect you, Patty," the young man said. "But when it really mattered, I wasn't there for you. I'll always regret that."

Several people around Joe broke into sobs, and the brother solemnly walked to his seat beside his parents.

A few young women got up and spoke next, friends and cousins; and many of them told funny stories that made everyone realize that, in the lives of many people, a bright light had been put out.

When no one else wanted to speak, the minister went to the podium again and led the crowd in the Lord's Prayer. Joe mouthed the words along with the crowd, speaking only one line aloud, "Deliver us from evil."

Then the minister announced that a reception would follow in the hall around the side of the church. The Miller family stood up slowly and followed one another through the side door, and then the crowd started to stand and shuffle out between the pews. Joe stayed in his seat, waiting for the crowd to thin out. He watched nervously as Autumn walked by. She had been crying, her eyes puffy and bloodshot; but in that tight, low-cut black dress, she was strikingly beautiful. With her head bowed, she glanced at Joe briefly but then made a point of turning away. He stood and stretched then made his way to the front of the church. People nodded as he passed, solemn in their grief.

The picture of Patricia Miller had been taken at the time she graduated from college. It could have been the same photograph as the small black-and-white photo he had seen in the online newspaper article. This professional portrait showed Patricia, head tilted to one side, hair smooth, light brown, combed in waves to frame her face; her complexion perfect, her eyes dark, and her lips full and sensual. She had been a beautiful woman.

"She was lovely, wasn't she?" said a man standing behind Joe.

"Yes, she was," Joe said. "Did you know her well?"

The man shook his head. "No. You don't recognize me, do you?"

Joe looked more closely. "I'm sorry, no."

The man held out his hand. "I'm the officer who stopped last Monday to help you."

Out of uniform, the CHP officer looked completely different.

"I'm sort of surprised you came," the officer said.

Joe blushed a little. "Well, I have a daughter myself. I feel bad for the family," he said. "And I was the one who found the body, after all."

The officer nodded. "I know what you mean. That stretch of freeway is part of my beat."

Joe nodded. His eyes began to tear up.

"I have two daughters myself," the officer said.

Just then, the side door opened, and the minister and brother strode toward Joe and the CHP officer. "Come join us in the reception hall," the minister said to both of them. "We're moving Patty's picture there."

The brother picked up the large framed photograph, and the minister grabbed the tripod.

"Do I know you?" the brother asked Joe.

Joe blushed again and extended his hand, but the brother's hands were full. "My name is Joseph Conrad. I'm the one who found your sister."

The brother's face grew bright red, and he put the picture down flat on the floor. "You've got a helluva lot of nerve to show up here!" he said loudly. "Are you the psycho who raped my sister?"

Before Joe could answer, he saw the man draw back as if to throw a punch. Joe lurched backward as the CHP officer jumped between the two men, grabbing the brother's shoulders.

"No violence in the church, please!" the minister said.

"I had nothing to do with your sister's death."

"Get the hell out!"

"You'd better leave now, Mr. Conrad," the officer said, holding Patty's brother.

Joe glanced down at the photograph of Patricia Miller, whose eyes still seemed to stare at him even though the photo lay flat on the carpeted floor of the church. Then he hurried down the aisle of the church. Detective Dunn was standing in the shadows at the back of the church. Dunn stepped toward him, but Joe picked up his pace, pushing the doors open hard as he left.

It had gotten dark again outside, but a news camera's lights illuminated the front of the church. Joan Ngo was speaking into the camera, and as Joe rushed down the steps, she turned and saw him. She and the cameraman ran to follow him.

"Joe!" she yelled. "Professor Conrad! Can I have a statement please? How did you like the service?"

Joe jogged down the sidewalk toward the parking lot around the far side of the church. The street was filled with five o'clock traffic. Glare from the headlights forced Joe to cover his eyes. He was shaking so much, he had trouble fitting the key into the lock. Once he made it into the car, he reached over and punched down the lock, which stood like a chess piece at the top of the long door. Then Joe fumbled with the keys again, trying to fit one into the ignition, but he had the wrong key. "Damn it!" he yelled. The car finally started; but he only sat in the darkness, the engine running, resting his forehead against the cool steering wheel.

During the drive home, as he neared Tower Bridge, he fought the urge to drive his car straight into the Sacramento River. He imagined how it would feel to sit in the old Mustang as it filled with cold, murky water. How long would it take to drown? He couldn't remember the line exactly, but he was reminded of Hamlet's lament: "Had not the Almighty fixed his canon 'gainst self-slaughter." Besides, if he killed himself by drowning in this river, then the police would probably see it as an admission of guilt. They'd have their man and would stop looking for the real killer.

Until he had killed again.

But what if the killer simply stopped after Joe had taken his own life? That would seal Joe's reputation as a rapist and murderer. Katie would grow up believing her father had been a monster.

Joe merged in with other traffic on Interstate 80, driving east toward Davis across the causeway. Fog rose from the flat farmland on either side.

He could commit suicide anytime. He wanted to see his daughter. And if possible, he wanted to save his marriage.

After getting off the freeway, instead of going straight home, Joe stopped at the Valley Wine Shoppe. He needed a drink. He was tempted to get scotch or gin, but he decided it would be wiser to buy a wine he knew Sara would like too. The old clerk, a retired physiology professor who looked more like a librarian than a store clerk, recommended Holly's Hill Patriarch. "If you like Zinfandel, you'll love this," the bearded connoisseur said.

When he got home, he found Sara already cooking spaghetti and Katie in the living room watching television.

"I bought some wine," Joe announced, sneaking up behind Sara. He put his arms around her from behind, holding the bottle up to her face.

"Don't, Joe," she said, pulling away.

"Can't we at least make an attempt, Sara?"

"Suzy's coming by after dinner, Joe. She's bringing another attorney with her, a criminal defense attorney."

Joe's heart sank. He shrunk away, taking a seat at the table.

"A criminal lawyer? You think I need one?"

"Suzy thinks so. She says this guy's good, and he owes her a favor."

"Sara, do *you* think I need a criminal attorney? I mean, do *you* think I'm guilty of something?"

Sara turned around and leveled her gaze at Joe.

"We're all guilty of something, Joe."

"You know what I mean. You can't really believe I had anything to do with these crimes, can you?"

"I don't know what to think, Joe. I know I don't seem to satisfy you—sexually."

Joe shook his head. "For the last two years, you haven't seemed very interested in me, Sara. When's the last time we made love?"

"It's been a couple of weeks."

"It was Halloween night, Sara!" Joe said. "It's been over a month! Before that, it was maybe three weeks."

"I'm tired, Joe. I work hard. I pay the bills while you go off to strip clubs!"

"At least those girls make me feel desirable!"

"Yeah, if you pay them!"

"You see sex as another chore. Do the cooking, do the dishes, do Joe!"

Sara shook her head. "Let's not get into this now. Suzy's going to be here at seven-thirty, and I want to get Katie bathed and in bed."

"So early?"

"Yes! Do you want your daughter to hear you talking to a criminal lawyer?"

From the doorway, Katie asked, "Are you a criminal, Daddy?"

"Oh my god," Sara said.

Joe stood and picked up Katie, saying, "No, honey. Of course not."

"Why's Mommy yelling?"

"Mommy's mad at Daddy for not helping with dinner, Katie. You go back into the living room and watch cartoons until we call you for dinner."

Joe carried her in and plopped her down in front of the television. An episode of *Family Ties* was starting.

In the kitchen, Sara was opening the wine. "We've got to be more careful, Sara," he said, getting two wineglasses down. Sara filled each glass, and Joe lifted his glass for a toast.

Sara looked at him, still angry and upset, but then she shook her head and grinned. "You're unbelievable, Joe!" she said as they clinked glasses.

They sipped the red wine, looking at each other. "That's good," Sara said.

Joe took another long sip.

The spaghetti sauce smelled heavenly. Joe realized how hungry he was. The smell of burnt garlic bread caught their attention, and Sara bent down and opened the broiler. Smoke rolled out.

"Damn it!" she said.

Joe laughed. "You always burn the bread!"

"I know! I've got to set the timer."

She set the pan down by the sink and used a knife to scrape the burnt layer off the garlic bread. Then she tossed the hot pieces into a basket, lined with a red-and-white cloth napkin, and grabbed her wineglass, which she nearly drained.

"Pour me some more, Joseph."

Joe filled both glasses again, took another long sip of wine, and followed Sara to the table. She had the breadbasket in one hand and the sauce bowl in the other. Joe blocked her with his face and forced a kiss on her mouth. At first, she pulled back, but he forced it again, and she gave in. He kissed her softly, and her lips parted. He could tell she had smoked today, but their tongues chased each other inside Sara's mouth until she finally pulled away.

"We need to do that more often, Sara."

Sara simply went back to the stove and drained the pot of angel hair pasta at the sink. She rinsed it and then piled heaps on all three plates already on the table.

"Get Katie, Joe."

Joe sipped his wine then put the glass down and went in to find Katie hypnotized by the old rerun. He lifted her up, still in her cross-legged sitting position, and carried her into the kitchen as her legs slowly came uncrossed.

During dinner, Katie told about her day while Joe and Sara finished another glass of wine. The doorbell rang as they were clearing the table.

"I'll get it," Katie yelled.

As Joe and Sara dried their hands with a towel, Katie led Suzy and a well-dressed man into the kitchen.

"Aunt Suzy's here," Katie said.

Susan Taylor, Sara's older sister, was dressed in a flattering light gray business suit. She looked tired but alert. Her hair was pulled back and piled up stylishly. She was as attractive as Sara, but more mature. The man with her was older, in his early forties, and also dressed in a suit; but his red tie was loosened and the button-down collar of his powder blue shirt—the same kind of Ivy League shirt that Joe usually wore—was open.

"Sara and Joe," Suzy said, "this is Bill Morgan. I've asked him to look into this trouble Joe's having."

Joe shook his hand. Morgan closed his grip like a vise, and Joe pulled his hand away without trying to reciprocate. He disliked this lawyer already.

"Would you like some coffee?" Sara offered.

"Sure," Suzy said. "Let's sit here at the table."

Sara started the coffee and then excused herself to get Katie bathed and to bed, leaving Joe alone with the two lawyers.

"I'm a corporate attorney, Joe, not a criminal defense attorney. So I've asked Bill to help. He's one of the best in Sacramento, Joe. He wins."

Bill moved closer to Joe, like a salesman trying to close a deal. "I owe your sister-in-law about two hundred billable hours, and she's called in the favor."

"That's great," Joe said. "I'm trying to remember the name of the Shakespeare play where he wrote, 'First, kill all the lawyers.'"

Bill Morgan ignored the comment. "The point is, you probably won't have to pay me unless the police actually bring charges, and this thing goes to trial."

Joe blushed. "Well, we can certainly afford to pay you if we need to."

"No, you can't," said Suzy. "I know how much you and Sara make. Let's be honest here."

"Okay, Suzy," Joe replied. "Let's be honest. I honestly don't think I need an attorney. I didn't do anything!"

Suzy and Bill glanced at each other knowingly.

"Look," Joe said. "You might think I'm in denial or something, but I didn't hurt anybody. I had nothing to do with the rape and murder of Patricia Miller or the disappearance of the Vietnamese girl from Lodi or those other bodies they found. I'm completely innocent."

"Then that's all the more reason you do need an attorney, Joe," Morgan said condescendingly. "If you were guilty, this would be easy. I'd advise you to confess, and they'd lock you up, and that'd be that."

Joe stood and poured coffee for all three of them. Bill Morgan opened his briefcase and took out a yellow legal pad. Joe looked toward the hallway, hoping Sara would join them again.

"At your sister-in-law's behest, I had a long conversation this afternoon with one of the detectives who's been investigating these murders."

"Which one?" Joe asked.

"Detective Dunn. Look, Joe, when it was just Patricia Miller, the police had four strong suspects." Morgan drew four boxes on the yellow paper laid out like a baseball diamond. He wrote as he spoke. "They had you because you found the body. They had an ex-boyfriend. Patricia broke up with him about six months ago." Morgan wrote "you" at second base and "ex-boyfriend" in the box at first base. At home plate, he wrote "waiter."

"Detective Dunn also learned that one of the waiters at Patricia's restaurant had been harassing her for a date," Morgan explained. "And this is going to surprise you. Dunn was also looking into Patricia's brother." Morgan wrote the word "brother" in the box at third base.

"Her brother? Why?"

"This is interesting," Morgan explained. "I guess when Patricia was in high school, her brother used to intimidate any guy who tried to date her. Dunn learned that the parents of a boy who took Patty to the prom filed a restraining order against him. He had threatened this kid a number of times. He's been arrested before on charges of assault and battery. He's a real hothead."

Joe snorted in agreement. "I found that out today. I made the mistake of going to the memorial service for Patricia."

Bill glanced at Suzy. "Joe," Suzy admonished, "you must not have any contact with the Miller family. Don't try to visit them, don't call them, don't even write them a sympathy card."

"All right," Joe said. "But what about the reward money?"

"No contact whatsoever, Joe. Promise us."

"All right. I promise."

"When the time is right, when the real killer is found, we will contact the family for you and ask about the reward. In the meantime, cool it. Now listen, Joe. When the police found the other two bodies yesterday, that tends to rule out the brother." Morgan drew an *X* through the box with "brother" written in it. "That also tends to rule out the boyfriend and the waiter," Morgan said, drawing two more *X*s. "That just leaves one suspect."

Joe laughed. "Why? That doesn't make any sense!"

"Because these other three suspects were only suspects because they are closely linked to the victim. Once the other victims were discovered, it becomes less likely that any one of these suspects is viable."

"You said it 'tends' to rule them out. But they're still suspects, right?"

"They aren't at the top of the list, but yes, they're still on it. But you're at the top of the list."

"So what makes *me* a likely candidate?"

"According to Detective Dunn, a few things," Morgan said. "The fact that you were not intimately connected to Patricia Miller means that her attack wasn't a planned, targeted attack. The fact that you regularly drive up and down Interstate 5 where all the victims were found."

"Along with about a thousand other people!" Joe snorted.

"And the fact that you were found with one of the victims," Morgan said bluntly.

"But why would I report finding the body if I was guilty of killing her?"

"According to Detective Dunn, you didn't actually report finding the body."

"But I was going to."

"The story you gave the CHP officer who discovered you could have been made up on the spot to cover up what you were really trying to do."

"And what was I really trying to do, according to the police?"

"You stopped to check on how well hidden the bodies were. When you discovered that one was floating downstream out in the open, you were trying to hide it from view or maybe weight it down with some rocks."

"This is really beyond belief!" Joe said.

"Or possibly, you went down to the body to have a little more fun."

"What?"

"Some rapists go back even when the victim is dead and, you know, rape again. Ted Bundy, for example. He had sex with the some of his victims' corpses."

"That's disgusting," Suzy said.

"I'm . . . I'm just not capable of that kind of sick act."

"Well, Dunn's been in contact with the detective from Stockton."

"Marino?" Joe asked.

"Yes, Marino. I don't know much about him," Morgan said.

"Do you know much about Dunn?" Joe asked.

"As a matter of fact, I do. I've worked with him many times over the years. And I helped him some years ago when he was in a little trouble. He's a good man and a straight shooter."

"A straight shooter? That's comforting," Joe said sarcastically.

"I mean, he's honest," Morgan said.

"If he's such a straight shooter, why was he in trouble? Why did he need your help?" Joe asked sarcastically.

"Obviously, I can't go into that," Morgan replied. "Suffice it to say, he found himself falsely accused of something. I was the police union's defense attorney at the time. With my help, Dunn was cleared."

"He should be a little more sympathetic toward my case, then," Joe huffed.

"Anyway, this student of yours—"

"Autumn Smith?" Joe asked.

"No. This character, Gary Grimes. He did attempt to file assault and battery charges against you yesterday."

"Attempted?"

"Yeah, Marino got interested and took the interview with him, trying to build a case against you."

"Well, that's comforting as hell!"

"Now listen, Joe, according to Dunn, Detective Marino was able to figure out pretty quickly that Grimes attacked you first. Grimes has a record, it turns out."

"For what?" Joe asked.

"This gets interesting. He's been arrested twice for assault and battery and once as a peeper. A Peeping Tom."

"Maybe he's the killer!"

"Maybe," Morgan said. "But Marino doesn't seem to think he's a good suspect, and neither does Dunn."

"Why not?"

"I'm still looking into that."

The lawyer drew another box on the legal pad.

"Detective Dunn hinted that there's someone else they're looking at, someone who's had contact with Patricia through her work, a bartender who tried to date her."

"Who is it?" Joe asked.

"A student of yours, coincidentally, named Marco Hernandez."

"Marco!" Joe snorted. "Why?"

"Dunn didn't go into detail, but he told me that this guy Marco was known at the restaurant and asked Patricia out a few times. Whether or not she actually dated him isn't clear."

Joe shook his head. "He doesn't seem the type. Not to me, at least."

"Well, someone murdered those women. I'll try to look into both these characters, Marco Hernandez and Gary Grimes."

"So with Grimes, where do I stand on the assault and battery charge?"

"No charges were actually filed. Marino talked him out of it. You're scot-free on that one."

"Thank God," Joe said.

Suzy spoke up again after sipping her coffee. "Tell him about the other girl."

"This is where it gets sticky again," Morgan said. "This former student of yours, Autumn Smith."

"Yeah?" Joe asked. Sara had come back into the kitchen and was pouring herself a cup of coffee.

"Are you sure *you* want to hear this, Mrs. Conrad?" Morgan said to Sara.

"Yes. I have to know what he's been up to," Sara said, tilting her head in Joe's direction.

"Are you sure, Sara?" Suzy asked.

"Well, how bad is it?" asked Sara.

"This girl says it was more or less Joe's idea that they have dinner. According to the girl, Autumn, Joe said that was the only time he was free, which we know isn't true because he doesn't teach on Tuesdays until the night class."

"Yeah, but *she's* in class all day Tuesday," Joe explained. "It was her call. Really. She was the one who made it sound like dinner was the only time we could meet."

"At any rate, she's telling the police you made her uncomfortable after the dinner. She says, and I quote, you 'lingered by the door expecting to be kissed.' Those are her words."

"I didn't linger by the door!"

"Did you expect to be kissed?" Sara demanded.

Joe looked at her. She was angry. Suzy was watching, looking aloof and professional.

"I *always* expect to be kissed," Joe said. He chuckled. "C'mon. That was funny."

"He's unbelievable! How can I stay with a man who won't take life seriously?" Sara asked her sister. "He's probably facing murder charges, and he's joking about kissing one of his students?"

"This whole thing is absurd, Sara," Joe argued. "If I don't laugh at this farce, I'll probably kill myself!"

"What's the bottom line on this business with the girl, Bill?" Suzy interrupted.

"The bottom line is this. Her story doesn't help Joe. Her impression that Joe expected something in return for his assistance—something sexual, I mean—makes Joe look more like the kind of guy who regards women as sex objects."

"That's enough," Joe said. "I'm not going to take this. I teach literature written by women. I teach my students about civil rights. Hell, they're studying Martin Luther King right now. I use feminist writings in my classes. I preach gender equality."

"But do you practice what you preach, Joe?" Suzy asked.

Joe's face suddenly burned with anger. "Are we about done for tonight?"

"Yeah," Bill Morgan said. "I guess so. Just a few more things on the plus side."

"Good news?" Sara asked.

"Yes. Very good news," Morgan responded. "So far, the police don't have any physical evidence that directly links Joe to the rape or the murder. Forensics did find a few of Joe's hairs on Patricia Miller's body, but no pubic hairs."

"Well, hell," Joe said. "Break out the champagne!"

"There was no evidence in the Mustang that linked Joe to Patricia Miller. There's no semen, but there is evidence that a condom was used."

"Well, that clears me right there!" Joe announced sarcastically. "I *never* wear a condom when I rape women!"

"Joe, for God's sakes, be serious," Sara said.

"What about the other bodies, Bill?" Suzy asked.

"It's too early. They're both badly decomposed, but one is definitely older than the other, according to Dunn. That is, one was dumped months ago, probably during the summer. The bodies were found just east of the freeway, off a frontage road, in a pretty isolated spot. If Joe hadn't found Patricia's body where he did, then police wouldn't have searched that area when they were looking for Lilly Nguyen."

"Have they found this girl Lilly yet?" Suzy asked.

"No. They searched the same area again today, and they'll broaden the search tomorrow."

Bill Morgan fell silent, and the four of them looked at one another.

"Joe," Bill asked. "Is there anything you need to tell me as your lawyer?"

"No," Joe answered. "As I said, I'm innocent."

"Innocent?" Sara queried.

"Well, not guilty of rape or murder. Let's put it that way."

"If there's anything at all, better to tell me about it now."

"Really," Joe said. "There's nothing."

"I'm going to leave my card. If you think of something later, give me a call."

With that, the two attorneys packed up and started to leave.

"May I peek in at Katie?" Suzy asked.

"Of course!" Sara answered. The two of them disappeared down the hall.

"Joe," Bill whispered. "I know how it is. If there's something you need to talk about in private, call me. I'm here to help you. Maybe there are some matters you don't want to discuss in front of Suzy or Sara."

Joe shook his head. "Honestly," he said, staring into the clear blue eyes of the attorney, "I have nothing to hide."

Chapter Fourteen

That night, Joe and Sara climbed into bed together again for the first time in three nights. Joe had reopened the wine and poured two glasses, draining the bottle. They sat up in bed together, leaning back against their pillows, sipping the wine. Joe was shirtless, with only his pajama bottoms on, and Sara was wearing one of Joe's old T-shirts. The wine warmed her cheeks.

"Thanks for bringing Suzy into this," Joe said. "I didn't like her friend, but I think he'll be a great help, Sara."

Sara sipped her wine quietly, staring straight ahead. "Joe, I'm still going ahead with my plans for the divorce."

Joe looked at her profile. Even without makeup, she was lovely.

"Give it some time, Sara." Joe pleaded. "Let's try to have a nice holiday. Things are bound to look better in the spring."

Sara sat quietly, listening. Joe looked at her. She drank the rest of the wine and then carefully reached over, setting the glass down on the nightstand. As she rocked back toward Joe, she leaned over and kissed him gently on the lips. She kept her face close to Joe's and kissed him again more fully. Her eyes were closed, and her cheeks were warm. Joe kissed her back, parting her lips with his tongue. She opened to him slowly, responding to every probe of his tongue. Then her mouth moved down onto his chest. He stroked her hair and back.

When she brought her face back up to his, Joe set his wineglass down on his nightstand, turned off the lamp, and rolled over toward Sara. Sara lay back as Joe kissed her neck. Then she reached over and turned out her light. Joe watched the shadow of her pull the T-shirt off over her head. His mouth found her breasts as she writhed with pleasure. Joe kissed her stomach as she lowered herself into the bed. He moved down, parting her legs. Her initial gasp was intense. Then she clenched the sheets in her fists. Sara reached the edge of the waterfall where Joe kept her a moment longer; and then over the edge she went—falling, writhing, and falling. Her fingers gently pushed Joe away, but he returned to take her over the waterfall again.

Finally, she would let him play no longer, and he climbed on top of her. She shuddered. He kissed her neck and shoulders. Her soft moans were music until it was his turn to fall into darkness. Sara's hands pressed his buttocks as he collapsed. He lingered then rolled over slowly. She rolled toward him, resting her damp cheek and cool hair on his chest. As his breathing slowed, Joe fell into the deepest sleep he had known in weeks.

Sometime during the night, Joe felt Sara move away. He watched her shadowy figure rise out of bed and pad down the hall to the bathroom. He was almost asleep when she returned. She had put on perfume, and she leaned over to kiss him on the mouth. Joe tasted her lipstick, and he was aroused again. Her hand took control of him, and then she mounted his body gently, kissing him deeply. Their bodies moved together until she hastened the pace, and again, she undulated with intense pleasure. Joe could take it no longer. He rolled her over, and for the second time that night, he rose to the edge of a cliff where he lingered as long as he could before plummeting downward and collapsing once again.

When Joe awoke in the morning, Sara was already out of bed. He smelled the coffee in the cup on the nightstand beside the bed. For a moment, he thought it was Saturday and was about to roll over to go back to sleep. Then he heard Sara's voice from the kitchen. "Hurry up, Katie. We're running late."

It was Friday, and he had classes.

Joe sat up in bed and glanced at the clock. It was almost seven. Sara walked into the room briskly, and Joe smiled.

"Last night was wonderful, Sara." He sat up, reaching for the coffee.

"Goodbye, Joe. I'm running late. I'll send Katie in to say goodbye in a minute. She's brushing her teeth."

With that, Sara turned to leave without bending down to kiss Joe goodbye.

"Sara, wait. What about last night? What did it mean?"

Her back to him, she stood in the doorway.

"I was a little drunk, Joe. I'm not sure I'll let that happen again." She turned to face him. "I wanted one more time. I want to remember what it was like with you. But I'm still meeting with Suzy next week."

"Sara," Joe whispered. "Don't you still love me?"

"I love the memory of you, Joe. The way you were when we first met. I loved your intensity then. Now you're becoming someone I don't like."

"You seemed to like me just fine last night. I seemed to be intense enough for you then!"

Sara spun around and walked out.

"It helps, Sara, when *you're* a little intense too."

He was about to get out of bed to follow her, but Katie ran in, and Joe realized he had nothing on.

"Goodbye, Daddy," she yelled gleefully. "Mommy says we're very late, so I must hurry."

"Goodbye, Katie-lou, my darling girl," Joe said, squeezing back as Katie threw her arms around Joe's neck and kissed him.

As quickly as she had run into the room, she ran back out and disappeared. Joe searched for his pajama bottoms under the covers but found them too late. He heard the car back out of the driveway and drive off down the street.

As Joe sipped his coffee, he struggled to make sense of the week's events. He had been coasting through life these last two years. Professionally, he hadn't written a paper or attended a conference in two years. At LSU, he had been something of a star, the only graduate teaching assistant to win a Louisiana Endowment for the Humanities Lectureship. Thanks to his wonderful old mentor, Professor Jack Claire, the chairman of the English department at LSU, Joe had been awarded several honors. He was resting on his minor laurels far too early in his career.

What had happened? He'd suffered a few blows, to be sure. The doctoral program at Berkeley had rejected him—twice! The program at UC-Davis had accepted him, but the department had few stars and few courses he found appealing. They were still trapped in post-structuralism. "Intellectual masturbation," Joe dubbed it.

Joe realized he'd be late if he didn't get up and shower. As he washed, the fragrance of Sara greeted him.

"I don't want to lose you," he said aloud.

The sun struggled to break through the low-hanging clouds as Joe drove to work. Most were dark gray and heavy with moisture, but patches of clouds were billowy and white with seams of blue between. At Lost Slough, Joe glanced to the west, seeing only heavier storm clouds moving in. On the levee to the east, Joe noticed a ribbon of yellow crime scene tape flapping over the edge. Evidently, one of the bodies had been found on the other side of the levee.

Maybe that's where Patricia Miller's body had been dumped too, Joe speculated. Maybe it had ended up in the stream and had floated south and then east on the stretch of the stream that snaked under the bridge. Like a giant *S*, the stream ran south for a while east of the freeway then turned west under the interstate, coursing south again about three hundred yards from the western side of the freeway.

In the patchy sunlight, the swampy terrain looked far less gloomy and intimidating. He would hate to be out in such a damp, cold tangle of brush at night. Joe shivered just thinking about it.

On campus, he made it to his office without being stopped and questioned by any of the students who might have seen him led away in handcuffs. He checked his voice mail and ignored two messages from the department chair. He wanted to make it through the day and have the weekend to sort things out. Next week was the last week of classes before finals. If he could just finish the semester, then he'd be free to straighten out this mess he was in.

"You're back!" Cassandra said from the doorway. "I thought I'd have to visit you in jail!"

Joe hung up the phone and looked at Cassandra, who seemed genuinely distraught.

"I'm fine. The charges were dropped."

"Which charges?"

"The assault and battery charges that a student tried to file."

"What about the murdered student? Patricia Miller? Have they cleared you of that?"

Joe blushed. "More or less. It was getting so ridiculous, I finally called a lawyer. Once my lawyer got involved, the police backed off. I assume they're going after more likely suspects now. Even a couple of my own students have attracted their interest."

"Don't be so sure," Cassandra said, pouting. "A detective came here yesterday and interviewed me and a few other people about you."

"Oh, really? What the hell did he want?"

"It was a big Italian guy. Morrillo, I think."

"Marino?"

"Yeah. He wanted to know if you had done anything suspicious. He asked me if I had ever walked in on you doing something inappropriate with one of your students."

"What'd you tell him?"

"I told him, hell yes! You had orgies in your office with dozens of students!" Cass laughed nervously, but Joe could barely force a smile.

"No, I said you were a good teacher and a good colleague, and I didn't believe you could have anything to do with rape or murder."

Joe hoped she'd been as convincing yesterday.

Cass leaned in, folding her tall body toward Joe. "You didn't, did you?"

"What? Rape and murder a former student?"

"Well, did you?"

"Yes, of course I did. I rape and murder many of my students, Cass, but only the attractive ones. I'm picky that way."

Cass straightened up and stepped closer, shutting the office door behind her. "No, really. Give me a straight answer. I need to read your eyes."

"Cass, if I raped and murdered attractive women, you'd be the first to know."

"Or the first to go?"

"Yes." Joe smiled. "Why go to all the trouble of taking girls up the interstate when I could just go next door?"

Cass laughed.

"How's Sara taking all of this?"

Joe searched the carpet and Cassandra's flat shoes for the answer. "Not well. She's going to spend Christmas in Baton Rouge with her parents. I'm allowed to visit for three days."

Cass put her hand on Joe's shoulder.

"She'll get over it."

"She's talking about divorce."

Saying the word out loud made Joe choke up. Cassandra remained silent. Then she stepped toward Joe, kissed the top of his head. "It *will* work out, Joe. Give her space."

Joe looked up and smiled. "Thanks," he said, his eyes watery.

The phone rang, and Cass excused herself. Joe answered and listened to the chair's secretary. "Good. You're there. Professor Thorne wants to speak with you."

"Should I come downstairs?"

"No. Hold on. I'll transfer you."

Joe listened to classical music for a moment until Thorne came on.

"Joe?"

"Yes, sir."

"We weren't sure you'd be here today. You should've called."

"I would have called if I needed to miss work today."

"You can certainly understand why we're all concerned."

"Well, you needn't be. I finally brought in an attorney. I think everything's been straightened out now."

"I certainly hope so."

Joe waited, hoping Thorne was satisfied.

"Joe, would you like us to arrange a substitute to finish the last two weeks for you? Craig Richmond has offered to cover your lit classes."

"Isn't that nice of Craig," Joe said, straining to sound sincere. "No. As I said, now that an attorney is involved, the police are actually doing their jobs, I think."

"Well, the university doesn't need any more negative publicity."

"I know, Professor Thorne. I don't think there's anything else to worry about."

"Now, Joe, about next semester. We've already divided up your courses, so you just take that semester off. You'll need the time, I'm sure, to conduct a job search."

Joe's fist tightened around the handle of the phone. "I'd like to stay here next year. I was hoping for another three-year contract."

"I'm sorry, Joe. That's out of the question. It's not that you're a bad teacher. In fact, I'll be happy to write an excellent letter of recommendation for you. It's just all this publicity. It's going to hang over you for a while if you stay here."

"I see. The notion of innocent until proven guilty doesn't really mean much to the university?"

"No reason to be sarcastic, Joe. Conduct a job search next semester. We're arranging a paid leave. You'll get your full salary. Now you can't complain about that."

"No," he said. "I guess I shouldn't complain."

"You showed a great deal of potential when we hired you. Maybe you can use your free time next semester to get back in touch with that. Reignite the fires, so to speak."

"I'd better get ready for my eleven o'clock class, sir."

After Joe hung up, he slammed his fist down on his desk and wiped a tear away from his eye.

In class, his students seemed oblivious to the news, but one student did ask him about it. "Are you the I-5 Strangler, Professor Conrad?"

"The I-5 Strangler?"

"Yeah. That's what they're calling the killer in the newspaper."

"Which paper?" Joe asked.

"The Stockton *Record*. The article even mentioned how you were one of the suspects."

"Cool," another student said, nodding his head.

"It's all a stupid mistake," Joe said. "And we don't have time to get into it. We've got to finish preparing for the final."

"But, Professor! This is way more interesting!"

"Back to work," Joe said, trying to smile. "You don't want me to strangle one of you, do you?"

Several of the girls nodded no, but a few smiled and nodded yes.

"Let's get back to work," Joe instructed, feeling himself blush.

The afternoon class seemed oblivious to the news as they discussed *Hamlet*. Joe noticed Marco sitting in the back of the room, the student having missed the morning section.

"What actions does Hamlet take that reveal his determination?" Joe asked.

"Well, his play within a play," one student said. "He sets a trap for Claudius to see if his uncle is guilty."

"Very good," said Joe. "By the way, what's the title of this play within a play?"

"*The Mouse Trap*," Marco answered.

"But, Professor," another student asked. "Is the king's reaction to the play really enough evidence of guilt?"

"Combined with other factors, yes," Joe said. "It confirms what the ghost told Hamlet and what he himself suspected."

"Hamlet is pretty clever," Marco said.

"Indeed."

"But that's where the play gets phony for me," Jesus, a different Hispanic student, said. "I mean, who goes through all these elaborate tricks to catch a bad guy? Only in the movies."

"Well, what would *you* have Hamlet do to make the play more realistic, Jesus?" Joe liked the Hispanic pronunciation for it sounded as if you were beckoning a Greek god, "Hey, Zeus!"

"Word," Jesus said. "I'd just have Hamlet stab him right after he gets the 411 from the ghost."

"Word?" Joe asked.

"It means like 'for sure' or 'truthfully,' Professor," Claudia explained.

"Professor?" another student asked. "That reminds me. What's that part in the play when Hamlet's talking to the old dude, and he says, 'Words, words, words'? What's that mean?"

"Well, Hamlet is feigning madness and reading a book in the library when the old 'dude,' as you call him, Polonius, tries to investigate Hamlet's madness. What do *you* think Hamlet means in that scene?"

"I don't know. Will it be on the final?"

"Maybe. Perhaps you'll have an opportunity to discuss it in one of your answers."

"Maybe," said Marco, "maybe it means that other things, like books and words, seem trivial when you're thinking about a loved one's death."

Joe leveled his gaze at Marco. "Very good," he said. But try as he might, he simply could not picture Marco as a murderer.

Joe looked in on Cass as he was leaving, but she was with a student. Driving north on I-5, he looked east where yellow crime scene tape fluttered in the breeze. The clouds had grown darker. When he reached the Hood Franklin exit, Joe suddenly swerved off the freeway. He followed the road east for half a mile then took a frontage road south. The road curved back toward the freeway and paralleled it for a mile before coming to a dead end.

At the end of the paved road was a narrow gravel road that disappeared into the thick brush. Joe eased the Mustang off the pavement, downshifted into second, and followed the gravel road to a spot where it dead-ended at a circle wide enough to turn around. The gravel cul-de-sac was littered with beer cans and liquor bottles. Joe spotted an old water-stained mattress under a shrub.

He parked and climbed out. Tissues, used condoms, dozens of cigarette butts, and broken beer bottles littered the ground. Joe followed a dirt path up the side of the levee. From the top, he spotted the yellow crime scene tape on the other side of the stream. Joe walked southwest along the top of the levee, getting closer to the crime scene. The prickly brush thickened, and Joe had to stoop and strain to manage his way through the haphazard maze. Finally, he reached a spot where he could go no farther without climbing down one side of the levee or the other. He was closer to the crime scene tape, but it was still easily two hundred yards away. There must be another road on the other side of the stream that allowed access to the crime scenes, he realized.

Suddenly, a hawk flew out of the brush, screeching at Joe, sending him backward. "Jesus Christ!" he yelled. Then he laughed at himself.

A few raindrops struck his face, and he looked up at the darkening sky. He started making his way through the brush back to his car, the rain falling harder, soaking his shoulders.

When Joe returned to the gravel cul-de-sac, he was surprised to see a police car parked beside his Mustang. "I'm screwed," he said.

An officer stood between the two cars, blocking the driver's side of the Mustang.

"May I ask what you're doing here, sir?" The officer was wearing rain gear over his uniform, a plastic cover for his hat. Joe had a V-neck sweater and a tie.

"I was curious about that yellow tape I saw from the freeway," Joe admitted.

"May I see your license, please?"

"Look, Deputy, my name is Joe Conrad. I'm the teacher from CLU you guys have questioned about the murders. I'm the guy who found Patricia Miller's body."

The deputy put his hand on the handle of his pistol. "May I see your license, please, sir?"

"Of course," Joe said. He reached into his back pocket and pulled out his wallet, opening it as he handed it over.

"Take the license out."

"You can see my license through this little plastic window," Joe tried to explain.

"Please remove your license from your wallet, and pass it over."

"Of course," Joe said. He handed the license over to the officer, who held it up close to his face and inspected it carefully.

"Can I sit inside my car while you check it out?"

The officer handed the license back to Joe. "You're free to go, Mr. Conrad. I already ran your plates while you were gone. I just wanted to confirm you were driving the car."

"I'm free to go?"

"I have no reason to hold you. As far as I can tell, you haven't done anything wrong."

"I know," Joe said, "but that hasn't stopped you guys in the past." He regretted having said it immediately. The deputy gave him an unpleasant look.

"I actually saw you from the overpass earlier. I followed you in here and watched you with binoculars. Trust me, if I had a reason to haul you in again for more questioning, I would. Detective Dunn says not to detain you."

"You spoke to Detective Dunn?"

"By radio. We're keeping an eye on this area for reasons I'm sure you can appreciate."

Joe climbed into the Mustang and started the car. He was soaking wet. As he drove back up onto the paved road, he began shivering. He turned the car's heater on full blast and shivered as he drove back to the interstate. The wide black ribbon of wet pavement glistened with lights as he drove north into Sacramento, merging with five o'clock traffic, joining the crowd of normal commuters.

CHAPTER FIFTEEN

After putting Katie to bed and reading for a while, Joe and Sara lay in their bedroom watching the ten o'clock news. The news stations had linked the three bodies as murders probably committed by the same person, whom they had dubbed the I-5 Strangler. Joan Ngo said, "The identity of one of the two recently found bodies has been determined to be a twenty-year-old college coed who had left Los Angeles in early September to return to college in Oregon. News of her disappearance had been covered heavily in Los Angeles County and in Salem, Oregon, where the young woman attended Willamette University." A picture of her appeared behind the newscaster as she spoke. She had been a beautiful young woman. Patricia Miller's picture was shown again. The report ended with Joan Ngo saying, "While a few suspects have been questioned, no arrests have been made."

"In a possibly related story," Joan Ngo said, "no new evidence has been found in the disappearance of Lilly Nguyen, the high school senior missing out of Lodi since last Tuesday night. A spokesman said police are following several leads. Plans to search for the missing honor roll student will resume Saturday."

When Joe looked over at Sara, she was wiping a tear from her face. "At least they've stopped mentioning my name," he said.

"That's not the point, Joe," Sara said. "Three beautiful young women have been killed, Joe. Their lives stolen by some asshole who thinks he has a right to use their bodies for his personal pleasure."

"I hope you're not making a comparison between me and the guy responsible for these deaths?"

Sara shot him an angry look. "It's always some *man* who brutalizes these beautiful women, women who have their whole lives in front of them. Men like you who go to those places and pay women to degrade themselves."

"There's a big difference between watching women dance, women who choose to earn a living that way, and killing them."

"It's all part of the same systematic oppression of women, Joe."

"Sara! Men dance too, and women pay them to take off their clothes. Are those women oppressing the men who dance half naked?"

"It isn't the same," Sara said.

"It's exactly the same! It's entertainment! It's the human body, which we're supposed to be proud of. Basic human sexuality, Sara. One of Maslow's hierarchy of needs!"

"Don't use that sophomore psychology shit on me."

"Well then, don't use that freshman feminist crap on me!"

Sara shook her head in frustration. "Just think about this, Joe. You claim you love me, right? Well, how would you feel if I were one of those women who dance naked?"

"I admit, I wouldn't like it. That makes me hypocritical, Sara. It doesn't make me an evil oppressor of women. What if you wanted to dance in one of those places? Would I have the right to stop you?"

"No, of course. But, Joe, if men didn't pay for that kind of prostitution, women wouldn't degrade themselves that way."

"People should be able to have the *choice*, shouldn't they?"

"The choice to degrade themselves?"

"Yes," Joe argued. "If men and women want to pose in the nude for an artist, shouldn't they be allowed to? If women like their bodies and want to pose for photographers, shouldn't they?"

Sara did not answer.

"You and I used to swim in the nude in that apartment pool late at night, remember? We used to enjoy doing things like that, Sara."

"I'm not sure dancing topless in front of a bunch of drunks is freedom of expression, Joe."

"You didn't object in the French Quarter when we went into those bars on Bourbon Street. It seemed harmless to you then. You slipped dollar bills under the G-strings of those dancers too if I remember correctly. Girls and guys alike. Especially that guy."

"Jesus, Joe. We were both drunk. It was Mardi Gras!"

"Yeah. That's the point. We used to have fun. Not take things so goddamn seriously."

"How would you like it if Katie danced at a place like that?"

Joe blinked. "I wouldn't want my own daughter humiliating herself like that."

"All those dancers are somebody's daughter, Joe. They used to be sweet little girls whose fathers probably loved them as much as you love Katie."

"I'm glad you know I love our daughter."

"I've never doubted your love for Katie."

"Have you ever doubted my love for you?"

"Yes," Sara said without hesitation. "When you go to those bars, it's like you're cheating on me, Joe."

"Okay, Sara. I'll stop going. If you'll be my lover the way you were last night, I won't need to go."

Sara shook her head in disgust. "You don't know the effect that has on me. Your linking our lovemaking to that garbage makes me sick. It's extortion."

"Extortion?"

Deepening her voice, she said, "Give it up, baby, or I'll see other women!"

"That's not the way I meant it."

"What if I gave you a similar ultimatum?" Sara asked. Using her deepened voice again, she said, "Give it up every night, Joe, or I'll see other men."

Joe smiled. "I'd say, 'Great!' I'd love to be your sex slave."

Half laughing, Sara screamed, "You're impossible!"

"I'll be better, Sara," he said. Doing his best Jack Nicholson, he said, "You make me want to be a better man!"

On Saturday morning, the clouds finally broke, and sunshine glistened off of the tree branches and green grass. Joe mowed the tiny front lawn and tried to mow part of the backyard, but it was too wet and muddy. Sara and Katie baked Christmas cookies, filling the house with aroma. After lunch, while reading the *Sacramento Examiner* he had bought while jogging that morning, Joe suggested they go Christmas shopping.

"They're lighting the Christmas tree at the Downtown Plaza tonight at six," Joe said. "Let's do some shopping, have a hamburger at the Hard Rock Cafe, and watch the lighting ceremony."

At first, Sara was cool to the idea. "I've got papers to correct," she said.

"Grade papers tomorrow," Joe insisted. "Let's have some fun today."

Katie nodded in agreement.

The Downtown Plaza shopping mall ran for several blocks, grounded at the west end by a three-story Macy's and opening at the east end with a Hard Rock Cafe, with dozens of shops and restaurants on both levels in between. The K-Street Mall continued east, running past the Cathedral of the Blessed Sacrament Catholic Church to the Civic Auditorium and the downtown Hyatt Hotel, which were across the street from the California State Capitol building and grounds.

The plaza was filled with shoppers even though it was only the first week of December. Christmas decorations adorned the stores inside the plaza, and with his family, Joe soaked all of it in. Though the air was chilly, the sunshine made everyone smile and nod as they passed. For a while, Joe forgot about Patricia Miller, Gary Grimes, and all the trouble. Sara and Katie tried on clothes in Macy's, and Joe sprayed perfume samples on both of them. Outside of Macy's in the large circular opening between stores, a miniature train ride had been set up with an old-fashioned engine pulling five cars just big enough for four people to ride in. A smile on her face, Katie stared at the train as it went in a circle through a few fake evergreen trees and some miniature gingerbread houses.

"Let's take Katie on it, Sara."

"It's too expensive," Sara said.

"Then you two go. I'll just watch."

"No, you take her, Joe."

"Are you sure?"

"Yeah," Sara said.

Joe and Katie waited in line until it was their turn.

As they rode in circles, they waved at Sara, who stood by an outdoor glass elevator. Then Joe recognized two people who were just getting on the elevator. The couple turned to watch the train. Joe recognized Autumn Smith at once, wearing a tight-fitting white-and-red turtleneck sweater, but he couldn't place the tall young man with her at first. As the train went around the curve, Joe lost track of the couple; but as they came back around, Joe suddenly realized that Autumn was with Patricia Miller's brother. Joe turned away, hoping neither Autumn nor Patricia's brother had seen him. "What's wrong, Daddy?"

"Nothing," Joe said, smiling down at her.

Joe tried not to look up at the second level of the plaza, but from the corner of his eye, he could tell that Autumn and her date were watching the train as they slowly walked by the railing on their way to Macy's.

Autumn stopped and pointed, and Joe tried to look away; but as the train rounded the curve, he had to look in the opposite direction.

"What are you looking for, Daddy?" Katie asked. "Mommy's still over there." Katie pointed toward the glass elevator, and Joe had to look. Both Autumn and Patricia's brother were staring directly at him, their faces solemn. Autumn leaned over and said something in the large man's ear, and they walked away.

After the ride, Joe helped Katie out of the little train car.

"Was it fun, kids?" Sara asked.

"I want to ride again, Mommy," Katie said.

Smiling up at Joe and slipping her fingers into his hand, Sara asked, "Did you have fun, big boy?"

Joe tried to smile. "I'm having the time of my life."

"It's four-thirty. We should head down to the Hard Rock," Sara suggested.

When they reached the far end of the plaza, a small crowd had already formed around the three-story Christmas tree, which was unlit but decorated with colorful oversized ornaments.

Inside the Hard Rock Cafe, the young hostess said it would be a fifteen-minute wait. She gave Sara a vibrating pager, which Sara put into the front pocket of her jeans. Then they wandered through the restaurant examining memorabilia. Twenty minutes later, while they were looking at some rock star's broken guitar, Sara jumped and said, "Woo! Our table must be ready!"

While they ate, Sara broached the topic of where they would spend Christmas to Katie.

"Would you like to fly on a big airplane for Christmas, Katie?"

"Sure!" she said, looking up from her half-eaten burger.

"You and I are going to fly back to Grandma and Grandpa's house for Christmas in a couple of weeks, and Daddy's going to come just a little later."

"Why can't Daddy come with us?"

"Well, he has to work a little bit longer. But he'll come in time for Christmas. Won't you, Joe?"

Joe tried to smile. "Yeah, Katie. You two will go on ahead so you can visit Grandma and Grandpa."

"Okay," Katie said. She dabbed a french fry in ketchup and bit the end off.

"I made reservations yesterday, Joe," Sara said. "We leave the Tuesday after next at 11 p.m."

"At 11 p.m.?" Joe said. "What time do you get into Baton Rouge?"

"We have a three-hour layover in Dallas, and then we fly into New Orleans. We get in about 6 a.m. Mom and Dad will be there to pick us up."

"You won't get back to Baton Rouge until eight in the morning, Sara!"

"It's the earliest flight I could get that wasn't a thousand dollars a ticket, Joe."

"Did you make a reservation for me?"

"I wasn't sure what your schedule would be like, so I didn't."

"My schedule? You know my schedule. I'll give finals the week after next and then turn in grades."

"Well, I thought it would be best for you to check your schedule and book your own flight. Suzy told me you might need to speak to, you know, those other parties to see if it will be all right for you to leave town."

"Fine," Joe said. "I'll check with Bill Morgan next week and figure out when I can get away."

"Are you going to some other parties, Daddy?" Katie asked.

"What, honey?"

"Mommy said you were going to other parties. Can I go?"

"No, honey. I'm not going to any parties." Joe looked at his watch. "We'd better get outside. They're lighting the giant Christmas tree in fifteen minutes, Katie!"

From the porch of the Hard Rock Cafe, their view of the tree was blocked by pillars. Joe led them down into the crowd. Two local disc jockeys named Paul and Phil were acting as MCs, joking and tossing candies out to the crowd. Beyond the platform where the MCs stood, across the street, a small outdoor ice rink was packed with skaters who made slow circles around the colorful rink. Christmas lights hung from strings above the rink.

"Put Katie on your shoulders," Sara said into Joe's ear.

Joe hoisted her above the crowd.

Soon, the crowd was counting down with Paul and Phil; and suddenly, the colorful lights on the tree illuminated the darkness. Oohs and ahs from the crowd broke into "Oh Tannenbaum."

After the song ended, the crowd began to break up, and Joe led his little family away. They walked slowly, allowing other small groups to walk around them. Joe looked in the window of a video store. They passed a bath shop, and Joe smiled at Sara who was eyeing the window display so closely that she nearly walked into a couple in front of her. Katie was between them, holding their hands. A couple maneuvered around them, and Joe immediately recognized the white-and-red turtleneck sweater. Autumn and Patricia Miller's brother were holding hands.

"Why are you stopping, Joe?" Sara asked.

Hearing Joe's name, Autumn glanced up and gasped when she recognized her old teacher. Miller turned back too and froze when he saw Joe.

"What the hell are you doing here?" Miller said loudly.

"Shopping with my family," answered Joe. Miller was bigger than Joe, and even under his leather jacket, he looked well built. "Autumn," Joe said, "this is my wife, Sara, and my daughter, Katie."

Autumn was dumbfounded, but she tried to nod at Sara. Joe watched their eyes meet as Sara pulled Katie closer. People were giving the small group a wide berth.

"Sara," Joe continued, "this is Autumn Smith, one of my former students. Remember? I helped her with applications."

"I remember," Sara said, her voice shaky.

Patricia Miller's brother glared at Joe. Joe could see his jaws clench and unclench.

"And this is Patricia Miller's brother," Joe said.

"We don't want any trouble," Sara said.

"Do you know what your husband did?" Miller hissed.

"I know what he didn't do," Sara replied. "He didn't have anything to do with your sister's disappearance."

"I tried to help," Joe said, but he could not move out of the way fast enough. Miller's right fist caught him squarely on the mouth, the sledgehammer punch propelling Joe's head backward, knocking him out momentarily.

As he came to a few seconds later, he felt pressure on his chest and then a numb clubbing of his face. When he opened his eyes, he saw Miller sitting on top of him, punching him in the face. Two men were trying to pull Miller off, but he seemed as slippery as a fish. Joe saw Sara holding Katie's face against her legs, hiding her eyes. Sara was crying and screaming, but Joe couldn't hear anything very well. Autumn was standing against the wall of a building behind Miller, her hands up to her mouth, her beautiful dark eyes opened wide. Then Joe began to feel the punches as the numbness wore off. He struggled to his feet while the men held Miller back.

Weakly rocking back and forth, Joe felt his lips, which were sticky and wet. A rusty taste filled his mouth. When he pulled his hand away, he saw that it was soaked with blood.

Rage filled him suddenly. He drew back and swung at Miller's face, connecting powerfully. Being held by the other men, Miller could not protect himself, and Joe's hammering fist knocked Miller on his butt.

Leaning over him, Joe screamed, "I had nothing to do with your sister's death! Get that through your thick skull, asshole!" As he spoke, blood sprayed down on Miller, splattering his face and jacket.

Sara grabbed Joe and pulled him away. As he staggered through the crowd, which parted like the Red Sea, he glanced back in time to see two security guards reaching down for Miller. Then the crowd filled in behind him, and Joe let himself be led away by Sara. Katie sobbed uncontrollably.

They made their way back to a Carl's Jr. where Joe went into the men's room and examined his face in the mirror. Blood covered his lips and teeth, and red lumps were rising on both sides of his face. He washed his face off in the sink then used paper towels to clean himself. He dabbed at his sweater with a damp paper towel, removing some of the blood.

A frail old man stumbled into the bathroom, saw Joe's face in the mirror, and turned right around and left.

The bathroom door opened again, but this time it was Sara, holding Katie's hand.

"Here's some ice, Joe. Hold it on your mouth."

Katie started crying again when she saw her father's face. Sara pulled her away.

Joe stared at himself in the mirror. Outside, his wife was trying to calm his hysterical daughter, whose sobs he could still hear. "Merry Christmas," he said to his reflection.

CHAPTER SIXTEEN

That night, Katie cried herself to sleep while Sara lay with her. Joe pressed ice against his mouth and cheeks, watching television as he lay on the sofa in the living room. His front teeth were loose, and each time he pushed at them, a little blood trickled from his gums.

Joe watched the news, wondering if there would be a report about the fight, but nothing was mentioned, even when the tree-lighting ceremony was covered.

Joe was just drifting to sleep when Sara touched his hand. "How are you feeling?"

"Sore and tired."

Sara inspected his face. "I think you'll live."

Joe looked into her sad eyes. "I'm sorry."

Sara shook her head. "I can't live this way. I don't want this kind of trouble in my life."

"I know."

"I don't want Katie seeing things like this."

"I know, I know. Do you think *I* want to live like this?"

"God, I wish you'd never stopped that day!"

Later, they lay awake in bed together without talking, both staring up at the shadows playing on the ceiling. Joe's head was throbbing, and he could not sleep, so he got out of bed and padded down the hallway to the kitchen. He took two Tylenols and went into Katie's room. Pulling the covers over her, he listened to her steady breathing, the outline of her angelic face barely visible in the darkness.

Back in the bedroom, he could tell Sara had drifted to sleep. Joe sat on the edge of the bed, looking out the corner windows at the street. He could see the street through the thin slits between the blinds. A car he didn't recognize was parked on the street in front of his neighbor's house. Joe got up and leaned over his desk. He parted the blinds to get a better look at the car. A dark figure was sitting inside it. Joe saw the orange glow of a cigarette become brighter, and then smoke rolled out of the partly opened window on the driver's side door.

Joe's heart began to pound. He wondered who it was. Could it be Patricia Miller's brother? Maybe he wanted another round. Was it Detective Dunn? *Should I go out there and confront this guy?* He debated calling the police when the car engine started, and the car drove slowly out of view. Joe walked back into the living room, peeking out through the curtains of the picture window. He couldn't see the car. He went over to check the front door and was surprised to find it still unlocked. He locked the door, tugged it, and returned to his bedroom.

Sunday was gloomy. Katie played in her room while Sara did housework and graded papers at the kitchen table. Joe spent most of the day in bed watching old movies on television and reading a little. He kept ice on his face on and off most of the day, but it still looked bad.

He didn't tell Sara about the car he had seen during the night. In the morning, Joe was less certain that the man in the car had anything at all to do with him.

Sara brought him soup and crackers in bed for dinner. She and Katie had finished the leftover spaghetti. While he ate, Sara spoke, "Let's try to get through next week without incident, Joe. I want Katie to have a normal week."

"I want all of us to have a normal week," Joe said.

After giving her a bath, Sara brought Katie in to say good night.

"How does your face feel, Daddy?" Katie asked.

"It's okay, honey. It looks worse than it feels."

"That was a bad man," Katie said. "I'm glad you hit back."

"He's angry, Katie. He lost someone he loved very much."

Katie looked confused. "Who got lost?"

"It's an expression, Katie. It means someone died. That man's sister died, and he's very angry about it. I don't think he's a bad man."

"Why does he blame you, Daddy?"

"It's just a misunderstanding, honey."

"That's what Mommy said."

Joe pulled Katie up onto the bed, hugging her. "You don't need to worry anymore. We're going to get the whole thing straightened out."

"And then no one will hit you again?"

"Then no one will hit me again."

Joe hugged his daughter tightly, smelling the wonderful fragrance of baby shampoo. He nuzzled his nose into Katie's shoulder, and she giggled. Then Sara picked her up and carried her off to bed.

Joe slept fitfully. He found himself in the water again, holding Patricia Miller's body, her bluish breasts exposed. He pushed her away, but she stayed put, and he floated into a bog. Now in an open field surrounded by people, but he was sinking into quicksand. Soon, the wet sand was around his shoulders. Struggle as he might, he sank deeper and deeper. The mud was up to his chin, then it covered his mouth. He struggled to say "Help!" but he couldn't catch his breath. Sara and Katie turned their backs and walked away as did Autumn Smith and Patricia's brother. Professor Thorne walked away, and then Cassandra Johnson turned away crying. Craig Richmond winked and waved at Joe before he turned away.

Suddenly, Katie ran up and dropped to her knees. "You've got to fight, Daddy," her little voice said. As Joe's mouth slipped under the mud, he became aware it had to be a dream. But his daughter's voice was so real.

Joe awoke panicked, having trouble breathing. He turned to look at Sara, but she was not in bed. He sat up. The bedroom was darker than usual. He had closed the curtains over the blinds before going to sleep.

Once he was fully awake, Joe walked out into the living room where he found Sara sleeping soundly under the thick blue comforter he'd used a few nights earlier. Joe went to the kitchen and took two more Tylenol. Remembering *Richard III*, he spoke to the darkness.

"Now is the winter of our discontent."

Monday morning, Joe slept in. By the time he awoke, Sara and Katie were gone. He found a note on the kitchen counter by the coffeemaker. "Tried to wake you, but couldn't. Will call when I get to school. S." Not "love, Sara." Just "S."

In the bathroom mirror, Joe inspected his face. Swollen lips, bruised cheeks. Could he face his students looking like this? What difference did it make? This might be the last semester of his short teaching career. The phone rang while he was in the shower, so he didn't answer it. He counted four rings. Sara didn't give him many opportunities. Did she blame him for Patricia Miller's brother?

Sunlight shone through patches of clouds on his drive down I-5. The wetlands and bare boughs of the valley oaks looked beautiful in the sunlight. White cranes stood in the reeds along the shore of the sloughs. The grasses were rich deep green between the grapevines of the vineyards, but the grapes had already been harvested; so the vines were bare, black, and cut back for winter. To the west of Lost Slough stood four tall radio and Doppler radar towers, their strobe lights blinking incessantly. Farther west and south rose

Mt. Diablo, watching over the landscape. Thick gray clouds floated in from the west. Rain was on its way again. This was winter in the Central Valley.

Campus was quiet when Joe arrived. He made it to his office without encountering anyone though a few students gave him odd looks. As he sipped coffee, he wrote careful, deliberate comments in the margins of the papers, trying hard to offer encouragement and suggestions. He used a deep blue pen, not red ink, making corrections and offering suggestions in a respectful tone, his handwriting clear and clean. These might, after all, be the last comments his students would ever see from him. Somehow, they must count.

A familiar tap came from behind him; and when he looked up, he saw Cassandra Johnson's lovely eyes, her slender face framed by her straight black hair. She wore a long straight print dress, low cut in the front. Her bronze skin seemed radiant.

"Oh my god, Joe," she said, moving into his office. "Did the police do that?"

Joe laughed. "No, Patricia Miller's brother."

"Are you okay?"

"No broken bones. No concussion. A very bruised ego and a battered spirit, though. This happened in front of Katie." Joe choked up and started to cry. Cass came toward him, and he instinctively buried his face into her shoulder as she bent down to comfort him. It felt good to cry. Cass knelt down in front of him and held him.

After a few minutes, he drew away and wiped his eyes. Cassandra had her arms around him, and she looked into his eyes, tears filling her own dark eyes.

A shuffling noise behind Cass caused Joe to look up. Autumn Smith stood in the doorway of Joe's office.

"Am I interrupting something?" she asked in her most sarcastic voice.

Joe instinctively let go of Cass and sat back in his chair. Apparently undaunted by the interruption, Cass stood calmly and turned toward the student.

"No, not at all. Professor Conrad was injured over the weekend."

"Yeah," Autumn said sarcastically. "I was there."

"It was Autumn's boyfriend, Patricia Miller's brother, who hit me," Joe explained to Cass.

"Oh my god!" Cass sensed the tension in the tiny office.

"Did you come to see me or Ms. Johnson?" Joe asked her.

"I came to talk to Cassandra," Autumn said.

Cass pulled herself together and started toward the door. "I'll see you later, Joe," she said. As she left, she gingerly tugged the door closed. Alone again, Joe turned back around to face his work, but his heart wasn't in it.

He decided to make a fresh pot of coffee and try to recapture the dedication he had felt earlier. *Maybe we should teach each day as if it's the last.*

In the men's room, he inspected his face again in the mirror. His lips and cheeks were still swollen, but he did not look grotesque. He could face his students.

Joe worked in his office for another hour, sipping coffee and commenting on student papers. The work was a good distraction. In his first class, students asked what had happened to him. He told them that he had been involved in a fight, but for legal reasons, he couldn't discuss it. Then he reminded them that they had to finish their research papers and prepare for the final exam. Working hard at the board, Joe led the discussion and carefully wrote notes and outlines to help his students. The hour flew by as did his lunch and the next two classes. He observed Cass come and go from her office, meeting her own classes, and he avoided Craig Richmond whenever he saw him. By four o'clock, Joe was finished teaching and was sitting in his office trying to decide whether to critique five late essays or work on them at home. Cassandra Johnson tapped on his door and came in.

"How are you feeling?" she asked.

"I made it through the day."

Cassandra sat in the chair beside his desk. "I bet you're wondering what Autumn wanted," she said.

Joe nodded. "Yes, of course."

"She told me about seeing you and your family at the plaza in Sacramento on Saturday. She and Marty were Christmas shopping, she said."

"Marty?" Joe asked. "Is that Patricia Miller's brother?"

"Yes. Did you know that Autumn has been dating him for over a year?"

"No," Joe admitted. "Before I went to the memorial service for Patricia, I'd never seen her brother." Joe thought about it for a minute. "What kind of a lame-ass name is Marty Miller?"

"The point is, he knew about your visit to Patricia Miller's apartment the night you had dinner with Autumn. He used to stay with Autumn and Patricia, especially on the weekends. According to Autumn, he's been jealous of you ever since that night."

Joe nodded. "That explains his hyperactive aggression."

"Autumn says he's high-strung."

"He almost attacked me at the memorial service. Thank God a cop was there to stop him."

"Marty is convinced you killed his sister. He thinks you would have killed Autumn if Patricia hadn't been at the apartment that night."

"What does Autumn think? Does she believe I'm capable of killing anyone?"

"I can't tell. I don't think so. She admitted that she used to have a thing for you," Cass said. Then she smiled at Joe. "She thinks you and I are having an affair, so I guess she thought I would approve of her having a crush on you."

Joe laughed. "What did she want to see you about?"

"She wanted to talk about missing class and changing the work to be included in her poetry portfolio. She wanted to know how it would affect her grade if she didn't attend the rest of the semester."

"Not attend? Why not?"

"She says she's too distraught because of everything that's happened. She's thinking of transferring to another school."

"She's almost finished with her degree, though," Joe said.

"That's what I told her. If she can grin and bear it, she'll have four weeks off for Christmas soon. I explained all that to her."

"Where will she go?"

"Mills College in Oakland. UOP maybe. She's already spoken to someone over there."

Joe shook his head. "Pacific? That's our biggest competitor. Has she told anyone in the administration here about her plans to transfer?" Joe knew that this would be reason enough to get rid of him for good. If the administration could prove that students were leaving the university because of him, then that was a death knell. Small private schools depended on the enrollment of individual students whose parents, like Autumn's, paid full tuition.

"She hasn't yet, but she probably will tomorrow or Wednesday. She wants to check with her instructors first."

"What did you tell her?"

"I told her she should try to attend class. But I also told her that her grade will be determined by her portfolio more than by her attendance these last two weeks."

"What changes did she want to make in her portfolio?"

"Well, this is interesting, Joe. I told you about the poem that was dedicated to Patricia Miller?"

"Yes."

"That's the one change she wants to make."

"Really?"

"She said she didn't think it was appropriate because of Patty's death."

"What did you say?"

"I suggested it might be a nice tribute to her friend."

Joe eyed Cassandra carefully. "Is that what you really think?"

"No," Cass admitted. "I was thinking about you. I was thinking there might be something in that poem that might help you somehow."

Joe smiled. "A clue to the real killer?"

"It sounds far-fetched, but there was something about that poem that made it stick out in my mind."

Joe became intrigued. "Like what?"

"I can't remember exactly," Cass said. "But that's the reason I told her she still had to submit it with her portfolio."

"How did she react to that?"

"She wasn't happy about it. She told me that she would submit it only if I promised not to let anyone else read it."

"And did you promise?"

"Yes. She said she would submit it tomorrow as long as I swore no one could read it. No one. Especially you, Joe."

Joe nodded. "And do you intend to keep that promise?"

"I don't know," Cass said. "It depends."

"On what?"

"It depends on whether or not I think there's something in it that might be helpful to you or to the police. Of course, it might point a finger at you, Joe."

Joe was taken aback. "You can't believe I had anything to do with these murders, can you?"

"I certainly don't think you did," Cass replied. "You don't seem like a murdering rapist."

"I try to control my lust when you're around."

"But maybe you're schizophrenic," Cass said, grinning. "Maybe you are guilty, but your good side doesn't even know it."

"Yeah. *The Strange Case of Dr. Jekyll and Mr. Conrad.* That's my story, all right," Joe said.

"The students turned in most of their portfolio poems today. Autumn turned in about half and said she'd get the rest to me tomorrow. If I see something that can help you, I'll pass it along."

"Thanks, Cass."

"It's a breach of trust, you know," she said seriously.

"I appreciate the risk you're taking."

Cass nodded. "I hope you do. If something goes south, I could lose my teaching job."

"I know."

"I don't want to wind up in your boat."

"Yeah," Joe said. "My boat's sinking fast."

"Sorry, Joe, but it's all over the department. You won't be back after this semester. Paid leave next semester and no renewal of your contract. Craig cautioned some of us not to get too chummy with you."

"It's okay," Joe said. "I know where I stand here. Thorne's made that abundantly clear. I'm not surprised the younger faculty aren't backing me."

"We don't have tenure, Joe," Cass said. "We're vulnerable."

"Some of us are more vulnerable than others."

Joe left campus dejected. His conversation with Cassandra Johnson had weighed him down. At home, Sara and Katie were morose. The evening dragged. Sara graded math quizzes after dinner, and Joe put on sweats and took a long jog. He looked for Lisa Piante, a young woman he'd met while jogging—she sometimes ran with him—but she wasn't in her apartment. The windows were dark, making him feel lonelier. He ran north on F Street then west on Covell Boulevard. At the shopping center, he went to the newspaper stands and bought a *Sacramento Examiner*. A quick hunt through the pages of the paper showed no new articles about Patricia Miller, the other dead women, or the missing Lodi student.

By the time he got back home, Katie was already in bed asleep. Joe showered and graded papers at his desk, waiting for Sara to come to bed. Without saying anything to Joe, she had made up the sofa again and was asleep, or was pretending to be asleep, when Joe came out at eleven to check on her. He checked the front door, found it locked, and stood over Sara, watching her face before he turned off a light.

He was losing her. They'd been so in love in Louisiana, so hopeful about moving west. But leaving the doctoral program at UC-Davis had broken his confidence. And he'd been sliding ever since, trapped in a dark cellar without a way out.

Before he went to bed, he looked out the window to see if the car he had seen before was parked there again. The street, at least what he could see of it from his window, seemed empty. A middle-aged couple strolled slowly down the sidewalk, bundled up in winter coats. The man had a light beard, graying at the chin, and the shorter woman was laughing at something the man was saying. She wore a pink knitted cap and clung to the man happily. Joe wondered if he and Sara would stay married long enough to be like this couple, taking a lovers' walk late on a serene winter's night. Something about the scene reminded him of a poem by Robert Frost. "The woods are lovely, dark and deep." Of course, the neighborhood streets were not the woods, and it wasn't snowing, but the older couple looked as if they had promises to keep.

In the morning, he awoke to an empty house. It was almost eight-thirty. Sara had let him sleep. He disliked it when she left without saying goodbye. There was no reason to rush down to campus. He had caught up on grading his students' papers, and he didn't need to prep for his night class. He could do some Christmas shopping or maybe begin decorating the house. He lay in bed for another hour, dozing on and off, trying to figure out what he should do.

After eating breakfast in his bathrobe, Joe sat at the kitchen table sipping coffee. He went to the dresser Sara used as a sideboard and found a California map. He opened the map, inspecting the roads around Lost Slough, which wasn't marked. He knew it was north of Highway 12. The map didn't identify the roads but a line indicating a waterway did curve serpentlike through the bold I-5 line.

An hour later, Joe was in the Mustang, driving south on I-5. Before getting to Lost Slough, he took the Twin Cities Road exit and drove east for about a mile. He took a right on Franklin Boulevard. A mile later, he saw a sign for Willow Slough Trail; and he almost took it, but it had come up so quickly that he missed it. Slowing down to make a U-turn at the next wide spot in the road, he discovered a parking area called Lost Slough Wetlands Boardwalk. No one was parked there. He pulled off and parked, feeling a chill slice through his body. He wanted to see the scene of mayhem for himself though he wasn't sure why.

The overcast sky sent a chill down his spine. The even layer of gray clouds looked as solid as slate. Joe hadn't dressed for hiking, but he did have on a heavy winter coat, which he zipped up and buttoned. The damp air moistened his face. The trail was much more heavily used than the one he had followed a few days ago. A few signs identified plants by genus and species. As he got closer to the water, he heard gnats whining near his ears. It was too cold for mosquitoes, but something was buzzing around his head. Just then, he saw a small black snake slither across the path and disappear into the reeds close to the water. Though the trail was wider, it was still muddy from the recent rains and fog. His shoes would get caked with mud if he tried to hike to the place where the yellow evidence tape was located. Another day, he decided, walking back to his car.

When he came to his usual exit at Hammer Lane, he stayed on the freeway and drove to the March Lane exit to get a cappuccino and croissant at La Bou. It was late morning, so the crowd had thinned considerably. A few real estate brokers were discussing deals or golf games at a table in the front corner of the cafe, and an older couple Joe recognized from CLU was chatting at one of the side tables next to a window. A businessman in his late thirties, dressed in an expensive-looking suit, sat alone at a small table, reading through papers. At another table, facing the man, sat an attractive woman in her late twenties. Dressed in tight black pants, a pink shirt, and a cream-colored cardigan sweater, she was writing in a leather-bound journal. Joe noticed her immediately. She was very attractive; and as she wrote, from time to time, she glanced up and stared at the businessman as an artist might examine her subject while sketching.

With his cappuccino and almond croissant, Joe sat at a table in a far corner to observe the young woman from behind as she seemed to make her play for the man's attention. Joe imagined that both of them were staying at the hotel across the street, that the woman had noticed the man earlier and was hoping to be taken back to his room. She would want the man to make love to her passionately, slowly caressing her at times; but at other times, she would want to feel his power. Joe could imagine them together in the hotel room, making love throughout the afternoon, ordering food from room service, dozing and talking, just as he and Sara used to do in New Orleans when they were first dating. Sometimes, they would drive from Baton Rouge down to New Orleans and rent a room at a cheap hotel on the outskirts of the French Quarter. They would take a bottle of wine and cheeses and french bread and apples, and they would eat and talk and make love to each other and sleep and eat and make love again. Especially on rainy days, they would sneak away from their jobs and classes for their premarriage honeymoons. And in Louisiana, there were many rainy days. They had dreamed of the future together and hoped and planned. And those long muggy afternoons lazing under the coolness of the hotel sheets, their lives had seemed so full of promise.

The young businessman gathered up his papers, cell phone, and appointment book and left abruptly without noticing the woman. The attractive young woman watched the man leave, and then she wrote something in her journal. The woman glanced around and noticed Joe sitting behind her. With his mouth half full, Joe tried to smile without looking like a chipmunk. The woman neither smiled nor frowned; she merely turned back around and made a few more comments on the journal page. Now she seemed to be looking toward the table of real estate brokers, all of whom looked like former football players.

It was still early afternoon, and Joe didn't want to face campus yet. He'd probably run into Craig Richmond, and he didn't want to face any more snide comments. Thorne might ask to see him too, and he didn't feel up to playing politics. Joe decided to see what was playing at the movie theater on Pacific Avenue.

The lobby and the theater themselves were almost empty. Even before the coming attractions started, Joe fell asleep. He dozed on and off through the movie.

By three-thirty, the film was over, and Joe drove toward campus. He stopped at a Lyon's restaurant near CLU and ordered prawns and a chocolate milk shake, which he savored without guilt. He finished his early dinner with a cup of hot black coffee, paid the bill, and drove to campus through the gathering fog and darkness.

It was almost five o'clock. The campus looked empty. Joe made it to his office without seeing anyone. Under his door was a note.

> Joe—
> A. dropped off her complete portfolio.
> The work we discussed is quite interesting.
> See you tomorrow to discuss it.
>
>   Cass

Cassandra's cryptic note piqued Joe's curiosity. Evidently, there was something in Autumn Smith's love poem to Patricia Miller that might help him. But what? He wished Cass had slipped the poem itself under the door, but the janitor and the secretaries downstairs had keys to all of the offices, so Cass was being careful in case she got caught helping Joe.

A voice mail message also caught Joe's interest. It was from Detective Marino. "Please give me a call regarding a student in your evening class named Nicholas Adams. If he attends your class tonight, call ASAP. We're trying to question him regarding Patricia Miller since he used to work with her. I'm sure you understand how urgent this is."

Joe pictured Nicholas Adams in his mind. Nick was a quiet, almost shy older student. While a little odd, he had never done anything threatening or suspicious.

Twenty-four students for Joe's evening class showed up on time and proudly turned in their research papers, each typed approximately twelve pages long.

One student in particular did not show up on time—Nicholas. Then Joe recalled that it had been Nick who had left early the week before after hearing the news about Patricia Miller's death.

The stack of essays represented a half ream of paper—almost three hundred pages that Joe would read and comment upon. His days of luxurious cappuccinos, croissants, matinees, and daydreams were over for the next two weeks as more stacks of literature papers came in along with the final exams. Joe realized this might be the last semester he would teach for a long time.

Although he'd assigned Martin Luther King's "Letter from Birmingham Jail," he knew that few students would have finished the ten-page essay while working to complete their research papers. He enjoyed reading parts of the letter out loud to his students, pausing to elaborate on a point here and explaining a historical reference there. King's rhetoric was masterful, and students appreciated the music of his prose and the imagery of his figures of speech.

Turning to the board, Joe wrote, "The Qualities of Effective Argumentation" at the top of it as he said, "The Greeks taught us, remember, that arguments are most effective when they balance three types of appeals." After writing "3 Types of Appeals" on the board, he said, "Appeals to ethics, appeals to logic, and appeals to emotions, such as empathy." He wrote "Ethics, Logic, Empathy" on the board.

"Of course, the Greeks called these three appeals *ethos*, *logos*, and *pathos*," he explained. Joe wrote "Ethos, Logos, Pathos" on the board and repeated the words aloud to the class. "The Three Musketeers of Argument," Joe announced, and a few students laughed. "As we read King's 'Letter,' look for examples of these three kinds of appeals, and compare King's use of these appeals to the way Socrates might have used them in *Crito*."

As Joe read the letter aloud, he stopped from time to time and highlighted passages that would help his students detect the qualities he had outlined.

Halfway through the "Letter," Nicholas Adams rushed in.

"Sorry," he said, out of breath. "Had some trouble with my printer."

"That's okay, Nick. Take a seat."

The student looked disheveled and confused as he walked between two rows of desks and plopped down in a seat.

"Here is where King makes arguments about obeying the law, and this is where you can find specific arguments that can be compared to Socrates' arguments in *Crito*."

Students underlined parts of the essay. "Notice that King divides laws into two categories, just and unjust laws. He says we have a moral obligation to obey just laws. Who agrees with him?" Joe asked.

Most of the students raised their hands, but Joe noted that Nicholas did not. "But notice what he says next. He says we have an equal obligation to disobey unjust laws. Who agrees now?"

Only a few students raised their hands, including Nick, this time. "Make your case. Why should we disobey laws that are not just?"

"Well, King says that an unjust law is, and I quote, 'no law at all,'" one student said.

"Did King actually say that, or is he repeating what someone else said?" the teacher asked.

Another student announced, "Saint Augustine said it."

"Right!" Joe said, pointing to the student. "Do you agree or disagree?"

A student raised his hand. "Well, if we can pick and choose which laws we obey and which ones we think are unjust, then wouldn't that lead to anarchy?"

"Perhaps," Joe answered. "What do the rest of you think?"

An older Hispanic woman raised her hand. "But King gives us some pretty clear guidelines to follow when we're trying to decide which laws are just and which ones are unjust."

"True," Joe said. "And those guidelines are important. Think about how King's guidelines compare to the ones Socrates offered in *Crito*."

"Is that what you expect us to do on the final exam?"

"Of course," Joe said, grinning. "By the way, what type of appeal is Dr. King making here?"

"Logical?" a student asked.

"Yes, he does use logical arguments here. But what type of appeal is it when one refers to qualities such as justice and morality?"

"Appeals to ethics," Nicholas said.

"Yes!" Joe said, pointing to him. Nicholas squirmed in his seat. He seemed uncomfortable with Joe pointing directly at him. But why? Joe tried to read the student's eyes, but Nick looked down at his book, so Joe continued with the lesson. "What would the Greeks call it?"

"*Ethos*," said several students.

"Correct," Joe affirmed. "Don't forget to refer to the Three Musketeers!"

"Is that going to be on the final exam?"

"Which?" Joe asked. "*Ethos* or the Three Musketeers?"

Some of the students laughed. "*Ethos*?" asked the student. "Are we supposed to use those old Greek words?"

"Yeah," Joe said. "You should be able to use those 'old Greek words.'"

Joe finished the lecture by 8:40, nearly an hour early; but he could see that the students were exhausted, having worked hard on their papers. He let them go.

As the students filed out of the classroom that night, they wished him luck reading their papers. "You don't have to read my paper, Professor," one student said. "Just give me an A!"

Nicholas avoided Joe's eyes as he walked by.

"Nick, can I speak to you?"

"No. Sorry, Professor Conrad. I've got to get to work."

"It's kind of important."

"Catch me another time, Mr. C," Nick said.

"It's about Patricia Miller."

The blood drained from the young man's face, and he hurried by the other students to leave before Joe could grab him.

Maybe Nick *was* guilty of something—stalking Patricia, perhaps—but he just didn't seem capable of anything more serious. Joe felt a sudden pang of sympathy for Nick, the bashful student might have to go through the same kind of interrogation Joe had recently experienced. He wasn't sure Nick could survive it—the young man seemed painfully shy, even though he mustered the courage to speak up in class sometimes.

One of the female students, Heather, a redhead with short hair, was slow and deliberate in gathering up her books and papers.

"Don't you know about Nick and Patty?" she asked Joe. "They used to date. Nick used to work at Murphy's with Patty. He was a waiter there."

"When was this?" asked Joe, surprised. His students seemed to know more than he did.

"Oh, about two years ago, I guess. They were pretty hot and heavy for a while."

"Really?"

"Yeah," Heather said as she strolled by Joe. "In fact, it was Patty who got Nick to come back to school."

"How do you know all this, Heather?"

She stopped dead in her tracks directly in front of Joe.

"Because I started dating Nick after Patricia Miller dumped him. She really did a number on him."

"What do you mean?"

"She made him feel, I dunno, unworthy or something. He's still sort of crushed by it."

Heather started to leave again.

"Are you still dating Nick?"

She looked back, smiling. "No, not for a few months."

"Why not, Heather?"

She shook her head. "I think he was hoping to get back with Patty."

With that, the redhead walked out of the classroom, leaving Joe alone in thought, staring into the darkness of the doorway. *Should I call Dunn or Marino about Nick Adams?* he wondered. He considered reporting the new information to the detectives as he gathered up his lecture notes.

He needed to erase the board. With his back to the room, Joe had the feeling someone was watching him. He glanced around, but no one else was in the classroom. After erasing the board, Joe looked out the door before entering the darkened hallway.

Back in his office, Joe listened to the old building creak and groan as he gathered his papers together and put them in his briefcase. He glanced around nervously as he turned off the computer and the light and locked his door. He walked down the stairs quietly, stopping a few times to listen. He thought he heard someone else's footsteps upstairs. Suddenly, he half trotted down the rest of the stairs, clutching the railing with one hand and his briefcase with the other, glancing back to make sure no one was following.

Outside, the campus was very dark. Patches of fog shrouded the old-fashioned lampposts that adorned the college sparsely. Students and faculty had often complained that the campus was poorly lit. As Joe walked along the brick pathways, sometimes between high walls of shrubbery, he felt certain that someone was following him. Once, after rounding the corner of a building near the parking lot where his car was parked, he looked back. There was someone behind him, but the large dark figure was too far back to be seen clearly. Whoever it was had stopped and turned to walk in a different direction, and soon, the mysterious person disappeared into the fog.

Joe made sure he had the correct key in his hand as he found the driver's side door of the old Mustang. He quickly got into his car, tossing his briefcase in the passenger's seat, and he reached over to lock the door. He looked at the same spot where he had seen Gary Grimes peeping into a dorm window the week before, but no one was there, at least no one he could see through the fog.

Driving north on the interstate again, Joe calmed down and reflected on his class. It had gone well. He had conducted a good class. In many ways, a college professor is like the conductor of an orchestra, Joe felt. A good, focused lecture builds and builds to a crescendo and leaves students, who contribute just as musicians do, feeling accomplished.

As Joe made it to South Sacramento, he felt too exhilarated to go straight home. Besides, what would be waiting for him at home? Katie would be asleep, and Sara would be either smoking or sleeping.

"What the hell," he said out loud. Instead of turning west to head toward Davis, he headed east and drove to Highbeams, the topless bar in the middle of Sacramento.

When he arrived, Joe did not pull into the parking lot. He drove around the block, thinking about the arguments he'd had with Sara, trying to imagine Katie when she was grown. He pulled into an open parking space and sat in the dark remembering his last visit to the bar the Tuesday before Thanksgiving.

The bar had been very dark that night, the music loud, and the place packed with men. Joe had taken a seat in the back at a small table by the wall. On two small stages, young women danced under black lights, their string bikini bottoms glowing. Near Joe's table, a petite blonde was giving a lap dance to a man who was a little older than Joe. She stroked the young man's face with her hands as she danced in front of him, leaning forward and whispering in his ear.

She used her hair to stroke the man's smiling face, and sometimes, she danced with her breasts so close to the man's lips they almost touched his mouth.

After the blonde had finished dancing for the man, she sat beside him for a while and put her bikini top back on, chatting as she worked. When the next song blared from the speakers, the dancer looked around. She smiled at Joe and walked straight toward him.

The skimpy pink bikini top barely held the woman's breasts, the bikini bottom, only a thin strip of fabric. Her long blonde hair framed her heavily made-up eyes and her full lips, which were the same shade of pink as her bikini. Bending from the waist, she had leaned over and whispered in Joe's ear. "Do you come here often?" she'd asked, speaking into Joe's ear. The loud music made it impossible to hear otherwise.

"No," Joe had said, speaking into the dancer's ear. Her heavy perfume had been intoxicating. "What about you?"

The dancer laughed. "Yeah," she'd said loudly. "About five times a week!"

"You must really like it here!" Joe had yelled.

"Yeah," she yelled back over the music. "Like being at a party every night!"

"Not like the parties I go to," Joe said.

She'd laughed again, touching Joe's thigh. "What's your name?"

"Richard," Joe had lied. "You can call me Rich."

She'd laughed again. "Are you? Rich, I mean?"

Joe remembered the idiot grin on his face. "I try to hide it," he'd told her. "Can't you tell?"

"Sure," she'd said, playing along. "At the next song, two dances for fifty, okay?"

Joe had pulled two twenties and ten out of his wallet and placed them on the table. The dancer nodded and patted Joe's thigh, a little higher up.

Sitting in his car alone, Joe remembered the woman's erotic dance. When the next song began, Jasmine stood up, pushing her way between Joe's legs. She rocked up and down, brushing his face with her hair, then pushing him back against the wall with her hands. She crouched low, tilting her head nearly inside his crotch, then pushing her head up his stomach and chest. Then she turned around, her muscular back toward Joe, and she reached back to untie her bikini top. The routine was exactly the same as it had been for the other man. When the top was untied, she turned back around, holding the top to her breasts with one hand and putting the other hand flat against her mouth, feigning embarrassment.

Suddenly, she pulled the top away, and her large breasts swayed back and forth in front of Joe's eyes. She leaned down as if to whisper in Joe's ears, but she only moaned as if in ecstasy. Her moans had made Joe squirm.

Between songs, she'd just stood in front of him, looking down and smiling at him, knowingly. When the music started again, she pushed her knees into Joe's crotch and rubbed back and forth, smiling. She moved and rocked and danced more closely than she had before, moaning in mock ecstasy in his ears. Joe had closed his eyes and imagined making love to her, to Sara, to her, to Sara. And then the music ended.

When Joe opened his eyes, the young woman's face was directly in front of his. "Would you like two more dances for the same price?" she'd asked.

"No," Joe had told her. "I don't think I could take it. I might swoon to death."

"You might do what?"

"Swoon," Joe repeated. "Haven't you ever swooned?"

The dancer sat down, putting her top back on. "Not that I know of," she'd said.

Joe recalled saying to her, "Too bad. There's nothing like a good swooning."

The young woman had picked up the money and stood up, scanning the room for another customer. She'd left without even saying goodbye as if Joe no longer existed.

While sitting in the chilled darkness of his car, a steady stream of car lights driving past, he remembered Patricia Miller's cold, stiff body.

"Jesus," he said out loud. He looked at his own eyes in the mirror and shook his head. "What were you thinking, Joe?"

He put the car in gear and looked for an opening in the traffic so he could drive home. He desperately wanted to be with his daughter and wife, the women he loved.

By the time Joe made it home from Sacramento, Katie and Sara were asleep. He checked on Katie, pulling the comforter up to her chin. She seemed to sleep on her back straight through the night. Sara was in bed, not on the sofa, the lamp on Joe's desk turned down low. Her face was toward the lamp, and the soft light warmed her features. Joe went back to the bathroom, undressed, and took a quick shower. When he climbed into bed, he rolled on his side facing Sara, who opened her eyes halfway. Joe kissed her gently on the cheek. She did not pull away, so he kissed her cheek again, closer to her lips. She rolled over on her back, her eyes still closed. When he kissed her mouth, she parted her lips and allowed his tongue to find hers. His hands explored her body under the covers as he kissed her mouth and neck. When he slipped his hand between her thighs, he found that she was already moist.

As Joe made love to Sara, he watched her face. She never opened her eyes, but by the end, she had put the knuckle of her finger into her mouth and bit it as she moaned softly. Joe stayed on top of her for a few moments, kissing her earlobe and temple. When he rolled off, she stayed on her back and rested her hand on Joe's stomach. Before he dozed off, Joe rolled over and turned off the little lamp whose gentle light had warmed them both.

CHAPTER SEVENTEEN

Wednesday morning, he smelled the coffee on the desk next to the bed even before he opened his eyes. The clock showed it was quarter to seven. The coffee was in a Christmas cup, and to Joe, this was the first sign that life was getting back to normal. He sat up in bed and sipped the hot coffee. As he rearranged the covers, the odor reminded Joe of their lovemaking, which made him smile just as Sara came into the room. She was wearing a white blouse under a colorful sweater vest with a Christmas tree on the front.

"Good morning," she said, smiling.

"Good morning," Joe answered.

Sara walked over and sat on the edge of the bed, putting her own coffee cup down on the desk. She leaned forward, kissing Joe's ear. "Do you remember last night?"

"Of course I do," he said. "I was wondering if you would. You seemed to sleep through it."

Sara kissed his ear again. "Your timing was impeccable. I was having a great sex dream."

"Oh?" Joe said, surprised. She rarely admitted to dreaming at all. "Was it about me, or someone else?"

Sara drew back and smiled. "I'll never tell."

Joe cocked his left eyebrow.

"I might have been dreaming about somebody else," Sara said, leaning over to kiss Joe on the mouth. She picked up her coffee and stood. "But I woke up to you." As she walked out of the room, she said, "I'll send Katie in to say goodbye in a few minutes. She's finishing her oatmeal."

Joe sipped his coffee and looked over at his desk. The previous summer, he had started work on an article about John Updike's influence on John Irving; but after a dozen pages, he had lost interest. The draft had sat on his desk all semester, practically untouched. Sipping his coffee, Joe picked up the manuscript and began reading it. It suddenly occurred to him that he should focus on the two authors' treatment of women and sexuality. *That* would make an interesting article!

Katie appeared in the doorway, holding a small tray with a bowl on it and a glass of orange juice. "Look, Daddy!" she announced, stepping carefully into the room. "Me and Mommy made you breakfast!"

"Mommy and I," Sara corrected, walking behind Katie.

"Great!" Joe said. "I'm starving."

Joe took the tray and examined the bowl. An island of oatmeal with cinnamon on its peak rose out of a sea of milk. "Thank you, Katie," Joe said. He ate a spoonful of oatmeal and said, "Yummy. Did you make this all by yourself?"

"No, Daddy. Mommy helped." Katie jumped onto the bed by Joe's legs, almost causing the glass of orange juice to tip over. "Look, Daddy! Mommy and me are wearing Christmas clothes!"

Katie had a red turtleneck jersey on under a green jumper.

"I see that," Joe said.

"Mommy says we have to start getting ready for Christmas even though we're going to Grandma's house."

"I think Mommy's right," Joe said. "Maybe we can get a Christmas tree this weekend."

"Should we spend the money, Joe, since we won't be here to enjoy it?"

"We'll see. We can talk about it tonight."

"Maybe we can get a little tree," Katie suggested, sounding too grown-up.

Joe laughed. "That's a Solomon-like compromise! Good girl!"

"Kiss Daddy goodbye, honey," Sara said. "We have to leave."

Joe hugged and kissed his daughter and then released her. Sara came over to the bed, and Joe pulled her closer. She laughed but then settled in and kissed Joe back fiercely.

"See you tonight," she whispered into his ear.

Joe listened as they left, hearing the car back out of the driveway, and the sound of the engine faded down the street. When he finished his coffee, he threw the covers back and hopped out of bed. Standing at the desk, a row of books shielding him from view, he opened the blinds and looked at the day. It was sunny for a change though the light disappeared from time to time behind a cloud. Suddenly, Lisa Piante jogged by wearing white mittens and a light gray sweat suit. She glanced in Joe's direction and waved, and Joe instinctively waved back before realizing that he was naked. Lisa smiled as she disappeared from view. Joe half expected the doorbell to ring. He went into the hallway and listened, but after a few minutes, he went into the bathroom and took a shower.

The drive to campus was lovely. The grasses in the farm fields and between the rows of grapevines were different shades of deep green, and the sky was mostly blue although large heavy clouds, looking like battleships, floated by. Joe was listening to light jazz as he drove, and he passed Lost Slough without even thinking about it.

He parked and walked across campus just as classes were letting out. In the cold sunlight, the students bustled through campus from building to building, chatting and laughing, many talking on cell phones, mostly ignoring Joe. He nodded at some of the young men he recognized and said good morning to the girls.

Cassandra Johnson was walking down the hallway when Joe got to his office. Her eyes brightened when she noticed him. "Oh, good," she said. "You're here! I've got something for you. I'll be right back."

Joe unlocked his office and went in, setting down his briefcase and turning on his computer. After taking off his coat, he took his coffee cup and coffeepot down to the restroom and rinsed them out. By the time the coffee was ready, Joe was sitting at his desk, reading a few e-mail messages. Cass bounded into his office holding a piece of sturdy paper, lavender in color.

"Lock the door, Joe," she said. "I've got Autumn Smith's poem!"

Joe turned the bolt and closed the blinds as Cass placed the poem on the desk and took a seat.

"You'll find this very revealing," Cass said, conspiratorially.

Joe took the heavy lavender paper into his fingers and began reading.

Fantasy Lover
Dedicated to Patricia Miller

You climb out of the shower while I do my eyes
With make-up, eye-liner black while I watch the muscles
Of your back glisten in the light.
The scent of you wafts in my direction
My eyes caress the contours of your breasts
As I imagine my hands on your body.
"It's all yours" you say,
While my mind's eye plays
With your nipples and lips.
We are two and then one, lying on the deck
In the nude in the sun.

I feel the power of you both,
The male and the female
Controlling, caressing, guiding, toying,
Always taking me, and taking me,
Both of you using me
Until I'm done.

Autumn Smith

"Wow!" Joe said. "She never wrote like that in *my* class!"

Cassandra laughed. "I know! Pretty sensual, huh?"

"What's your analysis?" Joe asked.

"Well, it's pretty typical free verse, sophomore stuff," Cass said, slipping into the role of literary critic. "It's not very accomplished. Some of the internal rhymes are effective, but some feel forced. It's not well balanced. I had encouraged her to rework it more, to try to balance the structure—it seems top-heavy."

"True," Joe agreed. "But it's not awful."

"No," Cass agreed. "There are some images that capture the speaker's emotions in a way that arouses similar responses from the reader. Autumn is definitely learning and growing. If she worked at it, in time, she might become a good poet. But I was struck by the implications that might relate to *your* issues."

"What do you mean?" Joe asked.

"Some of it seems too authentic to be mere fantasy," Cass continued. "But what's most striking is the use of the male and the female as images of a controlling lover."

"How do you interpret that?"

"Well, with lesbian poetry—and I'm not an expert, let me assure you—there are usually two ways of reading those types of descriptions. The first is pretty standard, that the lover plays a dual role, sometimes acting like a passive female during sex but acting like a more aggressive male at other times."

"Yeah, that's my reading," Joe said. "What's your second interpretation?"

"That they allowed a man to share their bed. That there really was a male with them." Cass noted Joe's reaction. "Every guy's fantasy, right?" she laughed.

"I suppose," Joe admitted.

"You know, of course, what the second interpretation could mean, don't you?"

"Maybe," Joe said. "But you go first."

"Well, based on what I know, I'd say there's a good chance that Autumn has gone to bed with Patricia and her brother Marty at the same time."

Joe tried not to imagine it. He had always pictured Autumn as virginal.

"Furthermore," Cass continued, "from the way this poem is written, Autumn felt manipulated by the two of them."

"Wow," was all Joe could manage. "That's possible."

"Of course, I'm just speculating here, but Patricia and Marty are both older than Autumn. And they're more experienced. In fact, if Marty has been having an incestuous affair with his younger sister Patty for a long time, then this whole routine might be something they've done before."

"What do you mean?"

"Well, think about it, Joe. If Marty seduced his sister when she was much younger, say in their early teens, then they'd been having a love affair for almost ten years. In many respects, they were practically married!"

"That would explain why Marty got so jealous and so protective when Patricia was with other guys."

"Exactly!" Cass said. "And over the years, they've probably both brought other people into their relationship."

"You mean there may have been times when Marty brought another guy to have sex with his sister?"

"Quite possibly. Assuming, of course, that they were really having an incestuous relationship."

"Right."

"I mean," Cass said, "we need to remember the first word in the title of the poem."

Joe glanced down at the paper. "Fantasy," he said aloud.

"Yes. This could all be exactly what the title suggests. Nothing more than a young girl's lesbian fantasy, inspired perhaps by the affair she's having with Patricia's brother."

"Right, right," Joe said. Yes, it could all be a rather innocuous fantasy written in response to an instructor's assignment to "think outside the box," so to speak. Or it could be a powerful admission that Autumn was caught up in a threesome.

"But how does this help *me*?" Joe asked. "Even if Autumn and Patty and Marty *were* sexually involved, how does that point guilt away from me and toward someone else?"

"It shows that Patricia was involved with someone else," Cass said. "And if an ex-lover found out that he'd been tossed aside for another woman—or worse, Patty's own brother—then couldn't that make somebody angry enough to kill her?"

"Yeah, I suppose," Joe said. "But that doesn't explain the connection between Patty and the other two women whose bodies were found near Lost Slough."

Cassandra Johnson knitted her eyebrows together. Then she perked up. "Unless Patricia's scorned lover just happened to be the same guy who killed the other two women?"

Joe wrinkled his brow. "But that could still be me, couldn't it? I mean, that's the way the police are going to see it."

"Maybe," Cass said. "Let me think it through."

Joe picked up the poem again. "I don't know," he said. "I was hoping there'd be something more obvious here."

Cassandra laughed that loud, lilting laugh of hers. "Did you expect the poem to say, 'Patricia was killed by Joe Blow'?"

Joe laughed in return. "I don't want the killer to be named Joe anything!"

"Well, I still think the poem offers some insight."

"Yeah," Joe said. "Thanks for letting me see it. Maybe the detectives can make something out of it. Can I make a copy?"

Cass looked surprised. "I don't feel comfortable letting the police see this yet. I don't want Autumn to feel I betrayed her trust. That wouldn't be good for my teaching career."

"No," Joe admitted. "I understand. It's just that they might be able to put this poem together with something that we don't even know about. I mean, this could be the missing piece that solves the jigsaw puzzle."

Cass turned the lavender page around and looked at it again. "No," she said. "I can't betray a student's trust by letting you make a copy and giving it to the police. Not yet," Cass said. "But if the police could somehow discover it for themselves, then that would be different."

Joe gazed at her. "You mean, I should somehow hint to the police that they should maybe look into other courses that Autumn is taking?"

"If you can do that tactfully without making it too obvious I've already shared this with you."

"Maybe," Joe said. "Let me think about it. There might not even be a need for me to talk to the police again. I haven't seen a cop in a few days now. At least, I don't think I have."

"That sounds cryptic. What do you mean?"

"Well, I've had the feeling someone's been following me. I can't be sure."

"I wouldn't put it past the police."

"Maybe they've moved on to other suspects."

"True," said Cass. She picked up the poem and stood to leave. "With those other two bodies, they must've found some DNA evidence or something."

"One would hope so!"

Cass unlocked the bolt. "I've got to get ready for class. See you later, Joe."

"Thanks for letting me see that poem, Cass. It might come in handy later on."

Joe sat quietly in his office thinking. He was tempted to reconstruct the poem as best he could, writing it out from memory. But he didn't want to betray Cassandra's trust any more than she wanted to betray Autumn's. Maybe he should pass the information on to his lawyer, Bill Morgan. Maybe Bill would know how to handle the situation.

He tried to imagine a scenario that would explain how the poem and Patricia's murder were connected. Maybe Marty had fallen so deeply in love with Autumn that he had stopped the relationship with Patty, but she wouldn't take no for an answer. Maybe she threatened to tell their parents about the incest. If Marty had at first raped his little sister when she was young, then he could be in a lot of trouble should Patty tell the police what had happened. Maybe Marty killed Patty to protect himself from charges of rape and incest.

Maybe Marty and Patty broke it off with Autumn in order to go back to their own twosome. Was Autumn capable of murdering Patty in order to get Marty back? Probably not. Autumn was petite, much smaller than either Patty or Marty. Autumn could not have strangled Patty by herself. Maybe Autumn and Marty did it together. But that still didn't explain the other women unless Autumn and Marty had been involved with other women all along. Maybe their thing was picking up other women for a threesome and then killing the women afterward. Marty certainly seemed capable of such violence.

But there was nothing in Autumn's poem that hinted at sadomasochism or violent impulses, was there? Joe suddenly wished he had reconstructed the poem. There were some lines about "controlling" and "toying" with the speaker of the poem.

Joe shook his head back and forth, exasperated. "I'm going crazy thinking about this!" he said to himself. "Joe, you're becoming as sick and twisted as the real killer!" He began shifting papers around on his desk, straightening up the stapler and scotch tape dispenser, and then he opened his literature text to preview *Death of a Salesman* by Arthur Miller. It was time to move on.

Standing in front of the students, Joe began his lecture. "From Oedipus through Hamlet to Willy Loman, we have seen the metamorphosis of the tragic hero in drama," Joe explained. He wrote the names of the characters on the board, drew circles around each one, and connected the circles with lines. "What do you notice about the status of these protagonists?"

"They all had sex with their mothers?" Marco asked.

"No," Joe said. "We have no evidence that Hamlet actually had sex with his mother although the bedroom scene after he kills Polonius certainly implies a sexual attraction. And there's absolutely nothing in *Death of a Salesman* to suggest that Willy had sex with his mother."

"Except that his wife *seems* like his mother!" Marco said.

The class broke into laughter, and Joe smiled. "Okay," Joe said. "Yes. Willy's wife does, at times, seem to be mothering him. But why is that?"

A blonde girl in the front raised her hand. "Because he's losing his memory? It's like he's got Alzheimer's."

"Yes," Joe said. "That's probably her motivation. She's trying to protect Willy and help him. But what do you notice about the social status of these tragic protagonists?"

"Well," said a black student on the side of the room. "Oedipus was a king, but Hamlet was only a prince, so there's a decline in their status. And Willy's just an unsuccessful salesman."

"Exactly," Joe said. "In fact, Willy's described as an 'every' man. Miller was one of the first writers to use the elements of classical tragedy in describing a man of low status, elevating him to tragic proportions in some ways."

The students of the class stared at Joe, unmoved, as if saying, "So what?"

"Why do you suppose this is important?" he challenged.

"It ain't important, Professor," said Marco.

"It *isn't* important, you mean," Joe corrected. "In terms of the way it was written, though, it was important at the time. Why?"

A dark-haired girl raised her hand. "Because it changed the genre?" she asked.

"Yes, good," Joe said. "Even though that sounds like something out of CliffsNotes, explain what you mean."

"Well, if we look at the classic tragedies, like Oedipus and Hamlet and King Lear, we see that these were all men of high social standing and nobility."

"Good," Joe said. "What else?"

"Well, like you explained before, when a hero like a king or a prince realizes he's failed in some way, he falls pretty far. It's a longer fall, so it seems more tragic."

"Very good. But how does that relate to Willy Loman?"

"Willy *is* a 'low' man, just like his name," the young woman said. "So he doesn't really fall from a high status, the way a king would."

"But is his fall from being a mediocre salesman to a man who loses his job and can't support his family any longer, is that still tragic?" Joe asked.

"Well, yeah," one of the young male athletes offered. "I mean, he wasn't a king or a prince, but he did go to work each day and make enough money to raise a family and pay for a home. So when he loses the job, it sucks!"

"Yes, it does!" Joe exclaimed. "And remember, in his own mind, Willy had inflated his status, especially in front of his two sons."

"Right," Marco said. "So in his mind, he was just as great as King Oedipus or Prince Hamlet."

"In his own mind," Joe said. "At least he felt that way sometimes. Maybe that was his flaw."

"His fatal flaw? You've mentioned that before, Professor," Marco said. "What's it mean?"

"Well, in classical literature, the protagonist is believed to have some serious character flaw that leads to his downfall."

Marco raised his hand. "It's easy to see with Oedipus. His pride. He thought he was hot shit and could solve any problem, right, Professor?"

"Yes, more or less, Marco. The Greeks called it hubris."

"Yeah. Hubris. I've heard that before." Marco nodded. "So Willy had hubris too, right?"

"Do you think he did, Marco?"

"Hell yeah. He was always telling his neighbor how to do things, and he was always braggin' about his son, sayin' he had greatness."

The dark-haired girl raised her hand again. "So that's how Miller was able to incorporate some of the same character elements and themes that were used in classic tragedy?"

Joe smiled. "I think so," he said. "Whether a protagonist actually is a person of high standing or merely believes himself to be is not important to Miller. All of us, after all, imagine that our own lives are very important."

Marco threw up his hand. "So you're sayin' we all suffer from this fatal flaw, hubris, right, Professor?"

"Well, not necessarily hubris. What's Hamlet's fatal flaw?" Joe scanned the blank faces. "Let me ask it another way. Does Hamlet seem excessively arrogant, full of himself?"

The blonde put up her hand, saying, "Not really. Just the opposite."

"Explain what you mean," instructed Joe.

"Well, he's full of doubt and questions every move he makes."

Marco held up his pen to grab Joe's attention, saying, "So with Hamlet, it's the opposite of pride? But he's so proud of his father."

"True," agreed the blonde. "But he's also ashamed of his mother, and he despises his uncle."

"So what's his fatal flaw, Professor?"

Joe grinned. "Well, I could tell you, but then I'd have to kill you."

A few students laughed, but some of the female students glanced at one another nervously.

"It's a joke," said Joe.

"Bad timing, Professor," said Marco.

"You're right."

"Do all literary heroes have a fatal flaw, Professor?" asked the dark-haired girl.

"Well, most literary figures have flaws, yes," Joe said. "But usually the flaws are not fatal unless the work of literature is a tragedy."

"It's like a weakness in a superhero, right, Professor?" asked Marco. "Like Superman and kryptonite."

"That's one way to look at it, I suppose."

The blonde raised her hand. "You don't have to be a superhero or a tragic hero to have a flaw. I mean, we all have flaws, right?"

Some students nodded their heads.

"True. But fortunately, most of our flaws don't lead to our demise, so we wouldn't describe them as *fatal* flaws." The students squirmed, and Joe felt he was losing them. "As you continue reading *Death of a Salesman*, think about the ways it parallels more traditional tragic drama. Notice the clever ways Miller interjects those classical ideas while still creating a realistic modern dramatic play."

Joe glanced at the clock.

"That's all for today," he told them as they began closing their books. "We'll pick up here on Friday. I'm going to want some volunteers to read a few scenes out loud. And try to read with a little passion, okay?"

The blonde student stopped beside Joe's desk. "Is there anything to that idea about Linda being Willy's mother?"

"What do you think?"

"I hope not. That part in Oedipus grossed me out!"

Joe grinned. "Yeah, it's pretty strange. But if you think that's weird, then see what Sigmund Freud had to say about the Electra complex."

"The electric complex?"

"No," Joe said, holding back his urge to laugh. "Electra. She was another character in Greek tragedy."

"What about her?"

"Well, she had a thing for her father."

The student's mouth dropped open. "Ooooh," she groaned. "That's disgusting!"

The student left reluctantly, Marco lingering behind her.

"Good lecture, Professor," Marco said. "Are any of these stories based on things that really happened?"

"Why do you want to know, Marco?"

"I don't know. I mean, don't get me wrong. You make this stuff seem interesting, but what good is it if it didn't really happen?"

"That's a good question, Marco. Maybe literature teaches us something about real life, even if the characters and events are manufactured."

"Yeah. That's the kind of answer I'd expect from a teacher."

Joe laughed. "How would you answer your own question?"

Marco looked down at the desk, thinking. "I guess we learn how to stay out of trouble. Maybe we learn how to appreciate our family. I dunno."

Joe nodded. "Good insight, Marco. Keep thinking about it, and let me know what you've come up with at the next class, okay?"

"Okay," said Marco. But instead of leaving, he lingered in front of Joe's desk, his head bowed.

"Was there something else?"

Marco looked up, looking straight into Joe's eyes. For a minute, Joe thought he might say something, but then Marco shook his head and turned toward the door.

"No, not really. Thanks, Professor," he said, leaving Joe perplexed.

Joe went to his office, ate lunch, and graded papers.

On the drive home, the sky grew darker as more rain clouds moved in slowly from the west. Joe noticed several police cars on the side of the freeway as he approached the Mokelumne River and Middle Slough. Down below the freeway on the right were half a dozen policemen walking through the brush of the flatland. Maybe they had found the body of the high school girl from Lodi. Seeing the police brought back the feelings of dread. He drove the rest of the way home with the radio turned up loud, trying to forget what had happened to him since Thanksgiving.

CHAPTER EIGHTEEN

From sleep, pounding and shouts. The room was dark when Joe and Sara awoke. Joe's heart thumped. Someone pounding on the front door of the house. The clock's green numbers showed 4:02. Sara bolted upright beside him.

"What the hell?"

Someone smashed open the front door, shouting unrecognizable syllables.

A home invasion!

People ran through the house. Men's voices. Many voices blurred together. Shouting "Please!"

Beams of light in the hallway.

Katie! Men going after Katie!

Joe wished he had a gun. He looked for a weapon. Sara's screams filled the room. What could he grab? On the desk were only books.

Joe threw the covers back to get to his feet. Large dark figures stormed down the hall, flashlights blinding Joe's eyes.

"Please!" the men shouted. "Please! Police! Police! We have a search warrant!"

Sara kept screaming. Joe looked over at her. Her hands were up in the air. "Don't shoot!" she yelled again. "We're unarmed! Don't shoot!"

Joe looked back as the men ran into the bedroom.

Before he could stand, they had him facedown on the floor, a knee between his shoulder blades, strong hands like vise grips twisting his wrists, then cold steel on each wrist.

As they lifted him to his feet, Joe twisted around in time to see a police officer dressed in black, S.W.A.T. stenciled in white across his chest, carrying Katie toward Sara as another officer held Sara's arms behind her and pushed her out of the room.

"What's going on?" Joe managed to say.

"Joseph Conrad?" the man yelled in Joe's ear.

"Yes!"

"You're under arrest!"

"What for?"

"You're under arrest!"

The men pushed and pulled him from around the bed to the hallway. Sara finally had Katie in her arms; and Katie's little face, terrorized, stared at Joe.

"Why are you arresting me?" Joe screamed.

"You're under arrest for the murder of Autumn Smith!"

Joe turned to look into the eyes of the man who had said the name of his former student.

"Who?" Joe asked, shocked.

"Autumn Smith."

"She's dead? She can't be dead!"

The officer stared at him incomprehensibly. His words had no effect on the cop, dressed in black, wearing a bulletproof vest and a helmet with a clear plastic face guard.

As they pulled Joe through the house, he saw his home filled with men similarly dressed. There must have been ten of them walking around, black M16-styled rifles pointed down to the floor. One of them turned on a light in the living room as the others led Joe out into a waiting van. There were several dark vans and cars parked at different angles on the street in front of Joe's house.

In the van, Joe's hands and feet were shackled to a bolt behind him. He was forced to sit bent over, and that's when he realized that he had on only pajama bottoms and a white V-neck T-shirt. Sitting between two officers dressed in full SWAT uniforms, across from two others, he felt naked. The ride to the police station in Sacramento seemed to take hours.

Joe found himself back in an interrogation room like the one he had been in on that Monday after Thanksgiving when he had first discovered the body of Patricia Miller. This time, though, his hands were cuffed, the handcuffs attached to a bolt in the table.

After sitting alone for half an hour, feeling the need to relieve himself, Joe yelled at the mirror, "This is ridiculous! I didn't do anything!"

The door opened, and both Detective Dunn and Detective Marino came in, Marino carrying an extra chair. Although Joe's heart was pounding hard inside his chest, he laughed as the men entered.

"This is absurd, Detectives! I haven't done anything!"

"You keep saying that," Dunn told him. "But women around you keep dying."

Dunn sat at the table directly across from Joe, and Marino placed his chair at the head of the table. Joe looked both of them in the eyes.

"What makes you think Autumn Smith is dead?"

"We found her body late last night, Mr. Conrad," Marino answered, his eyes filled with hatred. The intensity of Marino's expression sent a chill through Joe.

Joe shook his head back and forth. "Are you sure it's Autumn? I just saw her the other day."

"Yes. We're sure," Dunn said. "She was reported missing late Tuesday night by her boyfriend. She was missing all day yesterday."

Joe envisioned Autumn in his mind. He couldn't help but see her in the candlelight of the dinner she had served at the little table in her apartment. She was laughing, flirting, alive, and attractive. This was too real, too close to home. If she really was dead, then she was the first victim who could be linked to Joe.

"You have the wrong man! I haven't killed anybody."

"Where were you Tuesday?" Marino asked.

"I taught my class Tuesday night!" Joe said. "Check with my students! There were over twenty people in class who saw me there. I was there from six-thirty to almost nine, so I've got an alibi."

Dunn's eyes bore into Joe's. "The coroner estimates her time of death to be late afternoon Tuesday. That makes her murder *before* you met your students," Dunn said. "C'mon, Joe. You can do better than that. Don't you think we started checking you out as soon as we learned that Autumn was missing?"

Joe stared at the two hardened cops. In their eyes, he was certainly guilty. A feeling of dread settled over him.

"Let me think for a minute," Joe said. He tried to recall Tuesday. It was just the day before yesterday, and yet his mind went blank. "I know I was in class Tuesday night. After class I went to—" Joe looked up, realizing that he had to admit that he'd gone to the strip club. "I drove to Highbeams after class, but I didn't stay. I just parked outside."

"We know where you went after class," Dunn said. "One of Marino's coworkers was following you. Where were you *before* your class, Professor? That's when Autumn was abducted and murdered."

This couldn't be real. "Let me think," he said weakly.

"Yeah," Marino said. "Try to think up something good, Professor."

Then Joe remembered. "I went to a movie before class, and then I went to Lyon's for dinner. People had to see me."

Dunn took out a notepad. "What time did you go to the movie?" he asked skeptically. "Tell me the name of the theater and the name of the flick."

Joe described the movie, the girl who tore his ticket, and he described the waitress at the restaurant. Detective Dunn jotted notes carefully, glancing up from time to time. Whenever Joe looked at Marino, Marino glared back angrily.

"Where were you earlier in the day?" Dunn asked.

"I got a late start that morning," Joe admitted. "I drove to Stockton late in the morning and stopped at the La Bou on March Lane for a cappuccino."

"What time was that?" Dunn asked.

"About noon, I guess. I went to the movie theater on Pacific Avenue, just north of Delta College at about one in the afternoon. The movie ended at about three-thirty. I went to Lyon's afterward. I was on campus by five."

"Did anyone on campus see you at five?" Marino asked.

Joe tried to think. "I'm not sure. Someone must have seen me. It was getting dark by then. I was in my office preparing for class from about five until six-thirty."

Marino laughed. "You ain't as bright as you sound, Professor. You'd better come up with a better alibi."

Joe frowned at the detectives. "Why? What's wrong with my alibi? I've accounted for pretty much the whole day."

Marino laughed again though his eyes glared with anger. "Do you really think you're the first guy to go to a movie to try to establish an alibi?"

"What do you mean?" Joe asked again.

Dunn explained, "You wouldn't be the first perp to buy a ticket for a movie, make sure you're seen going into the theater, and then leave through a fire exit to commit a crime. It's been done so many times. It's a cliché in police work."

"I'll tell you what really happened, Professor," Marino said. "You spent your day thinking about how to kill Autumn without getting caught. You knew that trying to kidnap her after your class wouldn't be good because we might be watching you, and we were. You drove around town that afternoon checking your back to see if you was being tailed. When you thought it was safe, you went into the movie, waited for the lights to go down, and then left quietly, probably through a fire exit in the back. You found a way to get Autumn to meet you somewhere, probably north of Stockton where you raped and strangled her. When you were finished with her, you dumped her body like a bag of trash."

Joe laughed out loud. "That's bullshit."

"Well," Dunn said. "That's about the way we figured it happened. Autumn was in contact with people until about three that afternoon. She was supposed to head up to Sacramento to see her boyfriend."

"You mean Marty Miller?" Joe asked.

"Yes," Dunn answered. "Marty Miller. Autumn spoke to him by phone around noon. A woman in her apartment complex saw her doing laundry at about two. No one saw her after that."

"Have you checked out Marty Miller's alibi if he has one?" Joe asked.

"As a matter of fact, we have," Marino added gleefully. "He was at work and people saw him there."

"He's my top suspect!" Joe added. "He's a psychopath!"

Dunn chuckled a little. "He does have a temper, I'll give you that much."

"I'd double-check his alibi if I were you," Joe said.

Dunn looked at Joe and asked, "Will anyone at the Lyon's restaurant remember seeing you there?"

"The waitress should. I've gone there many times before, and I left her a big tip."

"I'm sure you'd like to give every woman you know a 'big tip'!" Marino said sarcastically.

Dunn didn't laugh, and Joe looked at Marino for a moment. "That's disgusting," he told the cop. Suddenly, the reality of Autumn Smith's death, her murder, hit Joe hard. She'd been a student of his, a girl he'd liked and helped. She was a bright, promising young woman, full of life, full of potential. Joe thought about Katie. Another pair of parents, like Patricia Miller's parents, would have to cope with the loss of their daughter. Joe choked back tears.

"Where," he started, "where did they find Autumn's body?"

"We found it at your favorite dumping ground, Professor," Marino said.

Dunn chimed in, "It was in the water at the Lost Slough overpass on Interstate 5. Exactly where you found the body of Patricia Miller."

CHAPTER NINETEEN

The image of Autumn Smith's beautiful body floating in the muddy waters of Lost Slough—covered by leaves, dead moss, cigarette butts the way Patricia's body had been—was too much for Joe. Unable to hold back any longer, he broke down and started crying in front of the two hardened detectives. Autumn's lovely, smiling face appeared in Joe's mind as did images of Patricia's cold, stiff body. Joe rested his face on his handcuffed hands on the tabletop and sobbed uncontrollably for several minutes. Finally, Marino said, "For Christ's sake!" and pushed his chair back dramatically. He stepped away from the table and stared down at Joe, who seemed not to care about anything anymore for he cried with abandon.

As Joe began to regain his composure, Dunn handed him a clean white handkerchief, which Joe took and used to dab his eyes. "Poor Autumn," he said. "Poor, poor girl."

"Yeah," Marino said. "Poor girl that you killed!"

Joe wiped his eyes some more with the handkerchief, looking at Marino. "No," he said firmly to the big detective. "No, I did not kill her. But somebody evidently did, and whoever killed her is still out there. It's got to be somebody who knows both of them. Both Patricia and Autumn."

"That would be *you*!" Marino said, almost laughing.

"But I didn't know Patricia," Joe said. "Even if she was Autumn's roommate, I never met her."

"What if I told you that you did?" Dunn asked. "Would that change your story?"

"No!" Joe exclaimed. "Because I did not know her! I never met Patricia Miller."

"Actually, you did," Dunn said. "You went to the restaurant where she worked at least twice that we can verify from your credit card bills. On one of the receipts, in your own handwriting, you wrote, 'Great Job! I'll come back for more.' Do you remember that?"

Joe vaguely recalled writing a message like that once in October around his birthday. "Yes," Joe admitted. "I recall writing something to that effect on a receipt one time."

"Yeah," Marino added. "One time about a month before you killed Patricia Miller!"

Dunn glared at the other detective.

"That was on a receipt for a dinner you had at Murphy's restaurant on a Tuesday night," Dunn told Joe. "You left a tip that was almost 30 percent."

"I was in a good mood that night if it's the night I'm thinking of. The service was good, and so was the food. I often leave big tips. Don't you?"

"Not really," Dunn said. "I've got a family to support, so I'm usually pinching pennies, like most married men."

Joe looked into Dunn's eyes. They were impossible to read. But the point of Dunn's statement was obvious to Joe. Dunn was telling him that his behavior wasn't typical, that little notes and excessive tips to waitresses made him look guilty. Joe tried to remember the waitress's face from that night in October. It could have been Patricia Miller, but he couldn't recall it vividly enough to know for sure.

"Joe, it's obvious that you feel bad about what happened to Autumn," Dunn said in a soothing, calm voice. "Maybe it's time to confess everything. You can end this entire nightmare right now. Just tell us exactly what happened."

Joe stared steadily into Dunn's eyes. Dunn seemed almost sympathetic as if he felt sorry for Joe. Marino was still angry, but he was hanging back. They clearly expected Joe to crack and confess. The room was dead silent.

Joe grinned. "You almost make me want to confess even though I didn't do anything."

Dunn's expression changed to a look of disgust, and Marino huffed and sat back down.

"I'm going to tell you this one more time," Joe said, suddenly feeling exhausted. "I did not kill Autumn Smith or Patricia Miller or the other women you've found. I haven't killed anybody, and I never will. I'm not going to confess to something I didn't do, gentlemen. You've got a serial killer out there, and you'd better find him before he kills again. It's not me, so stop wasting your time."

"We've got all day," Marino said.

"No you don't," Joe said. "I want my lawyer, William Morgan. I won't say another word without him."

Dunn and Marino looked at each other. Then Dunn turned to Joe. "We can help you, Joe, if you talk to us. We can help you plead out in a way that will save your life."

"California has a death penalty," Marino added.

Joe laughed. "Yeah, and we use it once every ten years! I'll take my chances with a good lawyer and a good jury."

Joe's statement obviously displeased the detectives. Marino stood up and walked behind his chair. Detective Dunn leaned in closer to Joe, asking, "Are you sure, Joe? If you are this killer, you need help. You probably wanted to stop a long time ago. We can help you end this nightmare right now."

Joe looked into the detective's blue eyes. He seemed sincere, like a parent who is pleading with a child for his own sake. It was the first time Joe saw Detective Dunn as a real person, a man whose emotions were not unlike his own.

"Honestly," Joe said. "I'm not the killer. You might have some reasons to think I am. You might have what you think is good evidence, but I'm telling you, I'm not the one."

Dunn pulled back, his expression changing to mild disgust.

"Really," Joe pleaded. "I'm not your man."

"We're finished here," Dunn said, standing. "You're going to jail, Mr. Conrad. Probably for the rest of your life."

Marino added, "Unless they put the needle in you."

Joe sat back, exhausted, and looked at the two men.

"The real killer is still out there. He'll kill again unless he's smart."

"What do you mean, 'unless he's smart'?" Dunn asked.

"If he's smart," Joe explained, "then he'll stop now that I've been arrested to make me look guilty. He probably chose Autumn because he knew I knew her. He's framing me."

"Of course," Dunn responded, "the more plausible explanation is, we've arrested the right man. So if the murders stop now, that confirms *your* guilt."

Joe shook his head. "I'm too tired to argue. Just call my lawyer."

Afterward, Joe was fingerprinted and booked. He was given an orange jumpsuit and taken in handcuffs through a long hallway with caged windows to another part of the building, the jail. More papers were filled out; and he was led into a modern white-walled facility, past a dozen cages with prisoners in their cells, watching through small windows in the solid metal doors as Joe walked by. He tried not to look nervous, but his stomach was churning, and he was afraid he would vomit before the officers got him to his cell. Before the officer unshackled him and pushed him into his cell, Joe asked, "What happens to me now?"

"You wait," the young officer said.

"How long?"

"Until you get arraigned. That could take a week or two," the officer said, closing the door behind Joe. "Or maybe three or four weeks, depending on how good your lawyer is."

The cell was the size of the walk-in closet in the master bedroom at home. It was all white with a thin mattress on top of a concrete slab that protruded from the wall. The toilet and sink were combined, and there was a window about as narrow as Joe's hand next to the toilet. Otherwise, the cell was as sterile as an operating room. A blanket and a small pillow sat folded at the foot of the bed. Joe tossed the pillow at the far end of the little bed, sat down, looked around the room again, then stretched out, pulling the blanket over himself as he rolled toward the wall. Thick white paint covered the pores of the concrete blocks in front of his face.

This can't be real, he told himself. *This can't be happening.*

And then the floodgates opened, and Joe cried as hard as a person can cry. Inside the cell, he could not be heard; and his loud guttural sobs echoed against the cold, bare walls of the cage. He felt childlike, his chest heaving with sobs that he could no longer control. All his life he had drifted from one thing to another, rarely taking a firm stance in one direction or another. He had drifted as if living his existence on a raft that floated almost effortlessly along with a current. It had been his way of coping after the death of his parents. This casual, directionless way of living had served him well enough, he used to think.

Until now. Now the stream had carried him to a place without hope. He was like the body he had found in the water that had wound its way through the Central Valley, carried along gently to a terrible dark, frightening place. As Joe's crying ceased, he felt the warm wave of sleep wash over his body, and he slipped into darkness.

For the rest of that day, he was not allowed out of his cell. In the afternoon, he heard the other prisoners being released into the great hall, which he could see somewhat from the little window in the door of his cell. Joe slept and thought until the cell grew dark.

During the night, he listened to the sounds of the building. It sounded like a great metal ship, its pipes groaning and creaking quietly all night long. His dreams were filled with images of bodies—Autumn's and Patricia's and other women's he did not recognize. Sometimes, he dreamed of the police grabbing him in his bedroom. He dreamed of the two detectives questioning him. In one dream, Katie was drowning in the bathtub, and Sara wouldn't let him go into the bathroom to save her. Joe awoke from that dream in a cold sweat.

On Friday afternoon, Joe was taken out of his cell to a room where he could speak to Bill Morgan through a glass partition.

"Katie and Sara are fine," Bill told him. "They're staying with Suzy in Sacramento."

"The cops didn't hurt them, did they?" Joe asked.

"No," Bill said. "But Sara was questioned for about five hours yesterday before they released her."

"Where was Katie all that time?" Joe asked.

"With Suzy," Bill told him. The lawyer took some forms out of his briefcase. "I'm going to have you sign these, Joe. These say that I'm officially representing both you and your wife."

"Why Sara?"

"Just in case. In some cases, the wife is an accomplice."

Joe laughed. "Sara? Sara couldn't kill anyone," he huffed. "Except maybe me. When all of this is over, she'll probably kill me." Joe started to sign the papers.

"No," Bill said. "But she probably will divorce you."

Joe looked at Bill, tears forming in his eyes. He felt a deep pain in his chest as though he had just learned that Sara had been with another man. He used the lawyer's expensive pen to sign all of the lines marked by little red arrows.

"We've advised her not to go ahead with the divorce until after the trial. You'll do a lot better, Joe, if you are seen as a married man with a young daughter."

"I *am* a married man with a young daughter," Joe snorted.

"For now. If the jury sees that your wife is staying by you and if they know that she feels comfortable letting a young daughter stay with you, that could help a lot. Sara has agreed."

"But then she's going to divorce me?"

"Probably, yes," Morgan admitted. "Joe, we've got to concentrate on your case. I'm pushing for an early preliminary hearing. Normally, you'd be in here for a week or more before we could get you scheduled for the prelim, but I pulled some strings and got your name added to Monday's schedule."

"Monday? I've got to wait until Monday?"

"You should be grateful, Joe. Most folks wait two or three weeks at the earliest. Sometimes, it can take over a month!"

"I guess I was hoping you could get me bailed out today."

Bill Morgan laughed, astonished. "For a smart guy, you don't know much about the legal system, do you, Joe?"

"I guess not," Joe admitted. He was trying to imagine three more nights inside the prison.

"I've got you on the schedule for Monday afternoon. The courts hold preliminary hearings on Mondays and Fridays, so if something happens, you might get bumped to next Friday. I want you to be prepared for that because it's a real possibility."

"All right," Joe said.

"I've got to tell you that this case has generated a lot of publicity. It's all over the news that the police have made an arrest in the I-5 stranglings, and they've named you. Your picture has been all over the news, along with stories about you."

"Oh god," Joe said soberly.

"The good news is that the police don't seem to have much hard evidence yet although they're still searching your house in Davis."

"Well, they won't find anything. I'm innocent. There's simply no evidence to find."

"Sometimes, things that don't seem like evidence to you can seem like solid evidence to a jury. For example, do you have any rolls of duct tape in your house?"

Joe's heart sunk. "Yeah," he admitted. "I've probably got two rolls in the garage and one in the junk drawer in the kitchen."

Bill winked at him. "So do I," he said. "Everybody's got duct tape. But when the jury hears that the victims were bound with duct tape and that the evidence technicians found duct tape in your home, that will tend to make you look guilty."

"You're talking as if it's a foregone conclusion that there will be a trial. What if the police find the real killer before my case comes up?"

"You have to understand how the police think," Bill explained. "In their minds, they have found the real killer. Therefore, all they're doing now is concentrating on finding evidence that helps their case against you. Unless they stumble onto some better evidence that leads them in a different direction, you are their only target. I've seen it a hundred times."

"Well, there's got to be evidence out there that exonerates me since I'm not guilty."

"Chances are, if the police do find some evidence that points away from you, they'll hide it. They won't want me to discover it. They'll assume that the evidence is invalid. That's the most serious problem with police work today. They put blinders on when it comes to seeing other possibilities once they've zeroed in on a suspect."

"You're saying that I'm totally screwed, then?"

"Not necessarily, Joe," Morgan stated. "A lot depends on the kind of evidence they find."

"Go on."

"Tell me, Joe. What kind of evidence *are* they going to find?" Morgan looked into Joe's eyes stoically.

"None!" Joe said. He thought Bill Morgan had believed him all along, but now he realized that even Morgan wasn't sure. "I'm telling you, Bill. I'm innocent!"

Bill Morgan smiled. "I believe you, Joe. Your wife doesn't believe you're capable of rape and murder either, but she does think you're guilty of screwing up your life enough to make you open to these kinds of charges. And *that* she cannot forgive."

Joe's eyes filled with tears. He almost couldn't control himself in front of Morgan. "What can I do, Bill? How do I get out of this mess?"

"At the prelim, the judge will decide whether or not he'll even allow bail in this case. Most of the time in capital cases, bail is denied, Joe. You've got to prepare yourself for that possibility. This case in particular is getting a lot of publicity as much as the Laci Peterson case. It could become a nationally televised case, like OJ or Robert Blake. Remember, Joe, they think you're guilty of raping and murdering at least four to five women in the last six months."

"Five women?" Joe asked.

"They still haven't found Lilly Nguyen, but the newspapers and television stations are speculating that she is one of the victims of the I-5 Strangler. They've moved their search south from the Lost Slough area to the Mokelumne River."

Joe sat quietly, barely able to contain his tears.

"Joe," Bill said, "They're going to kick me out of here soon, so let's get a few questions answered."

"Okay."

"First, when's the last time you saw Autumn Smith?"

"Let's see," Joe said, looking up at the ceiling, trying to remember. "I definitely saw her last Saturday. Her boyfriend made a powerful impression on me."

"Yeah," Bill said. "Sara told me about your encounter at the Downtown Plaza. Did you see her after that?"

"Yes," Joe said. "I saw her Monday. She came to my office on campus looking for her teacher, Cass."

"Cass?"

"Cassandra Johnson. Her office is next to mine, and she has Autumn in one of her classes. Autumn popped in for about five minutes, and Cass took her back to her own office. That's the last time I saw her," Joe said, his voice trailing off. It was hard to imagine that beautiful young girl dead.

"You did not see her at all on Tuesday?" Morgan asked pointedly.

"No, Bill. Not at all. I did not see Autumn on Tuesday or Wednesday."

"She was killed sometime Tuesday afternoon or early evening, probably between four and six. We'll know better after the autopsy. Tell me where you were during those hours on Tuesday. Don't leave anything out, not even the slightest detail."

Joe closed his eyes to concentrate. "I went to a movie at the Signature Theater on Pacific Avenue. I got out of the movie at about three-thirty, and I got into my car and drove to the Lyon's on West Lane near campus. That's where I usually go for dinner before my night classes. The waitress was a tall slender, attractive woman who's waited on me before. I think her name is Dolores, but I'm not sure. She should remember who I am, though, because I left her a big tip."

"What did you order?"

"I ordered what I usually have—six prawns, a chocolate milk shake, and coffee. Sometimes, I get a small dinner salad, but not that night."

"What time did you arrive at the restaurant?"

"About four o'clock, or a little before," Joe said. "You know, I told all this to Detectives Dunn and Marino."

"Okay, but now you're telling me," Morgan said as he wrote.

"Won't the detectives check it out? They'll see that I couldn't have killed Autumn. Won't they?"

Morgan didn't answer. He seemed irritated. "Did you see anyone at the restaurant you know? Anyone who might recognize you?"

Joe closed his eyes again to concentrate. "No," he said. "It wasn't very crowded. The waitress should recognize me, though. The bill was a little over ten bucks, and I left her fifteen. That's a pretty big tip. She's waited on me before, and I wanted her to be more friendly."

Bill looked up from the legal pad. "Why?" he asked.

"I don't know. I go in there sometimes as much for the company as the food. I'd like to be acknowledged."

"You weren't hitting on her, were you, Joe?"

"No! Of course not!" Joe tried to think about his actions with the waitress.

"Okay," Morgan said. "What time did you leave the restaurant?"

"It was a little before five. I left and drove the few blocks to campus, parked the car, and started walking to my office when the five o'clock chimes sounded from the cathedral's bell tower."

"Did anyone see you on campus at five o'clock?"

Joe shook his head. "No, not a soul. Because my face was still bruised, I was actually trying to avoid being seen. I didn't realize that I'd need an alibi later."

Bill finished writing and put his expensive-looking pen down on the pad. It made Joe envious.

"You see how it looks, don't you, Joe?"

"Explain it to me, Counselor."

"It looks like you targeted Autumn because her boyfriend, the brother of your earlier victim, beat you up two days before."

"Wouldn't I want to kill the boyfriend, though?"

"The prosecutor will argue that your revenge on the boyfriend was the rape and murder of his girlfriend. Through that act, you made the boyfriend feel impotent, and he will suffer the rest of his life knowing that you raped his woman."

"You should write a murder mystery, Counselor," Joe said. "That sounds like the kind of fiction you read in second-rate novels."

Morgan stared into Joe's eyes. "But it makes sense to juries. It's the kind of *Matlock* plot that they can relate to."

Joe swallowed hard and stared back into Bill Morgan's tense face.

"I get your point."

Bill started putting his pen and papers back into his briefcase on the other side of the glass partition.

"I've got a good private investigator who handles most of my cases. I'll get him started finding these people, especially this waitress. We've got to plug all the holes in your schedule that day to prove that you didn't have the time to kidnap Autumn Smith, rape her, strangle her, and dump her body."

Joe tried to imagine doing all of those horrible acts. "How much time do you guess all that actually took?" Joe asked. He could visualize it all happening to Autumn, and thinking about it made him light-headed.

Bill Morgan stood up. "Honestly, Joe?"

"Yeah. Honestly."

"A person could have done it all in less than an hour. The drive from Autumn's apartment complex to the I-5 bridge over Lost Slough only takes about fifteen minutes. If the killer met Autumn at a location closer to Lost Slough, it could have taken much less time."

"What makes you think someone met her near the slough?"

"The police haven't found her car yet. Patricia Miller's car was found about two miles from the slough. The woman from LA?"

"Yeah?" Joe asked.

"Her car was never found."

Joe shook his head, realizing that the killer was not careless.

"There's something else you need to think about, Joe."

"What's that?"

"If you aren't the killer, then the killer must have targeted Autumn Smith ahead of time, and he probably planned on committing the crime on Tuesday in order to make *you* look guilty."

"Yes, I already thought of that." Joe's mind swirled with possibilities. "It's got to be someone who knows me and Autumn and Patricia! Marty Miller fits that description!" Joe said. "Or—"

"Or what?"

"Have your private detective investigate Gary Grimes. He's got it in for me, and he might have known both Patricia and Autumn."

"We'll look into him too."

"I'm reluctant to mention this, but there are a couple of students in my classes who knew Patricia too."

"I know Dunn's been looking at one of your students. Give me their names."

"I hate to—I really don't think either of them could be killers."

"Joe, at this point, we're desperate. Anything might help."

"One is named Nicholas Adams, and the other is Marco Hernandez."

"Marco Hernandez," Bill Morgan wrote. "That name sounds familiar. Maybe that's the one Dunn mentioned before. I'll have to check my notes."

The guard had arrived behind Joe. His time was up. Joe stood.

"When can I see Sara and Katie?" he asked Bill Morgan.

"Sara will be at the preliminary hearing on Monday. If we can get you released on bail, you should be able to see Katie by Monday night or early Tuesday."

"How much will the bail be?"

"For a capital crime of this magnitude? If he grants bail at all, it's going to be a million dollars."

"A million dollars!"

Bill grinned. "Don't worry," he said. "You only have to post 10 percent of that."

"We can't afford a hundred thousand dollars!"

"Your sister, Suzy, has already taken out a second mortgage. She should have a check from her credit union by late Monday or Tuesday if we need it."

Bill Morgan walked away, dressed in his expensive dark suit, carrying his leather attaché case. Joe was led back to his cell where he sat on the edge of his bed thinking carefully about who could have murdered Autumn Smith, making him look guilty. Who could be framing him?

CHAPTER TWENTY

In the Sacramento County Jail, Saturday's breakfast was a box of cereal, a carton of milk, a small plastic container of orange juice, a fresh orange, and a bran muffin—all tied together in a plastic bag with a napkin and a plastic spoon. Joe ate everything, hungry and groggy after a fitful night's sleep where dreams mixed with nightmares. The trash, he was told by the guard who shoved the food through a small oblong opening in the door, was to be put back into the bag, including the spoon. "Be ready to hand me the bag in an hour," the guard told him.

Joe spent his morning dozing and thinking. Lunch was served as breakfast had been, through the opening in the door. Another carton of milk, a ham and American cheese sandwich, like those served in vending machines, a small green apple. After lunch, Joe tried to sleep again, but he wasn't tired. He got up and walked toe to heel from the door to the wall with the toilet. Nine and a half footsteps. He stretched out on the floor and began doing push-ups. It felt good to exercise. He rolled over and did fifty sit-ups. Then he stood and did jumping jacks until he couldn't continue. "This is why prisoners are so fit," he said aloud. "There's nothing else to do!"

Monday morning before breakfast, a guard walked down the line telling some prisoners to be ready to go to the courthouse right after breakfast. Joe was one of the inmates who was alerted; and before he was finished eating, a guard appeared at his window, and his door was opened. He was told to put on a wide leather belt, and his hands were then handcuffed to the front of the belt. A pair of large cuffs with a long chain between them were fitted around his ankles, and he was led over to six other men who had been similarly bound. They were attached to one another like train cars and led out of the jail to a waiting van.

At the courthouse, the prisoners were driven into an underground garage. When the van door was opened, it was facing another door; and four guards were forming a human hallway, two standing on each side. The prisoners were led into a basement room where they were stopped one at a time to do some paperwork with a clerk. Joe watched everything with interest. When it was his turn at the clerk's window, Joe looked inside and saw a dismal windowless office with rows of file cabinets and shelves filled with files.

"Joseph Lawrence Conrad?" the clerk asked.

"Yes," Joe answered.

The clerk had Joe sign a form, which he was barely able to do, straining against the handcuffs that were locked to his belt; and then the clerk explained that this was a preliminary hearing to determine whether should be held over for trial.

"You'll see your attorney inside the courtroom and you'll only have a few minutes to confer. You might see family members in the courtroom too, but you're not allowed to talk to anyone except your attorney and the judge. Do you understand?"

"Yes," Joe said, his mind racing. Things were happening so quickly now that he felt as if he was in a fog.

Each prisoner was released one at a time and allowed to go into the courtroom. They were not allowed to change clothes, having to appear in their orange jumpsuits. The courtroom was much smaller than Joe had expected, and it was devoid of the wood paneled grandeur of a Perry Mason show. In fact, the room was modern, like a business office. At first, Joe couldn't see Sara, but then he spotted her on the far side of the room standing in the back corner. He tried to smile at her, but she looked solemn and serious as if she had been crying. At least she was there.

Bill Morgan stood on the other side of a railing. "Don't say anything unless the judge asks you a question. Keep your answers honest and short. Understand?"

"Yes," Joe said.

He heard a clerk in the courtroom say his name and the word, "Four counts of murder." Next a woman in her thirties dressed in a suit, addressed the judge.

"We urge no bail be granted, Your Honor," she said. "This is a capital case. There are four victims that we know of, but there could be additional victims, and the defendant has not been a California resident for more than three years."

"Your Honor," Morgan said. "My client is a college instructor. He's married, gainfully employed, he has a child. There is no physical evidence connecting him to these crimes, Your Honor, so we ask for the lowest possible bail."

Joe looked up at the judge, an older man with a graying beard who seemed not to be listening to either attorney, so absorbed was he in reading papers. The two attorneys remained patiently silent while the judge read. Bill Morgan spoke up again, "Your Honor, my client has ties in this community. He has a relative who is an officer of the court, and she is willing to put up bail money, so confident is she of my client's innocence."

The judge continued looking through pages of papers. Then he looked up, ignoring Bill Morgan but looking squarely at the prosecuting attorney.

"Did I miss something here, Counselor? Is there any hard evidence linking this defendant with these murders? Because all I see here are some statements by a couple of witnesses who really aren't witnesses because they didn't witness a crime. Is that about right, Counselor?"

The woman looked down at her legal pad of notes. "Your Honor," she said, beginning slowly. "The police are gathering more evidence even as we speak, but we have eyewitnesses who put the defendant together with the most recent victim in the days leading up to her murder. We have a witness who was in the company of the victim just days before her murder who encountered the defendant in a hostile setting. We do have physical evidence that links the defendant to an earlier victim Patricia Miller and—"

"You've got a couple of credit card bills from a restaurant?" the judge said, interrupting the woman. "Have we ruled out all of the other customers who tipped this waitress?"

The female attorney looked up at the judge and said, "Are you asking me seriously, Your Honor, or are you being facetious?"

"I'm being facetious, Ms. Cantrell," the judge replied. Then he looked over at Joe. His eyes, behind thick steel-rimmed glasses, looked stern and impatient. "How did you like your weekend in jail, Professor Conrad?"

Joe was taken aback at the way the judge addressed him. It was so direct that Joe wondered if they had met before. "I didn't like it very much, Your Honor. I'd like to go home to my wife and daughter."

"You're being accused of some very serious crimes. Are you aware of that?"

Joe laughed. "Yes, Your Honor."

"If I set bail for you, are you going to run away or stay and fight?"

Joe blinked. The judge's question seemed absurd at first, but Joe suddenly imagined fleeing the country. Mexico, maybe.

"Don't think about your answer too long," the judge added, and some people in the packed courtroom laughed.

"Your Honor," Joe said. "I'm innocent, so I plan on staying and fighting. I want my life back."

The judge directed his attention toward the female prosecutor, pointing at her with the handle of his gavel. "Now you hear that, Ms. Cantrell? This defendant doesn't pose a flight risk. He's innocent!"

The crowd chuckled again at the judge's obvious sarcasm. "Being an old English major myself, I've got a weakness for English teachers. Bail is set for one million dollars."

Bill turned toward Joe and smiled. "Good job," he said. "We'll have you out by this afternoon."

Then Joe was escorted out of the courtroom, and another prisoner was escorted in. Joe was taken to a small holding cell. "It may be four or five hours," the guard told him. "So just relax."

He must have slept for a while. A little while later, a different guard handed him a plastic sack through the bars of the cell. "Your wife brought these. Change into them immediately. I'll come back for you in a few minutes. You made bail."

The sack contained a pair of dark green slacks, brown loafers, brown socks, and a blue shirt. As quickly as he could, he took off the orange jumpsuit and dressed in his familiar clothes, leaving the jumpsuit crumpled on the red concrete floor. He felt his face. That morning, he hadn't shaved with the tiny battery-operated electric razor they'd given him.

When the guard returned, he inspected Joe and the cell before opening the door. "Fold up that jumpsuit, and leave it on the bench," the guard instructed. Joe folded the suit.

Joe was walked through several corridors; and he had to sign yet more papers before finally being released into a room where Sara, Suzy, and Bill Morgan were waiting. He walked over to Sara trying not to cry. He put his arms around Sara, and she returned the embrace limply. "I didn't think I'd ever see you again, baby," he whispered in her ear. She stood unresponsive. Joe pulled back and looked at her. He had never seen her face so blank and sad.

"Let's go, Joe," Bill Morgan said.

"Honey, what's wrong?"

Sara blinked and looked at him. "Nothing, Joe. Let's just go."

"I gave her a Valium, Joe," Suzy said. "She's been very upset."

They walked outside and went across the busy street toward the parking garage. A Salvation Army Santa was on the corner ringing a bell, and it had drizzled earlier, so the streets were wet, and the city smelled damp. Joe followed as Bill and Suzy led the way. When Joe tried to hold Sara's hand, she pulled hers away. They came to a dark blue Dodge Intrepid.

"Whose car is this?" Joe asked.

"It's mine," Bill answered. "I drove Sara over from Suzy's apartment."

They climbed into the car, Bill in the driver's seat, and Suzy up front. Sara and Joe sat in the back together, and Joe tried to put his hand up behind Sara's neck, but she brushed it away.

"Where's Katie?" Joe asked.

Suzy turned back to face Joe, who was sitting behind Bill. "She's at my condo. I arranged a professional sitter to be with her."

"She's going to stay with me, Joe, at Suzy's place. You can't see her."

"What?" Joe said loudly. "Why not?"

Bill spoke, "Joe, we've been instructed by Child Protective Services that Katie will be taken away from Sara if you try to have contact with her before the trial is over."

"What?" Joe yelled.

"Joe," Sara pleaded. "They took her away from me all day Thursday. She had to spend all day Thursday and Thursday night with foster parents because the police questioned me for hours."

"Bill, you told me she was with Suzy! Why'd you lie?"

"I didn't want to upset you any more than necessary."

Suzy spoke, "Joe, I just managed to get Katie released in my custody on Friday. Otherwise, she might have had to stay in foster care until the end of the trial."

"Don't make this harder for me," Sara pleaded. "I've got to be able to stay with Katie."

"Can't we all go home?" Joe asked.

"Not if you want Sara to keep Katie," Bill said.

"Whatever happened to 'innocent until proven guilty'?" Joe asked.

"That's generally true," Bill said. "Except in the case of Child Protective Services. The courts err on the side of caution when it comes to the safety of children. For CPS, you're guilty until proven innocent. And even then, you're not always given custody of your children again."

Joe hit the armrest that divided him from Sara. "Goddamn it!" he yelled. "This is so unfair!"

"Calm down, Joe," Suzy instructed. "Blowing up won't help. It'll just get you in more trouble."

Joe sat fuming. It was late afternoon, and the streets were crowded. Suzy's condominium building was only twenty blocks away, but traffic was sluggish.

"When is my trial, Bill?"

"I'm pushing for as soon as possible. The DA's office will probably petition for a continuance, but legally, you're supposed to go to trial sixty days after you've been charged with a crime. That puts the date sometime in the middle of February, but my guess is March or early April."

"Why so long?" Joe asked.

"It takes time to process evidence and prepare a case, Joe. It takes our side time too. We want to move quickly, but not too quickly. Otherwise, the judge will be roasting my nuts over a fire instead of Sally Cantrell's."

Suzy looked over at Bill. "The judge gave Sally a hard time?"

Bill laughed. "Oh brother! Did he ever!" Bill caught Joe's eyes in the rearview mirror. "That kind of thing is rare, Joe. Usually that judge in particular—he's all business."

"But they've got no case, right?" Joe asked. "That's what the judge made it seem like anyway."

"Yeah. That's my fault," Bill said. "Sally knew she was going to take a hit, but she owed me a favor, so I got her to agree to a premature prelim. You ought to thank Sally Cantrell, Joe. Even though she wants to fry your ass."

"Does she think Joe's guilty?" Suzy asked.

"She thinks the detectives wouldn't have pushed so hard if they weren't sure they'd find enough to make a good case."

Sara looked at Joe with disgust.

"Sara!" Joe said. "This isn't my fault! I'm not guilty of anything!"

"The hell you aren't!" Sara said.

"You can't believe that I killed those women!"

"No, of course not. At least, I don't think so. But you are guilty of something, Joe," Sara said. "I think you must have slept with that girl we saw in the plaza, and I have a strong suspicion that you slept with that waitress too."

"Jesus Christ, Sara! I swear, I didn't!"

"Okay," Bill said. "Let's everyone calm down."

Bill drove the car into the parking garage that was under Suzy's condo. He found a parking space for visitors and parked the car. The four of them sat inside the dark car and talked quietly as if someone might be listening. From time to time, a car drove by, its headlights briefly illuminating the inside of Morgan's car. Sometimes, a car horn sounded while at other times, the sound of squealing tires could be heard.

"Joe," Bill said. "You go on home. Sara's car is parked out on the street in the front of the building." Sara handed him her keys and his wallet. "We can't do anything more today, and I've got other clients to meet tomorrow, so we'll meet Wednesday afternoon about two o'clock. I'll have my secretary give you a call."

Joe listened and nodded, but he was hoping to have a few minutes alone with Sara.

"Joe?" Suzy said.

"Yes?"

"You might find it impossible to stay at your house. There are bound to be dozens of reporters hounding you there. Once you get home, don't answer the telephone or the door. And if you can, slip out later tonight, and check into a cheap hotel somewhere."

"I spoke to Dr. Thorne on Friday," Sara said. "He'd already heard everything. It's all over the news that you're the I-5 Strangler, Joe, so you're going to find it hard to go anywhere without being recognized."

Bill looked back at him. "You might want to let that beard grow until it's time for the trial, just so it's harder to recognize you. Your life is very different now. You've become a celebrity in the worst sense of the word. You'll probably get death threats too, so be prepared."

Suzy added, "A lot of people don't need a trial to be convinced that you're guilty, Joe. You're going to be harassed in ways you can't even imagine."

"Anyway," Sara said. "Dr. Thorne has gotten substitutes to teach your classes for the rest of the semester. He says that you need to grade the final papers and turn in grades via the mail, but he doesn't want you to set foot on campus."

Joe laughed. "I guess tenure is out of the question, then, right?"

"Thorne was very serious. He says he needs those final papers and grades for your students right away. He told me to tell you not to take forever. He said he'll sue us if you don't get the students' grades turned in before Christmas."

"Well, Merry Christmas to you, Dr. Thorne!"

"He said you can call him if you have any questions. Just don't go back to campus, he said."

"Suzy," Joe said. "Can he do that? I mean, what good is it to be released on bail if you can't go about your normal business?"

"Did you sign an employment contract when you first started teaching at CLU?" Suzy asked him.

"Yes, of course."

"Well, it probably has a standard morals clause, which means that they can suspend you from teaching on campus if you do anything that they determine to be against the university's code of behavior."

The parking garage had grown very dark. Everyone in the car was a shadow from which a voice emerged. It was eerie.

"You'd better go now, Joe," Bill instructed. "Go home, keep the lights down low, get some rest, do your work, and take it easy. And whatever you do, don't talk to any reporters. That's my job now."

Joe turned to the dark figure sitting beside him, the woman whose face he could no longer see. "I wish you could come home with me, Sara," he told his wife. Sara's head went down, but she said nothing.

"My office will call you Wednesday morning, Joe," Morgan's voice said. "Be ready." Then he opened his door, and the interior lights came on. Sara hung her head and didn't look at Joe.

"Please go now, Joe," she finally said. "Let me get back upstairs to our daughter."

Joe opened his door to the cold, damp air and climbed out. He walked to the exit and went downstairs to the street. Around the corner was Sara's Escort. As Joe approached it, he noticed a parking ticket in plastic tucked under the windshield wiper.

"Great!" Joe said aloud. "Just fucking great!"

As he spoke, a couple walking on the sidewalk looked over, surprised by the outburst. Joe glared at them. "I'd better pay this ticket," he said to the couple. "Wouldn't want to go to jail again, would I!"

The couple ignored him. He stared up at the building at the lighted windows of the seventh floor, wondering which one was Suzy's apartment. He stared up, the damp air moistening his face, wondering if Katie was looking down trying to see her father.

CHAPTER TWENTY-ONE

Joe drove home the same way he had the night of Patricia Miller's memorial service, and he fought the same urge to drive straight into the Sacramento River and end his life. He felt imprisoned by what was happening—there seemed to be no way out of this nightmare. He no longer had any control of his life, and the overwhelming feeling of helplessness made him imagine what the last hour of life had been like for Autumn Smith, Patricia Miller, and the other victims of the I-5 Strangler.

The streets of Davis seemed unusually quiet that Monday evening. Where were people? Maybe the Monday night football game was something special. Joe hadn't been following football lately though he enjoyed watching it sometimes, having played a little in high school. He drove down B Street and slowed at Tenth, but just as he was about to turn down his street, he managed to see a half-dozen news vans parked in front of his house, so he continued down B until he got to Twelfth Street. Colorful Christmas lights outlined the roofs of several houses on this street. He turned and drove down about a third of the way, parking across the street from a larger-than-average blue house, which had two large teardrop-shaped windows under the eaves of the high roof. Lit from within, these windows looked like two large eyes watching him; and he was reminded of the billboard in *The Great Gatsby*, the ever-watchful eyes of Dr. T. J. Eckleburg that saw every adulterous, murderous sin Tom and Daisy and Jay Gatsby had committed.

Joe climbed out of the car, locked it, and walked east to F Street. He turned and walked two blocks to Tenth and turned west. He could see the news vans parked at the far end of the long block. Halfway down Tenth Street, he turned south and took the short street to Ninth Street. He had walked and jogged these streets many times, so he knew which house bordered the back fence of his house. The rundown house on Ninth seemed dark and empty. Joe looked around, saw no one following or watching, so he crossed the lawn and went around the house to the backyard. The back of the house was dark too. No one was home, evidently. Joe made his way through some brush to the back fence where he peered into his own backyard. No lights were on in his house, and the yard seemed empty. Reporters would have had to open gates to get into his backyard, and there were rules against trespassing. Even at a suspected murderer's house. He climbed over the redwood fence easily and made his way to the back door.

Once inside, Joe moved through the house carefully without turning on a light. All the blinds and curtains were closed, so the house was darker than he had ever known it. Such dead silence gave Joe a creepy feeling. He half expected Norman Bates to come running out of a closet wielding a long knife, *Psycho*'s soundtrack screaming in his ears.

At the front door, Joe peered out the peephole. A few reporters stood outside their TV stations' vans smoking, but the others seemed to be inside their satellite trucks. Joe could hear their muffled voices, but he couldn't make out what they were saying.

In the kitchen, he felt his way to the refrigerator and opened its door. Light filled the room, so he shut the door quickly and looked around. Even in this room, the vinyl blinds had been pulled down, so he doubted if the reporters had seen the light. Joe hadn't eaten since that morning in jail. What to do? "You're a clever guy, Joe," he whispered. "Solve this problem," he commanded of himself.

An idea came to him. He pulled the refrigerator toward himself, and it rolled easily away from the wall, exposing the plug, which he yanked out of the socket. He opened the door, grabbed the carton of milk and a jar of applesauce. Katie loved applesauce, so they always kept some in the house. He poured a glass of milk and dumped some of the applesauce into a cereal bowl, putting everything back when he was finished. Before plugging the refrigerator back in, he unscrewed the lightbulb inside.

From the freezer, he took out a frozen dinner, which he transferred to the microwave oven; but when he started the microwave, a light inside came on, so Joe quickly opened the door again. He grabbed a dishtowel and hung it over the door of the microwave, closing it inside the door just enough to act as a curtain. The light came on again, but it was barely visible.

While his meal was cooking, he searched through the junk drawer; and using his sense of touch like a blind man, he found a small candle and some matches. He put the candle inside a small juice glass and lit it. The candle, placed in the center of the table, produced just enough light so Joe could see. Under different circumstances, this might have been romantic. He'd have to remember this. If ever he got Sara back again, he would prepare a good meal for her and sit in candlelight across from her. Joe could almost imagine

Sara facing him, smiling and laughing, and looking seductive across the table. But her image quickly faded.

Joe ate his candlelit dinner quietly, reflecting on the events of the past four days. As hungry as he was, the more he thought about the circumstances of his life, the sicker he felt. He couldn't finish his food; and as he sat at the little table, alone in the dark, he felt as if he were back in the prison cell. This wasn't freedom.

"C'mon, Joe," he whispered to himself. "Straighten up. Get tough. Solve this problem. Think!"

He reviewed what he was doing to fix the problem. He had a lawyer, a good one, evidently, with some connections. The police couldn't have a strong case because there wasn't any solid evidence linking him to the victims. Even the judge had scoffed at the evidence! But the police had found enough circumstantial evidence to make him look like a possible suspect, and he did not have very good alibis for his whereabouts at the times of the killings. What else would the police find that might make him look guilty? He needed to know more.

Leaving his mess behind, Joe carried his little candle into the master bedroom. The blinds and curtains were drawn. Joe turned on the television, keeping the volume down very low. It was too late for the six o'clock news, but Joe wanted to test the brightness of the television to see if it was safe to watch later. He turned the brightness down on the screen and checked the walls. The light did not seem significant enough to show through the curtains and blinds, but Joe turned the TV off anyway. He placed the little candle on the desk beside his bed and blew it out. With blinds and curtains closed, the room was pitch black. Joe lay on his back, staring up at a ceiling he could not see.

Waves of exhaustion washed over him, and he fell asleep immediately. When he awoke, he checked the illuminated dials of his watch. It was 2:33 a.m. "Shit!" he said aloud, louder than he should have. He had missed the news at ten and eleven. Joe got up and went to the bathroom, leaving the light off. He splashed cold water on his face and patted his face with a soft towel that smelled wonderful, in contrast to the odors of urine and disinfectant that he had smelled in the prison. Joe then felt his way back to the front door where he peered through the hole again. All the vans were gone.

Still, Joe didn't want to risk being seen inside the house, so he kept the lights off and went back to bed. It took him almost an hour of tossing and turning to get back to sleep.

In deep black water, he embraced Autumn Smith, whose eyes and mouth at first looked seductive; but when Joe tried to kiss her, she began screaming hysterically, and her face dissolved into a mask of macabre decay. Joe pushed her cold, stiff corpse away, and it floated downstream in the water. He realized that he was back in the Lost Slough, but it was night, and the sky was black, without stars. Joe struggled and climbed up the muddy bank. Then he was running in a wooded field. The ground softened under his feet, trapping him, and he sank slowly.

Now he was in quicksand up to his chin, and he was freezing. The muddy sand around him was cold as ice. Dark silhouettes surrounded him—Sara, Suzy, Bill Morgan, Dr. Thorne, laughing, holding his mouth. Suddenly, Katie was kneeling in front of him, and Joe was terrified that she too would sink into this cold bog. "Go away, Katie," he pleaded in his dream. "It isn't safe here."

"Fight back, Daddy," Katie pleaded. But as she pleaded, Joe began sinking, and his sinking caused the ground Katie was on to give way. Now Katie started to sink, and the more she struggled, the faster she sank. Joe's mouth and nose were under the mud, and he could see that Katie was almost gone too. She fought vigorously, shaking her little shoulders and head back and forth, but her movements made her sink deeper. She was crying and screaming, and Joe began to cry. Joe cried as hard as he ever had, knowing his daughter was about to die. Just before Joe's eyes filled with mud, he jerked awake.

He was in bed, in his own room, in his own house. The room was odd, though, darker than normal; but some light showed around the edges of the window. For a few seconds, Joe was disoriented and terribly sad. His dream had been as real as any dream he had ever had, but as he grew more awake, he was thankful it was only a dream.

Groggy, Joe sat up and spoke to the empty room, "Dreams might not be real, but the feelings are. Too real, sometimes."

He rubbed his eyes and checked his watch. It was almost seven-thirty. Joe scooted down to the foot of the bed and turned on the television. He adjusted the brightness and found a local channel that gave local news until nine in the morning.

After several other news stories, the newscaster finally addressed what Joe was interested in.

"The main suspect in the I-5 Strangler case was released on bail, but his whereabouts are unknown at this time. Details next after these messages," the woman newscaster said.

Joe's heart pounded. After a few insipid commercials, coverage of a group of schoolchildren came on the screen and chanted, "Good day, Sacramento!"; and the morning show continued.

Photographs of both Patricia Miller and Autumn Smith appeared on the screen behind the newscaster as she spoke.

"The whereabouts of Joseph Conrad, the main suspect in the I-5 Strangler case, who was released on one million dollars' bail yesterday, are still unknown," she said. Videotape of Joe in his orange jumpsuit, standing beside Bill Morgan, played silently on the screen. The tape showed Bill turning toward Joe; and Joe, unshaven and looking dazed, was listening to something Bill had said. That was when Bill had said "Good job" to him. The report continued.

"Since being released sometime yesterday afternoon, Joseph Lawrence Conrad, the suspect who was arrested by police last Thursday morning, has not been seen. We now go to Kimberly Dalton, who's standing by outside the suspect's house. Kimberly?"

The picture changed, and Joe was looking at the front of his own house. It was a beautiful day outside, Joe realized. The sun was shining though the front porch of Joe's house was in shadow. A young woman stepped into the picture.

"There's no sign of the suspect here at his home in Davis, but his attorney assured reporters last night that Professor Conrad is still in the area. Conrad, who teaches at CLU in Stockton and who had at least one of the victims in his classes, hasn't been seen since the preliminary hearing yesterday morning. When asked to comment, a spokesman for the district attorney's office made this statement."

A man in a business suit appeared. Joe didn't recognize him. "We had urged the judge that no bail be given to this suspect," the man said irritably. "This is a person suspected in the deaths of at least four women. In the opinion of this office, he should not be walking the streets."

The main newscaster came back on. "Kimberly? Did the suspect return home last night?"

The reporter, standing in front of Joe's house, came back on the screen. "We were here with several other reporters until midnight, and there was no sign of him then, just as there's no sign of him now."

"Well," said the reporter in the station. "We can only hope he hasn't fled the country."

The man sitting next to her said, "Maybe it'd be better if he has!"

"Yes," the woman agreed. "At least he couldn't harm any more women in this area."

Joe shook his head. "Christ! They've already found me guilty!"

He turned off the television and sat on the edge of the bed, his heart racing, his face burning with anger.

"What the hell am I going to do?" He didn't care anymore if the reporters outside heard him. He was tempted to run outside and scream at them, but he could imagine how that would look. "What *am* I going to do?" he asked himself quietly, holding his head in his hands.

The answer came to him in the shower.

It was simple. As he reviewed his teaching plans for the day, he remembered Hamlet.

What would Hamlet do?

The answer was obvious.

He dried himself quickly and wiped off the mirror over the sink, grinning widely at himself, pleased by his decision.

From his closet, he took his newest powder blue shirt with a button-down collar, his best Ivy League tie, a pair of dark brown tweed slacks, and dressed himself as if for a job interview at Harvard. Inspecting himself in the full-length mirror on the back of the bedroom door, he was quite pleased with his professorial appearance. All he needed was a pipe clenched between his teeth!

In the kitchen, Joe carefully removed his coat, hung it on the back of a chair, put on an apron, and fixed himself scrambled eggs and toast with plum jam. He made coffee, drank a glass of milk and a glass of cold orange juice, and then sipped his coffee while eating his toast, smiling at his plan the entire time.

Next, he looked up the phone number for Suzy's condo and started to call, but the phone was literally off the wall. Joe found the telephone on a small bookshelf they kept under the window in the kitchen. He fitted the phone into its slot on the wall fixture and waited for a dial tone. After punching in Suzy's number, he listened to it ring three times, then the answering machine came on. Suzy's voice simply requested that he leave a message.

"Sara," Joe said. "Pick up. This is Joe. Sara, if you're there, please pick up. I want to say good morning to Katie. Please pick up," Joe pleaded again. He waited for a few seconds, but no one answered. "Okay. Maybe you aren't there. I just wanted to tell you both that I love you very much. I'm sorry for the trouble I've caused everyone, but it's not my fault. Not really. Anyway, Sara, I think I've found a way out. It might seem insane to you, but it's the only thing I can think of that might make this whole mess go away. Tell Katie that I love her very much. I had a dream about her—"

The machine beeped, and the tape ran out. Joe decided not to call back. He looked through his wallet and found a business card with a telephone number that he had never dialed before. He dialed the number carefully and waited.

"This is Joseph Lawrence Conrad," he told the woman who answered the phone. "Do you remember me?"

The woman on the other end of the line didn't answer at first. Then she said cautiously, "Yes. Of course, I remember you. What do you want?"

"I want to talk," Joe said.

There was silence on the other end.

"Do you want to hear what I have to say?" Joe asked, wondering if he had made a mistake.

"Yes," the woman said. "Very much."

"Good," Joe replied. "Meet me at the front entrance of Anderson Hall at the university at two o'clock this afternoon."

The woman asked Joe something.

"Yes, of course," Joe responded. "That's what I want. See you then."

Joe hung up without saying goodbye. He looked at the phone, wondering if he was doing the right thing, but then he smiled gleefully and turned toward the kitchen.

He had decided to clean up his mess, and he started by clearing the table.

CHAPTER TWENTY-TWO

After cleaning the kitchen, Joe put on his tweed sports coat and went out the back door, locking the bolt with his house key as he left. He wasn't certain when he'd be able to return. Things might not go as he hoped they would. He walked across the backyard to the fence, grabbed the top, pulled himself up, and hopped over. A frail elderly woman was raking leaves. Startled by Joe dropping to the ground, she gasped and dropped her rake.

"I'm sorry," Joe said. He walked over, picked up the rake, and handed it to her. "I didn't mean to frighten you."

The woman took the rake from Joe, confused and unsure what to do. Joe walked to the side of her house and made his way to the street. He quickly walked down to F Street, turned north, and walked as quickly as he could to Twelfth Street, realizing that if the police had been called, they could arrest him for trespassing.

In the daylight, Joe noticed Christmas decorations on many of the houses along Twelfth Street. Sara's car was still parked where he had left it the night before. He climbed in, warmed up the engine, and began his familiar commute.

He had about five hours to kill. Realizing that he might not get another chance after today, Joe drove to a shopping mall north of Davis and took his time buying gifts for Katie and Sara. He paid to have the gifts wrapped, and he labeled each one. He also bought a few small gifts for Suzy, Cassandra Johnson, Bill Morgan, and Sara's parents. No one in the mall seemed to recognize him though a few people looked at him carefully. At an Orange Julius stand, he bought a large drink as his lunch; and then after loading all the gifts in the trunk, Joe drove to Interstate 5 and headed south to Central Lutheran University—perhaps for the very last time.

Leaving the Christmas presents neatly wrapped and labeled in the trunk, Joe grabbed his briefcase and headed toward Anderson Hall. It was a beautiful sunny day. The air was crisp and clean, and only a few white clouds drifted overhead. It was almost two in the afternoon, and many students were leaving their one o'clock classes. Some students looked at Joe and whispered, others ignored him, oblivious to what had been happening; but others who knew him walked up to talk.

"Hey, Professor Conrad!" a young man said. "How ya doing?"

"I'm doing great!" Joe said, smiling back. "Glad to be back on campus!"

"We saw your picture on the news!" another student shouted. "Are you the I-5 Strangler?" the girl asked, laughing.

"I don't think so!" Joe yelled back. "But stay tuned."

When he rounded the corner of Anderson Hall, he saw the woman he had called, Joan Ngo, with her cameraman. They were alone as Joe assumed they would be. No other reporters were there. As Joe expected, Joan would want the exclusive interview. And there were no police—at least, none that Joe could see.

Joe smiled as he approached, but Joan and her cameraman looked very nervous. As Joe approached them, a small group of students crossed the lawn at an angle to intercept Joe.

"Hey, Professor C.!" Marco shouted. "You're a celebrity!"

Joe turned to greet the group of four. "Hello, Marco, Laurie," he said, shaking their hands when they stopped him. He noticed that Joan had instructed her cameraman to start videotaping. "How are you guys doing?"

"We're doing better than you are, Professor," Marco said.

"Yes, I suppose you are, Marco," Joe joked. The comment aroused suspicion in Joe that he did not want to reveal. "Although given the choice between going to jail and taking final exams, I think I'd rather go to jail!"

The students laughed.

"We know you're not guilty, Professor Conrad," Laurie said self-consciously. She was looking at the video camera from the corner of her eye.

"Thanks, guys," Joe said. "That means a lot to me." Joe shook hands with each of them, and just before they left, Laurie came back and hugged him sympathetically.

"Your students seem to be fond of you," Joan said, sounding more professional than she had on the telephone that morning. Joe realized she was getting this on tape.

"Most of them are," Joe said. "Of course, most of them earn good grades. A few students aren't quite as fond of me. Especially the ones who earn lower grades."

"Well, Mr. Conrad," Joan said into the microphone she was holding. "Tell us why you asked us down here today."

Joe motioned to the lawn. "May we walk?"

"Sure," Joan said. She caught up with him, and the cameraman scurried to get in front of them. He walked backward as they talked.

"Well, Joan," Joe said, speaking clearly, using his own professional voice. "I thought you might want to hear my side of the story in response to these outlandish charges that have been brought against me. And I thought that this beautiful campus would be an ideal setting."

They arrived at a bench along the path, and Joe motioned for Joan to sit down. He knew that Anderson Hall, with its classic redbrick walls covered by green ivy, would make a perfect backdrop for this part of the interview.

Another group of students walked by and, almost in unison, said, "Hi, Professor Conrad!"

Joe said hello even though he didn't recognize the students.

"Joan, I love teaching at this well-respected little university," Joe continued. "It's a truly wonderful place to teach because it has the most caring and compassionate faculty and administration I've ever worked with. This is truly a place of enlightenment, Joan. The administration here at CLU has told me that they are behind me 100 percent. They've said they believe in the ethical principle that a person is innocent until proven guilty."

"Very admirable, Professor Conrad," Joan said. "But tell us about your relationship with the victims of these horrible crimes."

Joe looked down for a moment and grew serious. "I did know Autumn Smith quite well. She was a bright, promising young student who took a couple of classes from me during her freshman year. A top student, Joan, like many of the bright, capable young people who find a home here in the CLU community. I recommended that she be a tutor in English, and I wrote letters of recommendation for her to attend graduate school elsewhere since CLU doesn't offer a doctoral program in English."

"Didn't you also have a relationship with Autumn Smith off campus, Professor?"

"As you yourself probably know, Joan, since you're a CLU alum, many of the faculty here meet students away from campus," Joe admitted. He could see Joan squirming on the bench. "I did meet Autumn at her apartment on one occasion to help her fill out some application forms for a scholarship. She was kind enough to make dinner for us. But I can assure you that nothing inappropriate happened. As with many of my students, I considered Autumn a friend as well as a student. And like most of the faculty who teach here, I wanted to help Autumn in any way I could. All of us here at CLU want our students to thrive."

"The police state that they have also linked you to Patricia Miller," the reporter stated. "What was your connection with her?"

"None really," Joe said. "Although she was a student here in the past, she left CLU before I was hired to teach at this wonderful institution. But it turns out that Patricia Miller was a waitress at a restaurant where I ate two or three times. Unbeknownst to me, she had been my waitress."

"Isn't that a bit of a coincidence, Professor?" Joan asked.

"Yes and no," Joe answered. "Stockton is still a fairly small community, so many people know one another here. That's one of the beauties of this town. It has a rich tradition of cultural diversity where people of all backgrounds interact and associate with each other. I'm sure that the police know of several other people who knew both Autumn Smith and Patricia Miller. In fact, Patricia Miller's own brother, Marty, was dating Autumn. I'm sure you'd agree, Joan, that he shouldn't be considered a suspect in the deaths of these women simply because he knew both of them quite well."

"Yes, that makes sense," Joan admitted.

"There are two or three other people, students here at CLU, who may have known both victims. Surely, we shouldn't automatically leap to the conclusion that one of them is guilty, should we?"

"Well, those kinds of coincidences do raise suspicion, especially for the police," the astute reporter added. She was beginning to catch on.

"As your professors must have taught you here, Joan, mere coincidence is not the same as evidence. We teach that in our first semester critical thinking courses for freshmen."

Joan laughed audibly.

"I'm sure the detectives who are working on this case have better training than a freshman-level course in deductive logic! Wouldn't you agree, Joan?"

"One would hope so, Professor," the reporter said.

"As to the other victims, I have no knowledge about them. One was from Los Angeles, I believe."

"That's correct, Professor. And as far as we know, the police have not been able to link you to either of those victims."

"Nor will they, Joan, since I am completely innocent of these crimes. The only mistake I made," Joe said as sincerely as he could, "was acting like a Good Samaritan and stopping to get water for my car when I discovered the body of a dead person floating in the slough. If I had not stopped that day, there would be no connection between me and these murders."

A crowd of students had gathered to watch, and a few were starting to get into the shot behind Joe and the reporter.

"Maybe I could show you my office and the classrooms where I teach, Joan," Joe suggested.

Joan ran her finger across her throat, and the cameraman stopped videotaping. Joan looked at Joe and smiled. "Nice job, Joe. You're a real pro."

Joe returned the reporter's smile. "Thanks. I'm fighting for my life here, Joan."

"Let's go upstairs to your office," Joan said. "We looked for you up there when we first got to campus."

"Trying to catch me off guard?" Joe asked.

Joan just smiled as they walked to the entrance of Anderson Hall. Then Joe saw Dr. Thorne standing just inside the doorway.

"Uh-oh," he said. "This could put an end to the interview."

"What is it?" Joan asked.

"That's my boss in the doorway, Dr. Thorne. He's the chair of the department."

Joan strained to look, apparently needing glasses. "That's old Thorne! He hasn't changed!"

Joe looked at the Asian reporter. "You remember him?"

"Yes," Joan laughed. "He was my professor in three courses. Talk about horny old men! He was always hitting on us back in those days. Thought he was a real charmer." Joan walked confidently toward him and motioned to the cameraman to start filming. "Hello, Dr. Thorne," she said loudly. "Nice to see you again. Joan Ngo, from Channel 8 news. Remember me?"

Thorne smiled nervously. He extended his hand, looking back and forth from Joe to Joan. "Yes, of course I remember you, Ms. Ngo. You were one of our favorite students here."

"You helped me get my first job in journalism, Dr. Thorne," Joan said, gripping Thorne's hand tightly. "I can't thank you enough," she said, still shaking his hand. "We're doing an interview with Professor Conrad here to try to shed some light on these outrageous charges against him."

"Yes, well—" Thorne said, but Joan continued.

"He's already told us how wonderful all of you in the administration have been, standing behind him this way when he needs the most support."

Thorne's expression changed. He realized that he must go along. "Yes," Thorne said. "Professor Conrad is one of our favorite instructors here at CLU. The students love him." Thorne realized he had committed a faux pas in light of the pending rape charges against Joe. Thorne turned bright red. "I mean, he gets a lot from his students." Thorne realized that his last statement sounded even worse.

Joe tried to rescue him. "We were just headed up to my office, Dr. Thorne. Joan wants to see where I work, and I do have to prepare for my night class, don't I?"

Thorne had regained his composure. "Yes, Joe," he said, resigned to accepting Joe back. "You've only got a few hours until your night class."

"Thanks," Joe said. He almost winked at Joan.

Thorne stepped out of the way and allowed Joe to enter the building, followed by Joan Ngo and her cameraman. Joe walked proudly up the stairs, almost expecting the victorious music from a *Rocky* movie to play in the background. Instead, he heard the echoes of his own footsteps on the old staircase. The footfalls were still music to his ears.

Upstairs, Craig Richmond walked out of his office reading a paper with his head down. The noise of Joe, Joan, and the cameraman arriving on the top floor startled Craig; and when he glanced up from his paper, he was shocked to see Joe looking so self-assured.

"Oh, Craig," Joe said. "I'd like you to meet Joan Ngo. This is one of my colleagues, Craig Richmond."

Joan held out her hand, but Craig was too stunned to react at first.

"You might recognize Joan from television?" Joe asked him.

"Oh, yes," Craig said, regaining his composure. "How do you do?"

"Nice meeting you," Joan responded, smiling.

"Craig has been very supportive in all this," Joe said, watching the other teacher's reaction. "As Dr. Thorne mentioned, when I've needed to miss class, Craig has been kind enough to take my place."

Craig looked over at Joe dumbfounded, still shaking the reporter's hand.

"You must be shocked," Joan said to Craig. "By the charges that have been made against one of your fellow professors here at CLU."

"Yes, it's all been surprising," Craig managed, withdrawing his hand.

"Well," Joan replied. "Nice meeting you."

Craig looked back over his shoulder as Joe led the reporter and her cameraman toward his office. Before they reached Joe's office door, Cassandra poked her head out of her office. The look of disbelief turned into a wide smile as she scurried from her office and hugged Joe.

"You're out?" she said in disbelief.

"Yeah," Joe said, returning her smile. "Haven't you been watching the news?"

"God no!" Cass said. "You know how I absolutely abhor television news!"

Joan laughed out loud. "I know what you mean," she said good-heartedly. "Too sensationalized."

"Too depressing!" Cass responded. "They all focus on the absolute worst of humanity!"

Joe released his hug and stepped aside. "Cass, let me introduce Joan Ngo to you. She's a reporter from the TV news. Joan," he said, "meet Cassandra Johnson. Poet in residence at the university."

Cass held out her hand and started to shake hands with the reporter when she realized what she had just said. "Oh my gawd!" she said, laughing. "I'm sure I didn't mean you." Cass could not control her laughter as she and Joe shared, it seemed, a private joke about the world of television.

"I'm sure you did," said Joan. "But I won't hold that against you. Poets shouldn't concern themselves with the mundane events of everyday life."

Cass released her hand from Joan's light grip. "Actually, it's the poet who immortalizes the events of everyday life in a way that makes them most meaningful."

Joe interrupted. "Joan is an alum of CLU. Of course, that was before our time. But she remembers Dr. Thorne quite well."

"Really?" Cass asked. "I imagine him to have been the dullest lecturer."

Joan laughed. "Not the dullest," she said. "But perhaps the oddest. He tried to be hip, but he was hopelessly stuck in the sixties and seventies."

"Interesting," Cass said. Turning toward Joe, she asked, "How are you out of jail? I thought you'd been locked up for the rest of your natural life?"

"The judge scoffed at the evidence," Joe said, almost gloating. "He released me on bail."

Cassandra grew more serious. "Are you still going to trial?"

Joan laughed at that question.

"I'm afraid so," Joe said. "But not for quite a while. I'm hoping they catch the real killer by then."

"Joe?" Joan said.

"Okay. We've got to finish this interview. She's got a deadline."

Joan's interview with Joe continued once they reached his office. The cameraman set up the camera in the doorway so he could focus mainly on Joe, but he was able to pull back and get Joan's profile from time to time.

"I want to ask you some tough questions," Joan said as the camera watched. "Did you kill Autumn Smith or Patricia Miller?"

Joe returned the reporter's gaze. "No, Joan, I did not. I'm completely innocent of these charges. I have a wife and a young daughter, and I would not want anything like this to happen to either of them. I love them both very much."

"Why have the police focused almost exclusively on you, then, if you're innocent?"

Joe shook his head. "I'm honestly not sure. I guess the fact that I knew one of the victims is enough in their minds to make me look like a suspect, especially since I was the person who found Patricia Miller's body."

"Let's change topics for a minute," Joan said. "Speaking of finding Patricia's body, some people have found it suspicious that you haven't made an effort to claim the reward. They suggest that this makes you look guilty."

Joe took a second to compose his answer. "It's not that my wife and I couldn't use the money, Joan. Believe me, we could. It just doesn't seem appropriate to ask something of people who have suffered the loss of a child. It just doesn't feel right."

"Isn't there some suspicion by the Miller family that you *are* the one responsible for Patricia's murder?"

"Of course there is," Joe admitted. "When the police arrest a person for a crime, all of us usually assume they wouldn't arrest someone without good reason. This experience has taught me an important lesson about the judicial process, Joan. Sometimes, the wrong people *are* accused of crimes. Just like those cases in Illinois where many men on death row were released because new forensic evidence proved that they weren't guilty."

"Good example," the reporter admitted.

"I only hope the public will keep an open mind. And I hope the police capture the real killer before he kills again."

CHAPTER TWENTY-THREE

He stood in a darkened bedroom at a tall dresser, photographs of a woman and two children in frames watching him though their faces were obscured by shadows. Soft black leather driving gloves rested together on top of this dresser, pressed together like a pair of hands in prayer. He pulled one of the expensive gloves over his left hand, working his strong fingers in forcefully, the expensive leather stretching over his hand like a second skin. Then using his gloved hand, he pulled the second glove over the fingers of his right hand, working them in slowly. When the black gloves covered his hands, he pressed the fingers of one hand down in between the fingers of the other to make sure each glove was on as tightly as it could be. The fragrance of the rich Italian leather reached his nostrils, and he breathed in this air as one would breathe in an intoxicant—slowly, sensually.

Walking through his dark house—he detested light when in this mood—he found the door to his garage and went in carefully in order to avoid scraping against the paint of his car. Even inside this Spartan garage, he kept the doors of his car locked. With a surgeon's care, he inserted the key into the lock of the door while making sure the other keys did not scratch the paint around the circular chrome lock. The door unlocked with mechanical precision, making a noise like that of the bolt action of a well-oiled rifle.

Climbing carefully into the Triumph Stag, he rested on the black leather driver's seat and checked his dark eyes in the rearview mirror. These simple rituals he always savored. The key slid into the ignition, and he turned the key slowly. The starter motor engaged quickly, and then the 3,000 cc British engine throbbed to life, its idle as steady as a heartbeat.

He punched the button on the remote control for the automatic garage door, and another motor rattled to work, raising the door to allow the noxious lethal fumes of the engine to escape into the afternoon air. The edge of a cassette tape protruded from the mouth of the cassette player he had had installed in the car years ago. His gloved fingers pushed the tape into the player, and Chris Isaak's deep, melancholy voice began singing "Wicked Game." The bass of the music pulsed through the speakers and throbbed against the interior of the car. He slowly backed out, pushing the remote control button again as he rolled backward down the slightly sloped driveway of the duplex. There was no traffic on the quiet street. Straightening out the front wheels after having backed into the road, he gripped the steering wheel with his gloved hands and drove slowly out of the neighborhood toward the interstate.

He had several hours to prowl before he would have to stop and return home in order to prepare himself for work. But the urge to drive was strong. With expert skill, he maneuvered the car through the streets, the new Pirelli tires gripping the pavement with ease.

As he drove toward the freeway on-ramp, he checked the sidewalks on both sides of the street. Few people were out walking. Fewer walked alone.

One young woman of the right size and age stood alone on the sidewalk in front of a fast-food restaurant. He slowed to examine her pretty face more closely. Her dark eyes and dark lips invited him. Her curly amber hair lifted and settled around her face in the breeze. The driver slowed and traced the outline of her body with his eyes. She seemed oblivious, staring absentmindedly at the traffic until she seemed to notice his eyes. Her expression altered ever so slightly. Her lips parted. The driver signaled to turn into the parking lot beside the little restaurant. Then a young man walked out of the restaurant door, and she turned around and reached for him.

The driver cancelled his signal and continued straight toward the freeway. His gloved fingers tightened around the wooden steering wheel.

Driving north on Interstate 5, he stayed in the slow lane through the heavy traffic on the west side of Stockton; but once north of all the new developments and just before the truck stop exit at Highway 12, he accelerated with head-jerking speed and whipped by several cars and trucks. As three lanes merged into two, he roared by the last car in the fast lane and tore up the freeway north for several miles until traffic forced him to ease the speedometer needle back down from one hundred to just under eighty miles per hour.

Now trapped behind a train of commuters, he was forced to drive the prevailing speed as he approached the Mokelumne River crossing. Next, he saw the bridge ahead that spanned Middle Slough. His eyes were drawn to the sight of a dozen or more people on both sides of the freeway who were walking side by side in lines searching the tangled brush of the ground between Middle Slough and Lost Slough. Police cars were parked on the muddy frontage roads he knew so well. As he drove by these searchers, a side of him shuddered; but that side was controlled, and a knowing smile drew his lips apart almost imperceptibly.

Gripping the steering wheel tightly with his left hand, he reached down to the console between the bucket seats. His right hand lifted the lid and reached inside where it searched out a small bottle filled with brown liquid. He brought the tiny bottle up to his neck, just below his right ear, and sprayed tiny particles of cool cologne on his flesh. He reached around and sprayed a small amount of Obsession on the skin just under his left ear. Then, without taking his eyes from the road, he carefully returned the little bottle of cologne to the console and shut the lid.

The fragrance aroused in him a strong feeling. His eyelids grew heavy, and he appeared sleepy. But he followed the traffic north, taking an exit south of Sacramento and turning east to drive his usual route. Through more boulevards and streets he drove, watching the edges of the road for cars that had stopped, watching the sidewalks where a few people walked in the chilly air of the afternoon.

He would know her when he saw her. She would appear to him as the others had appeared. Solitary. Easy. Maybe even willing. Though all before had denied it. If along these ribbons of concrete he did not find her, then he would turn south and join the evening traffic that plodded southward on Highway 99.

Highway 99 was not as good. It was too busy. Too many truck drivers who stopped for women who had broken down. No. He would not stop on Highway 99. He would continue on to Stockton and exit at the infamous Wilson Way. Along this road, women all too frequently walked alone. But they would not be alone for long. In the past, he had used these women. At the start of his new adventure, he had taken three of them. But they smelled foul. They were vulgar. His desires had grown beyond their expertise.

These days, he needed something younger. Something fresher. Something that did not fight back. Something too young to understand.

CHAPTER TWENTY-FOUR

Volunteers had concentrated their efforts on the east side of Interstate 5 as directed by police because the bodies of Patricia Miller, Autumn Smith, and the other two women had been found generally in that area. That Tuesday, the San Joaquin County sheriff directed them to search farther east, hoping that something new would be found. All morning, they searched just to the north of Lost Slough and to the south between Lost and Middle Slough, but nothing had been found. After a lunch break, the dozen volunteers, with their police escort, began searching the area between Middle Slough and the Mokelumne River.

Shortly after four, when the sun was growing closer to Mt. Diablo, two of the volunteers who had stayed back and were searching along the south bank of Lost Slough discovered a place where the reeds on the north bank had been parted recently as if a fisherman had pushed through them in order to find a suitable spot to fish. Using their walkie-talkies, they called command, the police officer chaperoning them, to tell him of their find.

The officer took three volunteers with him back to his police car, and they drove north on the interstate to the next exit and then east. From there, they drove until they found a dirt road that headed toward the slough. In a few minutes, they made it to a spot where fishermen probably parked frequently. Empty jars of bait, discarded packages of fishhooks, and other signs confirmed that this was a favorite place for sportsmen to park. After pushing through the brush along a narrow muddy path, the three volunteers and the police officer climbed the bank up to the levee that contained the river. Walking east for only a few minutes, they spotted the two volunteers on the north side.

The volunteers slid down the slippery embankment closer to the water. They made their way to the opening in the reeds, which looked like the part in someone's hair. Working backward from the part in the reeds at the water's edge, the volunteers seemingly retraced invisible steps as the police chaperone and third volunteer observed from the top of the embankment. They were losing light, so they walked quickly through the tall grasses, moving their hands back and forth over the grass as if wading in water. One volunteer stopped suddenly, and the other looked over at him and stopped as well.

At their feet was a depression in the grasses where two people had obviously lain. The larger flattened spot was almost a perfect outline of a body. Grass had been compressed in the shape of a person. A narrow wedge of grass between the legs was not as heavily compressed as the other shapes. Even in this dim light, it was clear that two people had lain here side by side.

When one volunteer looked up at the policeman at the top of the embankment to flag him down, he saw that the cop was already speaking to someone using the microphone on his shoulder. The officer flagged the volunteers back up to the top of the embankment, and they walked back to the car to wait for evidence technicians to arrive.

Thirty minutes later, a swarm of police, evidence techs, and volunteers carefully inspected the area. One volunteer, an Explorer scout, wearing a pair of wading boots he usually wore trout fishing, walked slowly in the water farther east than the others. Police had assumed that the gentle current of the water in the slough would carry a body west toward the ocean.

The Explorer, a student from Lodi High who vaguely knew Lilly, hoped he would not find her. But Lilly's long black hair was unmistakable, floating on the surface hidden within the reeds along the embankment.

As soon as the scout's flashlight beam landed on the young woman's hair, he screamed, "I found her! I found her!"

First one, then another, and then more flashlights pointed in his direction in the fading light of the cold winter evening.

Lilly's slender body had been pushed into the reeds and weighted down with a water-soaked log that had been laid across her back. With care and reverence, the evidence technicians lifted her nearly nude body out of the dark water and handed it up to others who were on the bank. They laid her lifeless body out on a piece of white canvas to make their inspection of it easier.

As he climbed out of the dark water with the help of two police officers, the Explorer was patted on the back and told, "Good job." Only then did the seventeen-year-old Scout begin to cry.

Under bright lights, the evidence technicians and the detectives examined Lilly Nguyen's delicate body. With rubber gloves on, one of the technicians lifted Lilly's right hand.

"See this?" the young technician asked. "This bruising probably happened shortly before her death. It's on the outside edge of her other hand too."

"What do you make of it?" Marino asked Dunn.

Dunn put his hands together as if to pray but then interlaced his fingers. "This girl fought back," Dunn said, making chopping motions with his hands. "She must have hit the perp hard several times to cause that kind of bruising."

Marino shook his head back and forth. "She's the tiniest victim, but she fought the hardest, looks like."

"Yeah," Dunn agreed.

The technician lowered the Vietnamese girl's arm slowly, reverently. He pointed to the side of her head that faced the detectives.

"Notice the bruising there?" he asked. "Whoever took her hit her hard on both sides of her head. There's bruising here around the temple that's real visible, but I suspect that when the coroner shaves her head, he's gonna find more bruising up in her scalp."

"Do you see marks around her neck?" Dunn asked.

The technician shone his flashlight on Lilly's bluish throat. "Not much," he said, the sadness of his voice evident. "There could be some, but it's not as pronounced as with the other victims."

"So she probably wasn't strangled to death like the others?" Marino asked.

"No," the technician said. "She was probably drowned. A lot of water came out of her mouth cavity when we lifted her."

"Are we sure it's the same perpetrator, then?" Marino asked.

Dunn pointed to her right wrist. "Red skin and less arm hair," he noted. "The evidence of duct tape is clear."

"Shirt opened, bra undone," the technician said. "No pants. No panties. We'll have to wait for the coroner to confirm, but I'd bet a month's pay that she's been raped."

"What's on her finger?" Dunn asked.

The technician reached down and rolled Lilly's hand over. He shone the beam of his flashlight onto the fingers.

"Looks like a school ring," the tech said. "Yeah. It's a Lodi High class ring."

Dunn leaned closer, almost touching Lilly's hand with his nose.

"Is that a hair?" Dunn asked.

The evidence technician nearly dropped Lilly's arm. "Where?" he asked excitedly.

"Caught in the ring," Dunn said calmly.

"Jeez, I hope that's what we think it is!" Marino's voice went tense with excitement.

"Bag her hands," Dunn instructed. "Let's get this girl back where she can tell the complete story."

Dunn and Marino straightened up. Standing next to each other, they looked at each other and smiled.

"I think we've got him!"

Dunn smiled. "I sure hope so," he said.

A technician working a few yards away at the place where the tall reeds had been parted called over, "Detectives!"

Marino and Dunn turned in unison and looked over at the other evidence technician. The two detectives walked over to the reeds.

"I think we might have something very good," the technician said.

"You got icing on the cake, son?" Marino grinned at the younger man.

"Not icing, Detective. Blood splatter, maybe."

"That's hard to believe after all the rain we've had," cautioned Dunn.

The technician pointed his flashlight beam at some of the reeds, which were about the same width as an index finger. Some had been bent over. Lifting one of the reeds carefully, he shone the light on the crease in the reed. A few dark spots, smaller than a pencil eraser, were on the underside of the bent reed.

"You evidence techs are amazing," said Marino. "Hundreds of reeds out here, and you find one with blood on it!"

The tech grinned. "It wasn't that amazing, Detective. We just retraced the obvious trail where they pushed through the reeds and examined the ones that were bent or broken. Usually, it's the bent or broken branch that snagged on a perp or vic's clothing. We found about a dozen broken reeds, so . . ."

Marino looked at Dunn. "You think we got him?"

"That could be the girl's blood," Dunn cautioned.

"Yeah," Marino replied. "But if we're lucky, it just could be the bastard's blood!"

"If Lilly hit him hard enough," Dunn said. He turned toward the technician. "Take good care of that evidence, son."

"It's a wonder it survived this long," Marino said. "Like you said, with all the rain we've had."

Dunn nodded. "Our boy is smart. He commits his acts on wet or rainy nights and leaves the bodies in the water as if he knows the water will wash away the physical evidence."

"Our boy *is* smart. He's a college professor, after all. Probably reads books on evidence collection and police work."

"Maybe," said Dunn. "The perp removes the duct tape from his victims because he knows the tape holds clues. He wears a condom so he doesn't leave DNA behind."

"What are you thinkin'?" Marino asked.

Dunn looked at him. "I'm not sure."

"I hope you ain't thinkin' what I think you're thinkin'," said Marino.

Dunn managed a grin. "Sounds like you're thinkin' enough for both of us," the weary detective said dryly.

CHAPTER TWENTY-FIVE

When Joan Ngo finished the interview with Joseph Lawrence Conrad, she felt confident that he was not the killer. Although she had interviewed only three other men who had been charged in murder cases, she trusted her intuition, which told her that Joe was as he claimed to be—an innocent man caught by circumstances that had wrongly turned the investigation toward him. Besides, she liked him. There was something disarming about him. Of course, this could be the very quality that made him an effective killer. Ted Bundy, after all, had been equally good looking and charming.

As her cameraman, Andy, checked the videotape and—satisfied with what he had seen—began to put the equipment away, Joan relaxed and smiled at Joe, feeling more like a colleague than a reporter. How often had she sat in an office just like this one with a professor just like Joe?

Joe sensed her ease. He was ready to announce the second part of his plan. "Joan," he began, "how would you like to win a Pulitzer Prize?"

Joan laughed. "What are you talking about?"

He sized her up. She was good at her job. She was competent. She was willing to take risks. And she was adventurous.

"I know the only way to clear my name is if the police find the real killer before I go to trial. I'm going to lose my wife and child, not to mention my freedom."

"Go on."

"I've got an idea. Just hear me out, and think about it before you say no."

"I'm listening."

Joe shifted in his chair, moving in closer to Joan. She did not move but kept her face dangerously close to his. She was very intrigued by this man's approach.

"This guy hunts at night, right?"

"Right," Joan allowed cautiously.

"What if we try to catch him ourselves? What if we set up a sting operation?"

"Go on."

"We wire you with a hidden microphone, maybe even a hidden camera if you have one. And we park you on the side of the freeway, with your car hood up, like you're broken down, about a mile or two from where they found Patricia Miller's car."

"This is insane," Joan said, grinning. "But I'm still listening."

"You'll be like a decoy out on the street. Meanwhile, your cameraman and I will be waiting back in the news van, listening and watching to see who stops to help you."

Joan laughed again. "Are you listening to this scheme, Andy?"

Without looking up from his work, the cameraman said, "Yeah, I hear him."

"Look," Joe said. "Andy can have a camera on you with a telephoto lens so we can see exactly who comes after you. We'll have a cell phone or a radio ready to call the police. If someone comes along who tries to pull you out of the car, we call 911, and we hightail it to save you!"

Joan simply stared into Joe's lips, smiling.

"That's a ridiculous idea," she said, still smiling.

"Ridiculous?" Joe asked.

Andy repeated, "Ridiculous."

Joe sat back in his chair. He sighed deeply. "I guess I'm going crazy," he said. "I shouldn't even think about putting you at risk like that. Forget I mentioned it."

"Putting my life at risk?" Joan asked.

"Yeah," Joe said. "This guy has killed too many women. We might not be able to get to you in time."

"*My* life wouldn't be at risk!" Joan announced, wagging her finger in the air. "That fucker's life would be at risk!"

Now it was Joe's turn to laugh. "Calm down! I didn't mean to rile you up so much!"

"You don't know Joan," Andy said.

"No," Joe admitted. "I guess I don't."

"She's got a black belt in Tae Kwon Do," Andy explained.

"I've got a third-degree black belt in Tae Kwon Do!"

"Sorry," Andy said. "Third-degree black belt."

"I've got something even better than that," Joan said.

"What?" Joe asked.

"I've got a gun and a permit to carry it!"

"You've got a gun?" Joe asked.

"She's got a gun," Andy said.

Joe was a little shaken. "I didn't mean to imply that you couldn't take care of yourself."

"I'll blow the fucker's head off if he tries anything with me!" Joan said.

"You're not saying that you'll do it then, are you?" Joe asked.

Joan closed her eyes and tried to think clearly for a few seconds. Andy stopped what he was doing and looked at Joan. Then he looked at Joe. Andy shook his head back and forth. Joe shrugged his shoulders.

"Please tell me you have more sense," Andy said to Joan.

"I could hold him at gunpoint until the police arrive," Joan said, her eyes still shut. "We could park the van on the overpass nearby. Andy, with the telephoto lens, you'd be able to see every move I make. I can park on the side of the northbound lanes facing you."

"This is crazy!" Andy said.

Joe tried to imagine how it might really happen. The reality of it frightened him. "I take it back," he said. "I withdraw my offer. It's a crazy idea like Andy says."

"It is a crazy idea," Joan admitted, her eyes still closed. "But you're right, Joe."

"I'm right about what?'

"If we pulled this off, I'd win a Pulitzer."

"Maybe," Andy said. "Or you might win a bullet in the brain."

"No," Joan said, opening her eyes and looking at Andy. "He doesn't shoot his victims. He strangles them. He likes to feel their necks in his hands. It gets him off."

"Jesus," Joe said. "You've thought about this guy, haven't you?"

Joan directed her intense gaze at Joe. She was serious now, very intense. "This guy thinks he has a right to use women as playthings and then throw them away like a used condom. I'd love to nail this fucker!"

"She can get pretty intense," said Joe.

"You have no idea," said Andy.

"When would you like to try this, Joe?" Joan asked.

"Tonight."

"*Tonight?*" Joan asked.

"Yeah. This guy thinks he's setting me up. He killed Autumn on a Tuesday because he knew that I'd been teaching my night class that night. Thanks to you people in the media, he knows that if he kills on Tuesdays, I'll be a suspect."

"Tonight's no good," Andy said to Joan. "We've got to get this tape back to the studio and edit it. You've got to be ready to go live at five and six."

"What about at nine-thirty?" Joe asked. "That's when he would strike anyway. Sometime later. Remember. They think Patricia was killed after 10:30 p.m."

Joan closed her eyes again to think about her schedule. Yes, if Andy was willing, they could set up on the freeway at nine and stay at it until after midnight if that's what it would take.

"Okay," Joan said. "Tonight at nine. Where do we meet?"

"Let's meet here," Joe suggested. "I'll let my class go at about nine, and then we can drive out to that spot. You can use my wife's car while Andy and I keep watch in the news van."

Joan looked at Andy. "Are you willing?"

Andy shook his head no for several seconds. "All right, yeah. I'll do it. But you'd better have that gun loaded and in your lap, Joan."

"That's a good idea," Joe added. "Put the gun in your lap under a sweater or something so you can keep your hands on it."

"Don't worry about my gun."

"She knows how to use her gun," Andy said.

Joe reached up and clutched his chest. "My heart's pounding hard!"

"So's mine," Joan said.

"Let's try to keep it that way tonight, folks," added Andy. "I want everyone's heart beating in the morning."

Joe stared at Joan. She looked back, smiling again.

"This is exciting," Joe said.

"Yes, it is," Joan replied.

Then Joe's expression changed as a new thought entered his mind. "Wait a minute," he said. "Are you two going along with this to catch the real killer, or do you think I'm the real killer and you're trying to trip me up?"

Joan smiled coyly. "You'll never know, will you?"

"Either way," said Andy, "it's a helluva story!"

That afternoon, Joe could barely concentrate on preparing for his night class. The minutes passed with intolerable slowness. He wanted to call Sara and tell her about the plan, but he knew that she would try to talk him out of it. If Suzy or Bill Morgan got wind of it, they'd stop it for sure. No. It wouldn't be wise to tell anyone about it.

Between four and four-thirty, Cassandra popped in and chatted with Joe a little, sipping water from a clear plastic bottle.

"You look like the Cheshire cat, Joe. What's going on?"

"I'm just very pleased with myself for pulling off this interview and manipulating the university this way. I thought I'd never set foot inside a classroom again."

"Yeah," Cass said. "You surprised the hell out of me by showing up here today with a reporter. You think she's going to do right by you?"

"I don't know. At five o'clock, I'm going to go into the classroom and watch the news on the television in there. We'll see."

"I'll make an exception and watch the news at home. What channel was she from?"

"Channel 8. You know, 'the News of the Big Valley!'" Joe said in a deep, mock announcer's voice.

"Right, right," Cass said, smirking.

She wished him luck and left. Joe fiddled with paper clips and a pen on his desk until five o'clock. Then he went into the classroom and watched the news on Channel 8.

Joan's exclusive interview with suspected serial murderer Joseph Lawrence Conrad was the lead story. There sat Joan, adjacent to the two news anchors, introducing her story. A shot of the CLU campus established the location as Joan's voice-over explained that Joe had invited her to interview him at her alma mater. The interview itself ran almost in its entirety, exactly as Joe remembered it. The first part outdoors showed several students greeting Joe, which made him look exactly as he had hoped—like a well-loved teacher. After the interview on the bench outside, the tape cut quickly to the questions and answers in Joe's office. It lasted a little more than four minutes.

In his mind, Joe compared it to the interview with Gary Condit about missing intern Chandra Levy, conducted a few years before. Condit, by contrast, had seemed nervous, evasive, and tight-lipped. Joe thought he looked much better—relaxed, confident, friendly, and open.

"Good job, Joan," he said to the television.

After the interview aired, Joe went back to his office. His phone rang, startling him. He debated answering it, suspecting that it was probably a news reporter wanting an interview.

Reluctantly, he answered. "Hello?"

"Joe?" Sara asked. "Is that you?"

"Sara, yes. Did you see the interview?"

"Yeah," Sara said. "So did Katie. I let her watch it, even though she's more confused now about what's happening with you."

"What did you think? Did I look okay?"

"You looked great, Joe," Sara said. "You looked confident and in control. And I loved seeing your students come up and say hello."

"Yeah. That was an unexpected plus."

"I didn't care for that one girl hugging you, though," Sara added, a note of jealousy in her voice.

"But it shows that young female students aren't afraid of me. I thought it was good that Joan left it in."

"Yeah," Sara added. "It helped."

"What did Suzy think?"

"I don't know. She's still at work."

"Did you hear from Bill Morgan?"

"No. He's probably still at work too," Sara said. "I don't think either of them will be happy with you, though. Remember what they told you, Joe? Don't talk to reporters!"

"I know, I know. But I don't think I'll listen to that advice."

Sara sighed audibly. "Joe, you're going to get yourself into more trouble."

"Perhaps," said Joe. "But, Sara, I feel like I've got nothing to lose. I'm already losing the two things that mean the most to me, you and Katie. I've got to do something to force this thing to a conclusion."

"What are you talking about?" Sara asked, a note of concern in her voice.

"I'm not sure exactly," Joe lied. "I just feel like I need to do something that will make the cops look for the real murderer."

"But how, Joe?"

"I'm not exactly sure. If you come up with a good idea, let me know."

Sara stayed silent for a moment.

"If I were in your shoes, Joe," she finally said, "I'd let the lawyers handle it, and I'd do exactly what they told me to do."

"That would be the sensible thing to do," Joe admitted.

Sara evaluated the tone of Joe's voice. "But you're not going to be sensible, are you?"

"I'll sure try to be," he said.

"Well, if you're not going to be sensible, at least be careful."

"It sounds like you still care," Joe said, half laughing.

Sara's voice choked. "Of course, I still care, Joe."

"I'm glad to hear it."

"I've got to go," Sara said. She was beginning to cry.

"Wait, Sara. Can I talk to Katie?"

"No," she said. "I've got to go."

She hung up before Joe could make another plea.

Joe massaged his temples for a while after the phone call from Sara, trying not to cry himself. After checking his watch, he went downstairs to the restroom; and on the way back, he stopped by the vending machines and bought some cheese-filled crackers and a diet soda.

"Two of the four food groups," he said, ascending the stairs with dinner in hand. The smell of hot food from the dining halls wafted in through an open window.

Joe was more a curiosity than a teacher in the evening class. His students listened politely and took notes diligently, but Joe could tell that they suspected him. These were older students, less naïve and less open-minded than the young freshmen he had encountered that afternoon. The mood of the class was tense and suspicious.

And Joe noticed another difference. Nicholas Adams was not there. Joe would have to remember to tell Bill Morgan to check on Nick's whereabouts.

The young security guard who had helped him to his car on the night that Gary Grimes had attacked him was now pacing the hallway outside the classroom, lingering noticeably in the doorway from time to time. The university administrators were sending a message.

Joe let the class leave early, explaining that he would return the rest of the research papers next week when they came for the final exam. The class of students left glumly, suspecting perhaps that they would not see their teacher again.

After the students left, the young security guard walked by the classroom and leaned inside as Joe erased the white board.

"Professor Conrad?"

"Yes?"

"If you were wondering why I was hanging around, I was told to keep an eye on you because the school had some threats phoned in."

Joe put down the eraser and looked at the guard. "Is that right?"

"Yeah," the guard replied. "I guess a lot of people called the school after some story appeared on the news. They said they were going to kill you."

Joe wondered if the guard was telling the truth or making up a story to cover himself.

"Well, thanks for watching out for me," Joe said finally. "I guess we made it through the class without incident."

"Yeah," the guard acknowledged. "I guess so. I'm supposed to walk you to your car."

Joe smiled. "I'll be ready in a few minutes," he said. Joe gathered up his books and papers and headed back to his office. It was ten to nine. He sat at his desk and filed papers away, placed some late research papers into his briefcase, and shut off his computer. Then he turned off the office lamp and turned to the guard. "All ready," he said, closing the door behind himself. He locked the door and headed toward the staircase with the guard. They descended the stairs side by side, the guard keeping his hand on the can of mace that was strapped to his utility belt.

When they reached the outside of the building, Joe turned to the guard. "It looks pretty quiet," he said. "I don't think you need to walk me to the parking lot."

"Are you sure? Someone could be waiting for you out there."

Disgruntled, Joe said, "If you insist."

They reached the parking lot just as the news van pulled in. Joe had hoped to ditch the guard and make it back up to his office to wait, but this worked out even better. He walked over to his car, unlocked the door, and pretended to get in.

"Thanks again, Officer," Joe told the young guard. "I'm safe now."

The guard turned and began walking away. The news van drove slowly toward Joe, and he smiled at the nervous faces of Joan Ngo and her cameraman, Andy.

Chapter Twenty-six

Joan climbed out of the van and walked straight toward Joe. "Are you sure you want to go through with this?" she asked him.

"Are you?" Joe asked. "You're the one who has to take the biggest risk."

"Yes, but if something goes wrong and you're involved, it could make you look even more guilty."

Joe looked down at the serious face of the female reporter, trying to read whether she was more concerned about him or herself.

"At this point," Joe explained, "I don't have much to lose. But if you don't want to go through with it, I understand completely, Joan."

"It's not that. I know I can take care of myself."

Joe waited for her to finish thinking out loud, but she needed to be coaxed.

"What's the matter?" he asked.

"All the way down here, Andy and Tony were telling me what could go wrong."

"Wait a minute," Joe said. "Who's Tony?"

Joan looked back at the van nervously. When Joe looked at the windshield, he saw another man's face in the van next to Andy.

"Tony's a security guard who works at the news station. We've used him a few times before—whenever we've done something risky."

Joe wasn't sure how he felt about another person coming along, but he decided it couldn't hurt to have another witness in case something terrible did happen.

"I suppose that's okay," Joe told Joan.

"You realize, of course, that there are about a thousand ways this could go bad."

"Yeah," Joe said. "I realize that."

Joan closed her eyes and hung her head for a few seconds, sorting the plan out in her mind.

"Okay," she said. "Let's do it. I'm going to drive your car, right?"

"Right," Joe said.

"You get in the van. Andy's going to follow me, and I'm going to pull over just north of Lost Slough. There's a freeway overpass about half a mile from the spot, and you three guys are going to watch me from it. Andy and I have worked out how we're doing it. Tony suggests that you stay out of the action if anything happens."

"And why should I listen to Tony?" Joe asked.

"Well," Joan said. "Like me, he's got a gun."

"Oh," said Joe. He gave her the keys to the Ford Escort.

Andy climbed out of the van with some equipment. "Hello, Joe," he said.

"Hi, Andy."

"I'm going to put this minicam on the dash of your car." He held up a statue of Saint Christopher. "It's got adhesive tape on the bottom of the stand, so it shouldn't hurt your dash at all."

Joan tossed the keys to Andy as he walked over; and without missing a beat, he caught the keys, unlocked the passenger's side door, and began installing the camera. While Joe was watching Andy, he felt someone's presence behind him. When he turned around, he was startled by Tony.

"Jumpy?" Tony asked him.

Joe clutched his heart. "I guess so."

Tony was the same size as Joe, but obviously well built under his tight-fitting black sweater. His black hair and thick dark eyebrows convinced Joe that Tony was Italian. Tony held out his hand, and Joe allowed his hand to be crushed in Tony's grip.

Tony stared sternly into Joe's eyes and said, "We're not going to let anything happen to this lovely lady, are we, Professor?" His grip tightened around Joe's hand.

"No," Joe managed to say through the pain. "What's your problem?"

"I don't trust you, Professor," Tony said.

Joe twisted and pulled his hand free.

"Down, boy," Joan said to Tony. "He's overly protective."

"I can see that," said Joe. He wondered if this was a good idea after all.

"Joan, sit in the driver's seat," Andy instructed.

Tony and Joe watched as Joan climbed in and made herself comfortable. She brought the seat closer to the steering wheel and adjusted the rearview mirrors. Andy walked back to the van.

"Can you hear me, Andy?" Joan said softly.

Joe looked at Andy through the windshield of the van. He gave a thumbs-up.

"Can you see me okay?" she asked, almost whispering.

Joe looked back at Andy, who held his thumb down then motioned toward the passenger's door. Looking back at Joan, Joe watched her turn the statue slightly clockwise. Looking back at Andy, Joe saw him motion to stop. Then he gave a thumbs-up signal.

"We're all set," Joan said. Then she started the car and closed the door, almost catching Joe with it.

"Let's go to the van," Tony instructed. He placed a hand on Joe's shoulder and walked him toward the van. "You ride in the back."

Joan led the way off campus and drove toward Interstate 5 while Andy followed. Tony sat up front, and Joe sat at a swivel chair in the back. There were three small monitors, one mounted up on the dashboard and two in the back. All three were tuned into Joan. Joe settled in to watch the television show that could have been called *Joan Ngo Drives Sara's Car*.

Exactly as planned, Joan pulled over about half a mile north of Lost Slough, and Andy drove by slowly, giving her the thumbs-up as they went past. Joe watched Joan return the thumbs-up sign on the monitor.

"I'm going to put the hood up once you boys are in place," Joan said over the speaker. Joe could hear her voice distinctly.

Andy took the next exit and, after stopping at the stop sign, drove back over the freeway to the other side where he made a wide U-turn and then drove back up to the top of the overpass and pulled over.

"I can see the van," Joan said. "Can you see me?"

Andy flashed the van lights on and off twice.

"Good," Joan's voice said. "I'm going to put the hood up now."

Joan disappeared from the television monitor, and the sound of the door closing came through the speakers. Joe strained to look out the passenger's window, around Tony's big dark head. He could easily see the Ford Escort in the distance, but a finger of fog was starting to form across the road. It swirled around a few cars that rushed through it. Otherwise, the freeway at almost 10 p.m. seemed virtually deserted.

Joan reappeared inside the car on the monitor. "Okay, boys, the bait is set. We just need to wait for Mr. Right to come along."

Andy climbed into the back of the van with Joe and started hooking up cables to another television camera. When the wires were attached, he opened the van door about six inches and positioned the camera on a tripod looking out from the top of the opening, just below the ceiling of the van. Andy switched on the camera and then two other monitors; and suddenly, images of the Escort, blurry and dark at first, came into view.

Andy then switched something on, and a weird whining noise hummed to life.

The images of the car on the freeway turned green and became much clearer.

"Night vision?" Joe asked.

Andy simply nodded as he worked. He zoomed in on the windshield of the car and was able to bring half of the windshield and the driver's side door window into focus. Joan could be seen in all the monitors now, shaded in grays from the minicam inside the car and illuminated in greens in the other monitors. She kept looking over her left shoulder.

"Relax," Andy whispered as if to Joan.

Andy took the swivel chair that Joe had been in and sat at the control panel, making fine adjustments to the images. Joe squatted on the carpeted floor, leaning to the side in order to look out of the open van door, even though all he could see was the top of the aluminum railing on the top of the guard wall that stood at the edge of the overpass. From where Joe sat, he could see all the monitors that Andy was looking at. Joan continued to shift in her seat.

"Oh," Joan said over the speaker. "I almost forgot."

She disappeared from view for a minute, bending down to pick up something from the floor of the car in front of the passenger's seat. They could not follow her movements clearly, but she was fiddling with something in her purse. Suddenly, the image of a handgun filled the screen as she held the gun up in front of the minicam.

"Can't forget this," she said. She placed the gun on her lap and pulled part of her sweater over it. Then she seemed to settle back and relax.

Joe scooted backward so he could lean against the other wall of the van, the wall without all the monitors and equipment.

"Here comes a car," Tony said. He had not taken his eyes from the freeway since they had first stopped. "It's slowing a little. No. Didn't even stop."

Joe closed his eyes.

"Thought we were gonna get lucky, boys," Joan's voice said.

The sound of traffic humming by under the overpass made Joe open his eyes.

"Five cars just went by going south, and not one stopped!" Tony said disgustedly. "What if she really was in trouble? That's like six people who didn't care enough to stop."

"Apathetic," Joe said.

"Yeah," Tony said. "It's pathetic all right."

Joe laughed a little at Tony's misunderstanding.

"It's getting foggy," Joan's voice said through the speakers.

"Here comes a couple of cars," Tony said. "Okay, Andy. Get ready. The last one pulled over behind Joan."

Joe moved forward and looked out of the door. Sure enough, a small car had pulled in behind the Escort that Joan was in. Joe looked over at the monitor. Andy was widening the shot so they could see whoever approached the car.

"I hope you're watching, boys," Joan said. "It looks like two people in the car, and one's getting out. I'm putting my finger on the trigger."

"I hope she remembered to take the safety off," Tony said.

Suddenly, a middle-aged woman came into view. She hurried up to the window, and Joan rolled the window down.

"Need help?" the woman asked Joan. The woman's voice was quite audible over the speakers.

"No, thanks," Joan said. "I've already called for a tow truck. He should be here any minute."

"Oh, okay," said the woman. "Want us to wait till he gets here? My husband's in the car."

Joan laughed. "No, thanks. It shouldn't be too much longer."

"Sure?" the woman asked.

"I'm sure. Thanks, though."

The Good Samaritan walked back to her car.

"Can you believe that husband?" Joan asked. "Makes his wife drive and makes her get out of the car to check on the stranded driver."

Andy and Tony stayed quiet.

"How do we know the husband *made* the wife drive or do anything?" Joe asked.

"We don't," Andy said.

Tony spoke, still looking out the window, "You think they could be our killers?"

Andy responded, "Wouldn't be the first time a husband and wife team was guilty of rape and murder."

"Who was that couple in Sacramento about twenty years ago?" Tony asked.

"I don't remember," Andy said. "Gilmore maybe? Guillermo?"

"Something like that. Used to kidnap young couples and hold the girls as sex slaves."

Joe asked, "What happened to the guys?"

Tony turned around to look at Joe, sliding his finger across his throat. "They cut their throats like they were slaughtering sheep," he said.

The sudden gruesome image made Joe shiver.

Tony turned back to stare out the window. "Here come some more cars," he announced. "And there go some more headed south. Trying to make LA before daybreak probably."

"Anybody stoppin'?" Andy asked.

Tony just watched for a few seconds. "Nope," he said. "Didn't even slow down."

Joe looked at his watch. It was a little after ten-thirty.

"It's getting foggier," Tony said, a note of concern in his voice.

They stayed silent for several minutes, reconsidering the wisdom of their scheme.

Joan's sudden voice startled Joe. "It's getting foggier, boys," she said.

Joe strained to look out over the overpass railing. Rising off the fields and vineyards on either side of the freeway, curtains of fog were forming slowly, hanging across the road.

"I assume you guys can still see me clearly," Joan said over the speakers. "When this fog gets to the point that you can't see the car clearly from the overpass, let's call it quits, okay?"

"Okay," Tony said out the side window, knowing Joan couldn't hear him.

Andy watched his monitors silently.

"Maybe this wasn't a good idea," Joe said. He could still see the Ford Escort, but just barely. Now the mist seemed to be falling from above.

"Remember that movie, boys?" Joan asked. "You know, the one set over on the coast. What was the name of it, Andy?"

"Which one?" Andy asked, knowing Joan couldn't hear him.

"You know. The one about the pirates who come after their gold. What's her name is in the lighthouse—Adrienne Barbeau. She's a radio disc jockey, and she tries to warn the town."

"*The Fog*," said Andy.

"Jamie Lee Curtis was in it too," Joan continued. "It was all about the fog, remember?"

"That's the title," Andy said aloud.

Joan said, "I know you're probably telling Tony the name of that movie, but for the life of me, I can't think of it."

"*The Fog*," Andy repeated.

"I wish she hadn't used that expression," Tony said.

"What expression?" Joe asked.

"For the life of me," Tony said.

"Guys?" Joan said, a note of concern in her voice. "There's a car coming."

"I see it," Tony said.

Joe kneeled and strained to look outside. He could not see Sara's Ford Escort anymore; the fog was too thick.

"Oh, I remember," Joan's voice said. "How could I be so stupid!"

"You're not stupid, baby," Tony said.

"Are you watching, boys?" Joan's voice asked. "This guy is stopping. He's pulling up right behind me. Jesus, he's pulling in close."

"I can't see a damn thing!" Tony said.

"I've got her," Andy said.

The view from the minicam was clear. Joan was straining to look in the rearview mirror. The green monitors were almost blank, the night-vision lens unable to find Joan's image through the fog.

"He's just sitting there," Joan said.

"I don't like this," Tony said.

"This could be the killer," warned Joe. "We should get down there."

"Let's give it a few more minutes," said Andy. "Joan wants this story."

Joe looked over at Andy. He was intently watching the minicam monitor.

"No story is worth a person's life, though, Andy," he said.

"By the way," Joan's voice said. She looked directly into the minicam lens. "The name of that stupid scary movie, which I will never, ever watch again is *The Fog.*"

Suddenly, bright red and blue lights lit up the fog behind the car Joan was in. The lights rotated steadily.

"A cop," Tony said. "It's a damn cop!"

"Maybe," Andy said.

"It's okay, boys," Joan said. "It's a highway patrolman, and he's getting out."

The minicam monitor showed Joan looking over her left shoulder as if she was expecting the officer to come to her window. Suddenly, a loud tapping could be heard over the microphone that Joan was wearing. The three men watched Joan on the monitors. She turned to her right and leaned over, her body moving back and forth as she rolled down the window of the passenger's door.

"Good evening, Officer," Joan said, straightening up and coming back into view. "I thought you guys always came up on the driver's side?"

"Much safer to be off the road," the officer's deep voice said off camera. "Do you need some help, Miss?"

"No, thanks, Officer," Joan said. "I've called a tow truck."

"Are you sure?" the voice asked. "We're usually notified if a tow truck's been called on the interstate."

"Yes, I'm sure," Joan lied.

"May I see you license and registration please, ma'am?"

"Why, Officer?" Joan asked. "I haven't done anything wrong."

"License and registration, please," the officer repeated.

"She's toast," Tony said.

"We're all toast," Andy agreed.

They watched the monitors as Joan reached for her purse.

"Stop!" the cop's voice yelled. "Don't move. Is that a gun in your lap?"

"Oh, shit," Andy said.

"Yes, Officer, but don't get worried. I have a permit for it."

"Very carefully, lady, grab the handle with two fingers and place that gun on the passenger's seat and then hold your hands up."

They watched on the monitors as Joan carefully placed her gun on the passenger's seat.

"This is loaded, lady," the cop said.

"Yes, I know," Joan answered. "Unloaded guns aren't much protection."

"You said you have a permit?"

"Yes, sir."

"I hope, for your sake, it's a permit to carry a loaded handgun."

"It is, sir," Joan said.

Tony said, "Don't give up your gun, baby."

"Give me your license, your permit, and your registration," the officer's voice said from off camera.

Joan could be seen on the monitors reaching for her purse, taking a wallet out, and removing her driver's license and another card. Then she handed the cards to a hand that briefly came into the view of the minicam.

"Oh, it's you," the officer's voice said. "Joan Ngo. I knew I recognized you from someplace. You're a reporter for Channel 8."

"Right," Joan said. She reached over to the officer, who was still standing out of view. "Nice to meet you, Officer . . . ?"

"Officer Harris," the cop's voice said.

The monitor showed Joan's arm being pumped.

"Uh-oh," Joe said.

"What do you mean 'Uh-oh'?" Andy asked.

"I think I know that cop."

"How?" asked Tony.

"I think that's the cop who found me with Patricia Miller's corpse."

"So?" Tony asked.

"I don't know," Joe said. "He wasn't very friendly the first time we met, that's all."

"The first time?" Andy asked.

"Yeah," Joe said, watching Joan's profile smile up at the officer. "I think he sort of rescued me at Patricia Miller's funeral when her brother almost punched me."

Tony watched the dashboard monitor since the fog had grown so thick that they could no longer see the car, only the flashing red and blue lights behind it.

The CHP officer's voice came clearly through the speakers: "Did you really call a tow truck, Ms. Ngo?"

"Well, Officer Harris," Joan said. "That was a little fib."

"I thought so," the highway patrolman said. "Now tell me what's really going on."

Joan looked into the minicam. "The jig's up, boys," she said. Then she turned back toward the cop. "I've got a camera crew with me. We were trying to catch the I-5 Strangler. That's why I had my gun in my lap."

"So you didn't call a tow company?"

"No sir."

"Where's this camera crew?"

Joan looked into the camera again. "Flash your lights, Andy, and honk the horn."

Joe watched as Tony reached far over, turned on the lights, and honked the horn several times.

"Well, I can hear the horn, but I barely see the lights," said the annoyed voice of Officer Harris. "This was a very foolish stunt to pull. I hope you realize that."

Almost with a pout on her lower lip, Joan said, "We do, Officer Harris. Can we go now? We promise to be good."

"Call me Rick, Ms. Ngo," the officer said. "Is your crew parked up ahead on the overpass?"

"Yes, Rick," Joan admitted.

"Well, follow me up there so I can have a word with all of you."

"All right," said Joan. On the monitor, a hand reached in and gave the driver's license and the gun permit back to Joan.

"I'll keep your gun until we join your friends," the cop's voice said.

"All right," Joan agreed.

Joan could be seen putting her license and permit back into her wallet. Then she started the car, and the men in the van watched her face as she drove up the ramp toward them. She pulled the Escort in directly in front of the van, their front bumpers practically touching. The officer kept the patrol car's lights flashing as he followed. Like Joan, the CHP officer drove the wrong way on the overpass and pulled in right behind Sara's Ford.

"You'd better stay here," Tony said to Joe.

Tony and Andy got out and met Joan and Officer Harris as they approached the front of the news van. From the darkness inside the cavern of the van, Joe watched as best he could through the misting windshield. Andy and Tony shook hands with the CHP officer, and the officer known as Rick patted Joan on the shoulder.

Joan was still wearing a concealed microphone.

"You'd better leave police work to us," the cop said.

"I will in the future, Rick," Joan said. She seemed relaxed now.

Joe watched as the officer expertly unloaded Joan's gun and handed it back to her. She laughed.

"Did you have permission from your news editor to do this?" the CHP officer asked.

"Not really," Joan admitted.

"We were going for a Pulitzer Prize," Andy added sarcastically.

"Whose hair-brained scheme was this, anyway?" Officer Harris asked good-naturedly.

Joan looked at Andy, who looked at Tony, who was looking at Joan.

"I can't really say," Joan laughed.

"In the future," cautioned the officer, "check with the police first so we know what you're up to. Less chance of someone getting hurt that way."

"All right, Rick," Joan said. "Can I ask a favor?"

"What's that, ma'am?"

"We'd like to salvage something from tonight," explained Joan. "Maybe we could do a quick interview with you right here, with the freeway in the background."

"No, I don't think that would be a good idea."

"We interview police on camera all the time," Joan added.

"No, I'd have to check with the boss," Officer Harris said.

"Maybe I could just ask you a few questions, you know, so I can update the story," Joan pleaded.

Officer Harris grinned. "Off the record?"

"Sure," said Joan. "If that's what you'd prefer."

"If you hurry. I've got to get back to my cruiser."

"Okay," Joan said. She took a notepad out of her hip pocket, which had a small pencil inside the rings. "Were you patrolling the freeway on the night that either of the recent victims were found?"

"Who do you mean?" Officer Harris asked.

"Well, let's start with Patricia Miller. Were you patrolling the night she went missing?"

"This is off the record, right? You can't use my name, okay?" asked the CHP officer.

"Absolutely not," Joan reassured him. "I'll refer to you as an anonymous source. I won't even say that you're a source inside the CHP."

"Okay," Harris said. "In that case, I'll let you in on a little secret. The CHP doesn't run patrols at night on long stretches of freeway where there aren't usually many problems."

"Why not?" asked the reporter.

"Budget cuts," the officer explained. "I was working a day shift when Patricia Miller disappeared. It wasn't until after the girl from Lodi went missing that headquarters switched me to nights."

"How do you feel about the budget cuts?" Joan asked.

Officer Harris smiled. "Now you're trying to get me in trouble with the governor, aren't you?"

Joan smiled. "Of course not, Rick."

"I've got to be getting back to work," he replied.

"Are you sure you don't want to do an on-camera interview, Rick?"

"Not with you," he said. "You're tricky."

Andy stepped in. "We'll put our stuff away and be out of here soon, Officer."

"Good. Call it a night, and head on home," Officer Harris ordered. "You're going to miss the eleven o'clock news."

The four of them laughed briefly, Joan rolling her eyes as she turned toward Joe. The police officer went to his car and killed the flashing lights. As Tony and Andy headed to the van, Joan lingered by the door of the Ford Escort, pretending she was about to climb inside. The CHP officer backed up his car and then pulled out and drove off.

As soon as the cop had gone, Andy went back to the Ford Escort and reached in to grab the minicam. Joe watched the jerky image in the monitor. Joan and Tony came up to the sliding side door and opened it fully.

"Come on out, Joe," Joan said brusquely. "No Pulitzer Prize story tonight."

"Get out, Professor," Tony said. He grabbed Joe's sweater at the shoulder and tugged Joe out of the van. Joe barely stayed on his feet as he jumped out.

"What the hell's wrong?" he asked.

"I've never been so embarrassed in my life," Joan said.

"We lost credibility, Joe," Andy said. "When the police catch us doing some stupid stunt like this, we lose a lot of credibility."

"And," Joan added, "the cops have something they can hold over us now."

"What difference does that make?" asked Joe.

"Let me explain it to you, Professor," Joan said bitterly. "An investigative reporter has little more than her press credentials and her reputation. This cop is gonna tell all his buddies in blue about the embarrassing little incident with the funny Asian reporter, and they're all gonna laugh their dicks off."

Joe stared at the woman, amazed by another side of her that he hadn't seen earlier.

She continued, "Now suppose I come up with a good story about a local cop in the future. Something real juicy, maybe even about this cop, Ricky Harris. These boys in blue can call me and say, 'Remember that night we caught you doing a stakeout? One of the other TV stations in town might like the details of that night. Why don't you pull that embarrassing story, girlie girl, okay?' See how it works now, Professor? For the next few years until it's too far in the distant past for anyone to care, I've got to watch how I deal with the police."

Joe listened silently.

"It means," Andy added, "she can't be as effective as she used to be."

"I'm sorry," Joe said. "But you knew the risks going in."

"Yeah," Joan said. "I knew the risks."

"It was a lame idea," Tony added.

"Your keys are in the ignition, Professor," Andy said.

Joan climbed into the passenger's seat of the van and fished a cigarette out of her purse. Tony got into the driver's seat while Andy climbed into the back to shut off the equipment and put it away, Joe assumed.

As Joe climbed into his wife's car and started the engine, he looked at Joan. She took a long drag on her cigarette, held the smoke deep in her lungs for several seconds while shooting daggers at him with her dark eyes then exhaled out the window of the door. The smoke disappeared into the fog, and Joe started the engine of the car. He backed away from the van then made a U-turn and found the on-ramp to the freeway. Soon, he was heading north toward Sacramento, driving carefully in the dense fog.

CHAPTER TWENTY-SEVEN

In the morning, Joe awoke in time to watch the local news at six. Channel 8 ran a shortened version of Joan's interview with him. Edited out were the background scenes of students greeting him. This edited version was less flattering. Joan came on camera once the tape of the interview ended.

"An anonymous police source informed me that night patrols have been stepped up on the usually quiet stretches of freeway," she explained. "This reporter for one is certainly glad that our men in blue are out there protecting us, and we wish them success in stopping these murders."

Joe smiled. "She's trying to mend fences," he said aloud.

The other channels didn't cover the story as far as Joe could tell. Maybe they had mentioned something during the time that Joe watched the interview, but he couldn't be sure.

Joe called Susan's place to speak to Sara and Katie, but the phone rang without being answered. He let the phone ring twenty times. Not even the machine answered. Joe decided he would call Susan at the office later to check on Katie and Sara.

He went through the rituals of getting ready for work with far less enthusiasm than he had only twenty-four hours earlier. The morning was overcast and cold. He passed by Lost Slough at about twenty minutes after seven. It looked quiet. No police. Only a lone white heron perched on the branch of a bare oak tree. As he drove the rest of the way to campus that morning, he decided on the spur of the moment to cancel his Friday classes, which would mean giving students the course evaluation forms today. He was supposed to give finals next week on Tuesday night and Wednesday, so he would have a nice long weekend to finish grading research essays.

Under gray skies, the campus seemed dreary and quiet that Wednesday morning, save for the tolling of the eight o'clock bells, and Joe noted how different a place could seem with the passage of only a little time. Students who had greeted him enthusiastically the day before merely nodded as they walked by. Yesterday he had been something of a celebrity, but today that he was merely another college instructor with personal problems. The students themselves seemed to have realized that final exams were less than a week away.

When he ascended the stairs and glanced up at his office, Joe was stunned by the word "killer" spray-painted in white across the lower part of his door. He immediately suspected Gary Grimes. As he walked closer, Joe noticed that the door window had been broken. Looking inside, he saw that nothing was out of place except for the broken glass on the carpet, but then an odor hit his nose. Unlocking the door, Joe stepped in just far enough to turn on the light switch. There on top of the shattered glass lay sausage-sized pieces of excrement. Stepping around the pieces, Joe picked up the phone and dialed the number of the campus police.

Dr. Thorne suddenly appeared in the doorway, a stunned and angry look on his face. "My god!" he exclaimed hoarsely. "What happened here?"

"I'm not sure," Joe said. "But I have some suspicions."

"This is intolerable, Conrad!" he shouted. Joe was shocked by the anger in Thorne's eyes. Dr. Thorne's complexion reddened, and his jawbones clenched repeatedly. For a moment, Joe thought the good doctor might throw a punch at him.

"I have campus security on the phone," Joe said. "Would you like to speak to them?"

Dr. Thorne grew angrier. "Just tell them to get the hell over here right now!"

"Did you hear Dr. Thorne?" Joe asked, speaking into the telephone receiver. "They heard you," Joe informed the department chairman.

"This is why you must leave the university," Thorne commanded. He spun around and stomped toward the staircase. Joe had never seen him this angry. It seemed out of character, and Joe suddenly remembered what Joan Ngo had said about Thorne when he was younger. Had he really been such a lecherous professor?

Within fifteen minutes, three campus police officers appeared at Joe's door.

"I haven't touched anything except the door handle and the telephone," Joe told them. "I'd like to get that shit out of here, though, as soon as possible. It's stinking up the place."

One of the policemen looked down at the excrement and laughed. "Vandals almost always leave a calling card like that behind. It must be in the *How to Vandalize Handbook*!"

The others laughed, but not Joe.

"Are you going to collect it as evidence, or can I dispose of it?" he asked them.

"Evidence?" another cop laughed. "No, we don't need it as evidence. You can throw it away."

"I'll do it right now if you're not," Joe said.

"Let me get a picture of it first," the older cop said.

One of the campus cops had a camera, which he opened up and turned on. It made a whining noise reminiscent of the night-vision lens that Andy had used on the camera the night before. The cop with the camera took two photos of the excrement, two shots of the broken window, and three of the word "killer" on the door.

"Do you recognize the handwriting?" the oldest cop asked.

"I'm not 100 percent certain, but it looks like the juvenile printing of a student named Gary Grimes. I've had trouble with him before, and he threatened to lie to the police to make me look guilty of those I-5 killings."

"Why would he do that?" the cop asked.

"I dropped him from a special course he was taking, and he's not happy about it. He's in danger of being dropped from the entire program now."

"No," the cop said. "I mean, why would he have to lie to make you look guilty? You've been doing a pretty good job of making yourself look guilty, wouldn't you say?"

The other two cops chuckled. Joe fumed.

"Well, tell me, Officer," Joe said. "How *is* someone supposed to act when he's been wrongly charged with a heinous crime?"

The cop ignored the question and pulled his walkie-talkie out of a holster on his belt. He called the campus custodial department.

"We need a cleanup on the third floor office of Professor Conrad in Anderson," he said.

"Roger that," a voice said.

Joe asked, "How soon will they be here?"

"What's your ETA?" the cop asked the radio.

After a pause, the voice said, "Thirty to forty minutes."

"Roger that," the cop said, sounding like Deputy Barney Fife from *The Andy Griffith Show* to Joe.

"Aren't you guys going to clean up anything?" Joe asked.

"No," the same cop said. "We just gather evidence and make a record of the crime against the university. Custodial does the cleanup."

"Are you going to dust for fingerprints or anything?" Joe asked, frustrated.

"No. It's probably not worth it."

"Are you going to question Gary Grimes?" Joe asked.

"One of us might give him a call. Even if he did do it, he won't admit it."

"He might," Joe said. "He's a psychopath as far as I'm concerned."

One of the younger officers laughed.

"What's so funny?" asked Joe, very annoyed.

"Well, obviously," said the young cop, pointing toward the spray-painted word, "whoever wrote that thinks the same about you!"

Joe stood up and faced the cop, and all three officers tensed up.

"Are you always so damn rude to the faculty?"

"No," the young cop said, his face growing red with anger. "I'm only rude to the ones who murder college girls!"

"I didn't murder those girls!" Joe yelled.

The young cop's jaws were clenching as he stepped closer to Joe. He put his face just inches from Joe's

"I knew Autumn Smith personally," he yelled. "So I'd love to be left alone in a small room with whoever murdered her!"

"Well, that wasn't me!" Joe yelled back.

The other two officers grabbed the angry cop by the arms and tugged him back, and as he stepped backward, the angry young cop stepped in the pile of excrement.

"Oh, shit!" he yelled before he could stop himself.

"That's just great," exclaimed Joe. "Now you've ground that crap into my carpet!"

The older cop chuckled. "Everyone just calm down," he said. "Calm down, Professor. It's not in your carpet. It's still on the glass."

The older cop pushed the other two back. Then he bent down and started picking up the pieces of broken glass with the flattened excrement on them, and he carefully tossed them into the plastic waste pail that was next to the door. The trash can was lined with a plastic bag, and when the officer had thrown away all of the large pieces of glass, he pulled the plastic bag out of the can carefully and stood up again.

"There you go, Professor Conrad. The worst is cleaned up now, and the janitor should be here shortly to finish the job."

"Thank you," Joe said.

The smell in the office was already subsiding, and the angry younger cop was standing out in the middle of the hallway.

Joe looked the oldest officer in the eyes. "I really didn't have anything to do with the deaths of those women," he said quietly. "Tell your friend that for me."

The older cop smiled maturely. "He's not my friend, Professor. I just work with him."

After the cops left, Joe sat back down for a minute to calm the beating of his heart. He had been sure that the cop was going to hit him. He hadn't been struck in the face so often since high school. His first two years of high school had been rough, and he had gotten into a fistfight with somebody about every other week, it seemed.

It was a quarter to nine, and he had only a couple of hours left before his first class. He grabbed the coffeepot and went downstairs to the restroom to get water. Upon his return, he found a middle-aged woman with short black-and-gray hair vacuuming the carpet in his office.

"I opened your window a little to let some fresh air in!" she yelled over the noise of the vacuum.

"Thanks," replied Joe.

He set to work preparing his coffee, turning on the computer, and getting the research papers out of his briefcase to grade. After about half an hour, two handymen came by to repair the window. They removed the rest of the glass and screwed a thin piece of plywood over the space where the window had been.

"What about the graffito?" Joe asked.

"The what?" asked one of the men.

"The graffito? The spray-painted word?"

"Ain't that called graph-feet-tea, Professor?"

"'Graffiti' is the plural form of 'graffito,'" Joe explained.

"Didn't know that," the man responded, rolling his eyes at the other worker.

"Are you going to cover it up?" Joe asked.

"No, we ain't the painters, Professor. The painters are busier than we are. One can get by here tomorrow, probably."

"Tomorrow? I don't want people to see that on my door all day."

The worker shrugged. "Just cover it up with paper till tomorrow," he advised.

After the men left, Joe took a piece of white paper and held it over the first part of the word. It barely covered the first two letters. Then Joe went to his desk and took out a blue Magic Marker. The door to his office was painted about the same shade of blue, and Joe went to work covering the letters with blue ink. He stepped back when he was done. The word was still visible, but it was far less noticeable.

At his desk, Joe stared at the telephone for a few seconds before picking up the receiver and dialing the number for Susan's office. Sara was at work by now, so Joe didn't even try the condo again. After three rings, a secretary answered, and Joe asked to speak to Susan Taylor.

"Who's calling please?"

"I'm her brother-in-law, Joseph Conrad."

"Please hold," the polite voice said.

Joe listened to classical music while he waited.

"I'm sorry," the polite voice stated. "Ms. Taylor is in a meeting right now. She'll have to call you back. Can I have your number please."

"She has my number. Please tell her it's urgent."

The secretary assured Joe that she'd pass on the message and then hung up.

After drinking coffee and grading papers for about an hour, Joe went over to Cassandra's office, only to find a note:

> Class cancelled Wednesday.
> Grading your portfolios.
> See you Friday.
>
> > Cass

Joe went back to his office and sulked as he graded more papers. Before he left for his first class, he went over and closed the window—his office had grown chilly. Looking outside, he saw a darkening sky, and the branches of the trees swayed in a wet breeze. Another storm was coming.

In the classroom, the students sat silently, jotting down a few notes, dark circles under their eyes. They were exhausted. The end of the semester was killing them. Too much work, too many papers and tests. A few students could barely keep themselves from nodding off. Joe tried to provide an overview of the three dramatic tragedies they had studied together to help the students put the stories into a larger perspective.

"Sometimes, we become so absorbed in the minutia of these characters' lives we forget to consider the grand, sweeping themes that these dramas reveal," Joe professed as students jotted their notes. He could almost hear the questions in their minds: "Will this be on the test?"

"The lives of Oedipus, Hamlet, and Willy Loman are lives punctuated by great deeds and noble motives. These characters live lives of intense drama with tragic results while we, by contrast, live mundane lives of routine and boredom. We are drawn to the intensity of a character's life, even while we ourselves read quietly and safely, snug and warm in our little beds. But through these fictions, we gain perspectives on the tragedies of life without risking our own lives. We hope we have learned to live like our heroes while avoiding the tragic flaws that lead to their downfall. Our lives are, in fact, a little better, a little richer for having witnessed our heroes' crises and conflicts. Should we ask anything more from literature?"

Joe watched as students finished paraphrasing his lecture, and he hoped that his words might inspire a few of them to appreciate the work they had done in his class this semester. As the students finished writing, they put down their pens, and a few looked around at the others conspiratorially. Then the students applauded.

Students had never applauded one of Joe's lectures before. He was moved almost to tears by the act of kindness and respect; and for a moment, he was at a loss, not knowing how to react. Finally, he regained his composure and held up his hands.

"Thank you," he said. "I can't tell you how much I appreciate that. With everything that's happened, your support means more than I can say."

A few seconds of uncomfortable silence passed, and then Joe remembered the course evaluation forms. He reached down and picked up the forms, passing the stack to the student at the front of the classroom.

"Well," he said. "Maybe you'll give me a good evaluation after all!"

Some of the students laughed.

"Okay," said Joe, picking up his books and papers. "I have to leave while you're filling those out, but I'll see you next Wednesday for the final exam."

With that, he left the classroom and went back to his office, hoping that the classes in the afternoon would be just as touching. With his door closed and the light off, Joe sat in the darkness.

CHAPTER TWENTY-EIGHT

During the afternoon class, the clouds opened, and a strong rainstorm pounded the trees outside the classroom windows. A few flashes of lightening brightened the walls, and nearby claps of thunder rocked the glass in the windows. It was hard to compete with Mother Nature's display of drama.

Joe tried to deliver the same speech in his afternoon; and though he delivered the same words, more or less, the emotion was not as strong. The afternoon class did not applaud.

The storm passed before Joe left campus, so he drove home through patches of sunlight. Once home, Joe called Susan's condo again. After a few rings, Sara answered.

"I tried to reach you this morning," Joe told her.

"We left early," Sara explained. "I put Katie in a new day care center near my school, so I had to sign her in this morning."

"Where is it?" Joe asked.

"I'll give you all that later, but here's the telephone number." Sara read the numbers as Joe wrote them down.

"What's the name of this place?"

"It's called KinderChild, and it's on Cottage Way just two blocks from my school."

"Sounds convenient," Joe said. "How's it look?"

"It looks fine. I dropped in unexpectedly yesterday after school to pick up the application forms, and all the children looked happy and well supervised."

"Does Katie seem to like it?" Joe asked.

"She was happy to be around other kids again when I left her this morning. She didn't cry or cling at all," Sara said. "This afternoon she was a little more tired than usual. They have more playtime at this place, and they don't allow long naps. I think Katie's going to sleep well tonight."

"Good," Joe said. "I'm glad someone will."

"I know," Sara agreed. "I haven't been sleeping well either."

"It's not supposed to be like this, Sara. I miss you. I miss having you in bed with me."

Sara stayed quiet for several seconds.

Joe asked, "Don't you miss me?"

"Don't ask me that," Sara said, and Joe could hear her voice cracking.

"Well, I miss you and Katie like hell," Joe said. "I miss holding you both, and I miss hearing her laugh, and I especially miss making love to you."

"There was never a problem in that area of our relationship," Sara said, her voice soft and warm.

Joe closed his eyes and imagined making love to Sara—her on top, her eyes closed, her faced relaxed and pleased, a smile on his face; and her lips slightly parted.

"Are you still there?" he asked.

"Yes, Joe," Sara responded softly. "I'm definitely still here."

"What are you thinking of?"

"What do you think?" Sara said.

"Me too," Joe said. "I've got an idea."

"I bet you do," Sara said.

"No, listen. I'm done with classes until next Tuesday night. I give one final Tuesday night and two the following Wednesday. Why don't we get away for a long weekend?"

"What do you mean?" Sara asked.

"Well, why don't you get a substitute for your classes tomorrow and Friday, and we can go away somewhere together."

"I can't do that, Joe."

"Why not?"

"Remember?" Sara asked. "Katie and I fly back to Louisiana Tuesday night. I've got to do my grades and get things wrapped up in case I don't come back after the break."

"What?" Joe said, alarmed. "When did you decide you weren't coming back after the Christmas break?"

"I haven't decided yet, Joe, but I'm going to consider it seriously while I'm back home. Especially if I can get a teaching job in Baton Rouge."

"Are you still going ahead with the divorce?"

"I told you already," Sara said, sounding a little annoyed. "I'll wait until after the trial. Bill Morgan and Suzy made it clear that you'll be helped a lot by having a wife and daughter on your side, even if it's just for show."

"I don't care about how it looks for the goddamn trial, Sara. I care about you and my daughter. I want to keep you in my life."

"Why?" Sara asked. "You have all your other girlfriends at the strip club and the students you evidently go out with. So why do you want to keep me in your life?"

"Because I love you, Sara," Joe said without hesitation. "I love you and Katie more than I love anything else in the world."

"But you don't always act like you love us, Joe," Sara said sadly.

"I know, Sara. But you have to admit, you haven't been acting very loving toward me lately either."

Again, Sara stayed quiet. Joe knew she had to think.

"I absolutely can't get a sub for tomorrow," Sara finally said. "But I might be able to for Friday. And Monday is just an in-service day when we're supposed to work on grades and cleaning up the classroom. I can miss Monday without even needing a sub. What did you have in mind, Joe?"

"I don't know for sure. Maybe we could drive up to Lake Tahoe and just get a hotel room. We could get a sled for Katie. What would you like to do?"

"Honestly?" Sara asked.

"Yeah, of course," Joe said.

"Honestly, I'd love to go to San Francisco and take Katie to a Christmas play. We could finish our Christmas shopping at Macy's and take Katie to see the store Santa."

"That sounds great, Sara," Joe admitted, "but it would be incredibly expensive. The room alone would probably cost two hundred dollars a night!"

"Joe," Sara said very seriously. "This might be the last time we spend anytime together as a real family. Suzy and I spoke to Mom and Dad, Joe. They really want me to move back home to Baton Rouge and stay there. You know my parents like you, Joe, but they want me to leave you."

"You used to say you didn't care what your parents thought," Joe said.

"I didn't. But now, with Katie, I understand their concerns a little better."

"With age comes wisdom?"

"Having a child to take care of puts your priorities in place. That's for damn sure."

It was Joe's turn to stay quiet and think.

"Okay," he said. "What the hell. It's only money."

"Oh, good," Sara said. "Besides, I just got a new credit card that has a credit limit of nine thousand dollars!"

"Well then, hell! Let's stay at the Ritz-Carlton!"

"No," Sara said. "But remember that place we went to for dinner near Union Square?"

"The Donatello?"

"Yeah. Let's stay there. I loved the food and the Mediterranean décor."

"Fine."

"And it's a block from Macy's."

"Great."

"And it's right around the corner from the theaters. I think *A Christmas Carol* is being performed at the Geary."

"Okay," Joe said. "Do you want me to make the reservations, or do you want to do it?"

"I'll do it," Sara said excitedly. "I'll put it on my new credit card."

"Can Suzy drop you and Katie off here Friday morning?" Joe asked.

"Maybe we should meet you away from the house, in case reporters are following you."

"Have Suzy drop you off in front of Mrak Hall on the UCD campus. I'll meet you near the law school."

Joe spent Wednesday night and all day Thursday grading research papers. At three o'clock, he remembered to call his attorney. He put the telephone back on the wall, and it rang immediately. Joe lifted the receiver as if to answer but hung it up right away. He dialed the number on Morgan's card. Once he was able to speak to Bill Morgan, the lawyer explained the law, "As long as an officer of the court knows where you'll be, you can go out of town. Just don't jump a plane and leave the state!"

Before dinner, Joe put on his sweats and took a jog. The sun was setting behind patchy clouds and the air grew chilly. As Joe ran through the park, he watched mothers and fathers play with their young children on the swing sets and monkey bars of the playgrounds. Joe left the park as it was getting dark and jogged down F Street as the streetlights were coming on. When he rounded the corner to Tenth Street, he saw Lisa Piante unloading grocery bags from her car next to her small apartment complex.

"Lisa," he called as he slowed down. "How are you?"

The beautiful young dark-haired woman looked at him nervously. "Oh, hi, Joe," she said, looking around. "How have you been?"

Joe was breathing hard, but he leaned against the car, smiling at Lisa in the fading light.

"Fine," he replied. "Or as well as can be expected with all that's happened. Have you seen the news?"

"Yes, I have," Lisa said nervously.

"Crazy," Joe said. "I used to have more faith in the police."

"I saw that interview at your school."

"Did you?" Joe asked, smiling. "How'd I come off? Guilty as sin or innocent as a newborn babe?"

Lisa laughed a little. "Somewhere in between, I guess. I've got to get these groceries inside."

Joe stood and came around the open door. "Let me help you."

"No, thanks," Lisa said, coldly, "I can get it."

"But you've got your arms full," Joe said, taking two bags away from her.

At first, it was clear that she did not want to let go of the bags, but she did; and then she reached into the car and grabbed the last bag of groceries, closing the car door loudly.

"I'm just upstairs," she said, walking quickly toward the staircase.

Joe walked fast behind her.

When she got to the door, she turned around and said, "You can just set them down here, Joe."

She looked into his eyes nervously, and Joe suddenly realized that she was afraid of him.

"Lisa," Joe said calmly. "Don't be afraid. I won't hurt you."

Lisa began to tremble. "Please don't hurt me, Joe," she said, her voice quivering.

"Lisa," Joe said. "You know me. I won't hurt you."

"It was on the news today," Lisa said.

"What?"

"The police found that other girl's body."

"What girl?" Joe asked.

"That Vietnamese girl from Lodi."

"Oh," Joe said. He didn't quite know how to react. He had hoped that she would not be found, that she would not have been a victim. He had suspected that this girl had probably run away.

"She was strangled like the others," Lisa said, almost crying.

"That's awful," said Joe. He suddenly thought about Katie. It sounded crazy, but he wanted this killer stopped before Katie got older.

"Please leave," Lisa said. "I don't want to end up like the others."

Joe was stunned. "You know I could never do something like that, Lisa," he said. He inched toward her, hoping to calm her down.

She closed her eyes, leaned back against the door, and started to cry. "I'm going to scream if you don't leave right now."

Holding the two bags in his arms, Joe looked at Lisa's terrified face. Now he knew how Autumn and Patricia must have looked when they were face-to-face with their killer. Joe put the bags down.

"I'm leaving," he said. "I'm sorry, Lisa. I didn't realize I was scaring you."

"Just go!"

He started to back away. He walked the rest of the way back to his house slowly, saddened by what had happened. Most people probably assumed he was guilty after all.

Before dinner, he showered and watched the news while he was drying off. A picture of Lilly Nguyen was shown with a picture of the stream where her body was found in the background. A handsome young well-groomed newscaster appeared on the screen. "Few details have been released about how the victim was found," the newscaster said. "But this case seems to be related to the others for which Joseph Lawrence Conrad was arrested and released on bail only last week."

Then a picture of Joe in the courtroom appeared on the screen. "The Central Valley has had more than its share of these types of homicides," said the newscaster over photographs of Chandra Levy and Laci Peterson. Joe watched as the faces of Patricia Miller, Autumn Smith, and, now, Lilly Nguyen appeared one by one. The Vietnamese girl looked so young, even younger than Autumn Smith. Then photographs of Scott Peterson appeared, followed by a picture of Joe, and Joe switched the television set off in disgust.

"Goddamn it!" Joe shouted at the blank television screen. "I'm not guilty!" He bent down, holding his head in his hands for several minutes, too enraged to move but feeling like he wanted to kill somebody. For a moment, he visualized his hands around the TV reporter's throat, choking the life out of him. He straightened up and took several deep breaths to relax.

After dinner, he made coffee and went back to grading papers at the little desk in the corner of his bedroom. With the curtains open and the blinds only partially closed, he could check the street between papers.

At eleven o'clock, Joe looked up and saw a car parked across the street that he didn't recognize. It looked as if someone was inside, but he couldn't be sure. He turned off the lamp, and his bedroom went dark. In a few seconds, when his eyes had adjusted to the light, he was able to see the car better. A man was inside, smoking. The man's shape was silhouetted by the porch lights of the houses behind him. Joe watched the figure who evidently had been watching him. *Is this a cop?* Joe wondered. *Maybe it's the killer.*

Joe got up and went to the kitchen where he removed a large flashlight from the junk drawer. He checked the backyard, which looked empty in the darkness. Joe opened the back door cautiously and went around to the driveway. He inched his way down the driveway until he could see the man inside the car through the bushes. Joe calculated that if he walked behind the bushes, he could almost reach the sidewalk before the man parked across the street saw him. Then what would he do? He would shine the light at the man's face and get a good look at him, that's what he'd do.

Dressed only in an old LSU sweatshirt and pajama bottoms, Joe crouched and crept closer to the sidewalk, keeping the bushes between himself and the man's view. The grass between the bushes and the driveway was cold and wet on Joe's bare feet. He began to shiver despite his desire to appear fierce. Once he reached the end of the row of shrubs, he dashed for the car, switching on the flashlight about halfway across the street.

The car's headlights came on at almost the same instant! Joe was blinded by the lights and slowed just a little. Suddenly, the car's engine roared to life; and the driver backed up rapidly, the engine whining as it increased speed. The man backed up until he reached the little cross street. Then the car turned down the cross street and disappeared.

Joe jogged after the car until he reached the half street too. Seeing that the car was gone, he waved the flashlight back and forth. "And don't come back!" he yelled defiantly.

A porch light suddenly came on at the corner, and Joe turned and walked back toward his house. When he reached the back door, he found it closed and locked. "Just great!" he said aloud.

Fortunately, he and Sara had hung a spare key on a little nail at the rear of the garage behind a shrub. Joe made his way around the garage and found the key. When he got back inside the kitchen, he turned on the light and looked at his feet. They were covered with wet grass, and his ankles were splattered with mud from the street. Joe shook his head, laughed at himself, and went to the bathroom to rinse off before going to bed.

CHAPTER TWENTY-NINE

Friday morning, Joe awoke early, showered, and packed a bag for a long weekend, excited to see Katie and Sara again. He ate a sweet roll for breakfast and sipped coffee from a travel mug as he drove to the UCD campus administration building. The campus was virtually empty. The ten-week quarter had already ended at UC-Davis, so only staff and a few faculty were on campus. Joe parked in front of Mrak Hall with a view of the two large egg-head sculptures that stood perched on two hills facing each other. In the shape of eggs about six feet high and four feet around, the heads had human faces with large ears. It looked as if the two heads were arguing with each other, and Joe often believed that the artist was secretly satirizing the university's administrators though this sculpture in particular was titled *The Debaters*, if Joe remembered correctly. Half a dozen of these egg-head sculptures appeared on campus, one with his large nose stuck in the binding of an open book in front of the library.

After half an hour of waiting, Joe saw Suzy's car turn in at the end of the lane, and he could see Sara sitting in the passenger's seat. She smiled when she spotted Joe resting against the fender of her Ford. Suzy, by contrast, was frowning and seemed very displeased with the entire escapade. Nevertheless, she pulled in to an open space next to Joe, and Sara got out quickly and immediately embraced Joe.

"I've really missed you," she whispered in his ear, kissing his earlobe softly.

"Daddy!" Katie shrieked, getting out of the backseat.

She ran over and jumped into Joe's arms, and Joe hugged her tightly.

"I missed you so much, Daddy," Katie said in Joe's arms.

"I missed you too, Katie-did," Joe said.

"Hello, Joe," Suzy said coldly.

She extended her hand, and Joe shook it while still holding on to Katie.

"Thanks for driving them here."

Suzy let go of Joe's hand. "Against my will," she said.

Though it had been cloudy and cold, the sun suddenly popped out from the puffy white clouds, and the sunshine was almost blinding. Then the sunlight disappeared again for a few seconds but reappeared between large patches of clouds and fog that seemed to be burning off.

"Mommy?" Katie asked. "Can I go over and see the egg heads?"

Sara and Joe glanced over at the grassy hill. No one was near the sculptures.

"Sure, but just for a few minutes."

Katie ran across the road and up the hill. Joe and Sara watched as Katie stood in front of one of the large white eggs, apparently waiting for it to say something. The egg was almost twice as tall as Katie. After touching it with a finger, she then began climbing on the face, putting one foot inside the opened mouth and trying to hold on to an eyebrow.

Suzy broke their silence. "I hope the campus police don't come by."

Joe laughed. "You think they'd arrest a four-year-old, Suzy?"

"I'll go get her," Sara said.

She strolled over to the knoll and flagged Katie down.

"Do you realize how much trouble you're in, Joe?" said Susan.

Joe shot her a stern look. "Hey, Counselor, I was the one in jail, remember? It's been my face all over the television. So yeah, I have a pretty good idea."

Pulling Sara along, Katie returned to the cars where Joe and Susan were standing. Joe tried not to show his anger.

"Let's get started," Joe said.

They transferred a few small suitcases from Susan's car to the trunk of Sara's Escort, and then Sara and Katie hugged Susan goodbye. Susan started crying.

"Hey!" Sara said, holding her. "Don't cry. This is going to be fine. We're going to have fun, the way families are supposed to at Christmas."

Joe stepped closer. "I promise I'll take good care of them, Suzy," he told his wife's sister.

She shot a cold look at him. "Just stay out of trouble, Joe!"

"I will."

"I mean it," she said.

Joe strapped Katie into the backseat, and they were off to San Francisco. By the time they reached Berkeley, the freeway traffic was stop-and-go all the way to the tollbooths on the Oakland Bay Bridge. The gray clouds had all but disappeared, and sunlight made the whitecaps of the water in the Bay sparkle. From the car, the three of them stared at the buildings of the city, the Transamerica Pyramid gleaming in the sunlight. Beyond the buildings stood the Golden Gate Bridge on the far side of the Bay. The Bay itself was filled with ships and sailboats of all shapes and sizes. On days when the weather was even halfway decent, it was as if the sailboats had been pent up in their stalls like racehorses aching to run. Alcatraz Island was ringed by boats with brightly colored sails.

As they neared the western end of the bridge, the smell of coffee filled the car from a coffee-packing plant that was just at the foot of the bridge. This was the city with its traffic like blood coursing through its arteries. Joe loved San Francisco almost as much as he loved the French Quarter in New Orleans. It was vibrant and glorious in the sunlight, and Sara and Joe simply looked at each other, smiling. Sara slipped her hand into Joe's, and for a time, Joe forgot about the murder case. Katie giggled from the backseat.

"This city is too, too big, Daddy!" she exclaimed.

At the Donatello Hotel, Joe pulled into the parking garage where they unloaded their bags and gave the car keys to a valet, who gave Joe a receipt.

As the valet drove the car deeper inside the building, Joe looked at Katie and said, "I sure hope that fella works for the hotel!"

Sara laughed, but Katie looked worried.

Sara walked up to the front desk in the ornate lobby of the hotel while Joe and Katie stood by the three small suitcases. In no time, they were riding the elevator up to the eleventh floor. The room was bright and airy, tastefully decorated in Victorian era furniture. Sara went to the window.

"Come look."

They could see part of Union Square far down below, decorated lavishly for Christmas and crowded with tiny shoppers.

"We're high up," Katie said, a little worried.

"Yes, we are," Joe said. "I hope there isn't an earthquake!"

Sara slapped Joe's shoulder. "Stop it, Joe!" she laughed.

"With my luck," Joe said, but he decided not to finish his statement.

The room held one queen-sized bed with a dozen pillows piled up against the mahogany headboard.

"Where do I sleep?" Katie asked. "Between you and Daddy?"

Joe and Sara laughed. "No, honey," Sara explained. "They're bringing a special little bed for you."

Almost on cue, there was a knock on the door, and Joe opened it to find a well-dressed bellboy pushing a rollaway bed that was folded in half.

Joe opened the bed and positioned it against the wall between a tall mahogany armoire and the foot of the bed. There was just enough room to squeeze by it. Katie immediately flopped on the bed and bounced a few times.

"This is comfy," she said, grinning happily.

The three of them set about unpacking their bags, and when they were done, Joe picked up Katie and asked, "Are you hungry, Katie-did?"

"Yes, Daddy. How did you know?"

"How would you like to go to a real New York-style delicatessen?"

Katie pondered the question for a few seconds. "Can't we just stay here in San Francisco?"

Sara and Joe laughed.

"Yes, honey. Right around the corner, there's a good delicatessen where we can get a great lunch," Joe explained. "Understand, Katie?"

"Yes," she said, but she still seemed worried.

Katie seemed to enjoy the elevator ride as much as any amusement park ride. Outside, the air was crisp and chilly, but sunlight poured down into Union Square, and the sidewalks were busy. A woman in a Salvation Army uniform was ringing a bell across the street. With Katie between them, Joe and Sara walked down the hill to Geary and then turned west and walked a few blocks up to the delicatessen, which was already filling with noisy people of all shapes and ages. A waitress walked them to the rear where they squeezed into a clean little booth. From the back of the restaurant, they could look out past the customers through the window and watch people walking on the sidewalk. All of the hustle and bustle of city life made Katie's eyes wide with interest.

A woman approached in a waitress uniform who looked exactly the part. Her hair was piled up in a beehive bun, she had a pencil behind her ear, she wore too much blue eye shadow and too much red lipstick; and although middle-aged, she still had a good figure with the buttons of her blouse undone just enough to show her ample cleavage.

"What'll ya have, hon?" the waitress asked Sara.

"I'll have the turkey and swiss cheese on dark rye with mayonnaise and honey mustard," Sara said.

"You want lettuce and tomato?" the waitress asked.

"Oh, yes please," Sara said, apparently delighted that the waitress had thought to ask.

"Yeah," the waitress said. "We gals like a little salad on our sandwich." Turning her attention to Katie, she asked, "And what will you have, sweetie?"

Katie, who was holding a menu as if reading it, said, "Can I have a hot dog?"

"I'm not sure they have hot dogs here, Katie," Joe said.

"Sure we do," the waitress said. "What'll you have on it, sweetie? The works?"

"What's the works?" Katie asked.

"Ketchup, mustard, relish, onions, chili, sauerkraut, peppers."

"May I please have a chili dog," Katie asked thoughtfully.

Sara told the waitress, "Everything but onions, peppers, and sauerkraut please."

"Very good," the waitress said. "And what would Madame like to drink?"

"Do you have chocolate milk?"

"We have the best chocolate milk on the West Coast," the waitress said, giving Katie a toothy smile.

"Yummy!" Katie said. "I'd like a big glass of chocolate milk."

The waitress wrote down Katie's order.

"And for you, sir?"

"I'll have a hot pastrami and swiss cheese on light rye with mayo and hot mustard," Joe said, his mouth already watering.

"Want me to throw a little sauerkraut on that too, sir?" asked the waitress.

"You must be a mind reader," Joe told the middle-aged woman.

The woman targeted her gaze straight at Joe. "Believe me," she said, "I've read the minds of many guys over the years."

Joe laughed. "I bet you have."

"Do Mom and Dad want a drink with lunch?"

"Sure," Joe said, glancing at Sara, who smiled back.

"It's not like we have to drive anywhere, I guess," Sara said. "I'll have rum and Coke."

The waitress wrote it down. "And for you, sir?"

"Read my mind, Dorothy," Joe said, noting her name tag.

She leveled her gaze at Joe once again. "A double gin martini on the rocks with two olives if I'm readin' you right," she said.

Though Joe usually only drank gin and tonics, he decided to go along with Dorothy's telepathy. "Perfect!"

When the drinks came, Sara proposed a toast. "Here's to a Merry Christmas for the Conrad family."

"Merry Christmas," Joe said, lifting his glass over to Sara's.

Katie carefully lifted her rather-full glass of chocolate milk and managed to tap both of the other glasses without spilling. While Joe and Sara sipped their drinks, Katie just put hers down without taking a sip.

"Oh, Katie," Joe said. "You've got to take a drink after a toast has been made. Otherwise, it's bad luck."

Katie looked worried as if she might be in trouble. Using both of her small hands, she carefully lifted the glass and drank a good portion of the milk.

After lunch, they walked to Union Square. Katie was disappointed. There was no ice-skating rink anymore. Joe and Sara had gone ice-skating there during the first year they lived in California, and it had been magical.

"I've got a better idea," Joe told Katie, who was beginning to tear up as if she were about to cry. "Let's ride the cable cars!"

They had already watched the cable cars go by a few times, so Katie's eyes brightened when she realized what her father meant. They walked several blocks down the hill to the cable car station where the cars were turned around, and Joe stood in line while Sara walked Katie along the sidewalk to window-shop at the tourist stores that held all things San Franciscan and Christmas.

By the time they were ready to board the cable car, the air had turned colder; so they found a seat inside, and Katie pressed her face right up against the glass of the window. When the cable car lurched to a start, Katie looked at her parents, startled; but reassured that the jerky motion was normal, Katie clapped with delight. They stayed on the cable car all the way over the top of Nob Hill—or Snob Hill as Joe called it—and at the other end of the line, down by the Bay, the wind whipped through their coats easily. They got back on the next car as quickly as they could and rode the cable car up over the hill again, getting off at Union Square. From there, they walked back over to the Geary Theater where they picked up tickets for the Saturday evening show.

Katie was fading fast. Joe and Sara coaxed her back to the hotel where Joe picked her up. She went limp in his arms as they rode the elevator to their room.

"Let's all take a nap before dinner," Sara said.

In the room, Sara managed to remove Katie's coat and shoes without waking her up. She positioned Katie on the center of the little rollaway bed, pulling a blanket up over her.

"She's out," Sara said as she lay down next to Joe on the bed.

Joe looked over at her and smiled. Sara rolled over and kissed Joe lightly on the lips. Then she kissed him again more forcefully. Reaching over to the nightstand, Joe turned off the bedside lamp; and with the curtains pulled shut, the room became almost completely dark. Joe and Sara undressed each other as they kissed. Hungry for each other, they climbed underneath cool sheets and made love fiercely. The darkness of a deep, peaceful sleep came easily to both of them when they had finished.

Katie woke them at six-thirty by turning on the television. The bluish glow and noise filled the hotel room. They dressed and went downstairs for dinner in the hotel restaurant.

"Look at these prices, Sara," Joe said, inspecting the menu.

"New credit card," Sara reminded him. "Let's just enjoy ourselves."

"Guilt free?"

"Yes."

The Italian food was delicious; and Joe savored every bite, recalling the bland, stale food he had eaten in jail. Sara reached under the table and rubbed the inside of his thigh. Sara wanted to splurge, he suspected, because she believed Joe would go to jail for the rest of his life. It was as if she owed him one last fling. If Joe thought about it too much . . .

Joe and Sara shared a bottle of red wine and watched Katie eat chocolate mousse for the first time in her life. After dinner, they decided to walk around the block outside. Well-dressed couples were being let out of limousines in front of the two theaters on Geary, and they stood and watched the parade of people for a while.

"Are those people rich, Daddy?" Katie asked.

"Well, Katie," Joe said, leaning down to whisper in her ear. "They're probably not teachers."

Back in the room, they changed into pajamas and watched *Miracle on 34th Street* as they lay on the bed drowsily. Katie fell asleep again before the movie was over, and Joe carried her over to her little bed.

Sara turned off the television just as the news was starting. Joe returned, and the two of them sat against the headboard staring at Katie as she slept.

"An odd thing happened last night," Joe said.

Sara turned to look at the side of his face. "What?" she asked.

"I was grading papers in our room, and when I happened to look up, I noticed a guy sitting in a car across the street. It looked like he was watching our house."

"What did the guy look like?"

"I didn't get a good look."

"Was it a cop?"

"It could have been," Joe said. "Or it could have been a reporter."

"Or someone else?"

"Yeah," Joe said nervously. "Maybe it was him."

"Did you call the police?"

Joe chuckled. "Hell no! The police probably would have found a way to accuse *me* of something."

"So what *did* you do, Joe?"

"I turned out the light and watched him for a while. Then I slipped out of the house with a flashlight and tried to get a better look at him, but he got away."

"Jesus, Joe," Sara said angrily. "That's the kind of thing that's going to get you into more trouble. Let the police handle it."

Joe laughed again. "I *have* let the police handle it, and so far, they're pointing their fingers straight at me!"

"Suzy said something interesting last night."

"What?"

"Well, don't get angry. She's my older sister, and she's a lawyer, so she's trying to look out for me," Sara explained apologetically.

"Go on."

"She was trying to talk me out of coming here with you this weekend."

"Why?" Joe asked. "Doe she really think I'm the killer?"

"I don't think so, Joe, but she does say you're on thin ice."

"Meaning what?"

"She thinks you *are* going to be found guilty of these murders based on what Bill Morgan has told her."

"Wonderful!" Joe said sarcastically. "My own lawyer thinks it's hopeless!" Joe could feel the anger rising inside. He wished he had that double gin martini again.

"Bill and Suzy were talking with me the other day. They talked about all the murders and abductions of young women in the past few years, starting with the three women at Yosemite. The people in this area want these killings to stop, and they want someone to be found guilty so they can relax."

"I agree," Joe admitted. "This area has seen more than its fair share of murders."

"Suzy says the only hope is if the police catch somebody else in the act, and that's not very likely."

The reality of it hit him again.

"Is there a minibar in here?" Joe asked. He needed a drink.

"No," Sara said. "But we can order room service if you want something."

"I need a drink," Joe said picking up the phone. "How about you?"

"Sure. Order another glass of red wine."

Joe ordered himself a double martini on the rocks and a glass of Pinot Noir for Sara. After he hung up, he decided to tell Sara about using Joan Ngo as a decoy. He had just started describing how the fog was obscuring their view of the reporter when a knock on the door startled both of them. Joe hopped up and took a five from his wallet.

The waiter, a young man from the Middle East, had both drinks on a small tray and brought the drinks straight into the room, placing them on the dresser. He tried not to look at Sara, whose nightgown revealed her cleavage. He looked at Katie instead, smiling at her as Joe signed for the drinks and handed him the five. Katie slept soundly, not moving a muscle while the waiter watched her. Joe showed him to the door and locked it after the stranger left. As he walked by Katie's little bed, Joe bent down and straightened the blankets just under Katie's chin. She was clearly out for the night.

Back in bed with the drinks, Joe finished the story.

"I can't believe you got a grown woman to go along with that scheme!" Sara said, half laughing. She sipped her wine.

"I was so scared when I saw those headlights come up behind the car!" Joe laughed, fishing one of the fat green olives out of his drink. He munched on the olive as he spoke. "And then when I saw that it was a cop, I think I got even more frightened!"

By now, Sara was laughing too in spite of herself.

"It's a wonder he didn't haul your ass off to jail, Joe!"

They were both laughing now despite their best efforts to stop. It was somehow a relief to laugh at all that had happened.

"Here's to being on thin ice!" Joe said, clinking his glass with Sara's.

"To thin ice!" Sara said, drinking more of her wine. "Except there isn't any ice this Christmas, Joe! No ice rink this year!"

"No," Joe said. "Our liability insurance doesn't cover ice-skating in Union Square."

Sara raised her glass and added, "Thanks to the lawyers!"

"If your child falls and cracks her head open, then you might sue the city!"

"Terrorists might attack us with ice skates!" Sara laughed.

"It's a wonder they still let the cable cars roll."

"Give 'em time, Joe," Sara said. "Pretty soon, the politicians and lawyers will shut down the cable cars."

"You know, Sara," Joe said, "your sister's a lawyer."

"What do you call a thousand lawyers at the bottom of the ocean?"

"A good start," Joe said.

Katie moaned and rolled over, and Sara looked guiltily at Joe, holding her finger up to her lips and trying not to laugh.

"You're makin' too damn much noise, sir," she said with a Brooklyn accent, trying to imitate Dorothy, the waitress from the deli.

Joe finished his drink, set the glass down, and leaned over to kiss Sara. In the middle of the kiss, Sara started laughing.

"Not tonight, dear," Sara laughed. "I've got a headache."

Joe pouted, and Sara leaned back toward him and kissed him on the mouth, still smiling. They both looked at Katie, who had rolled toward the wall and seemed to be deeply asleep again. Joe turned out the light, and the couple reached for each other in the quiet darkness of the room.

They made love again for the second time that day and then fell into a deep sleep as if there was nothing at all wrong in their lives.

In the morning, they ordered room service and had breakfast in bed. Katie took the entire process very seriously, working hard to balance her plate of scrambled eggs and french toast on her lap. Joe, eating eggs Benedict for the first time in years, watched Katie's struggle with amusement while Sara was perfectly happy with a croissant, fruit, and coffee.

"What are we going to do today?" Katie asked, taking a bite of french toast.

"We have a special treat for you today," Joe said.

"We came down to this big beautiful city this weekend because we heard that Santa Claus was going to be here," Sara added.

Katie's eyes brightened. "Can we go see Santa?" she asked excitedly.

"That's the plan, Katie," said Joe.

Katie began clapping and squealing, and her parents watched with delight. Then Katie put her plate to the side and started to get out of bed.

"Where are you going, honey?" Sara asked.

"To get ready for Santa, Mommy."

"But it's too early, dear. He won't be seeing children until after lunch."

"Does he have to see other children too?" Katie asked.

Joe laughed. "You wouldn't want to hog Santa Claus all to yourself, would you, Katie?"

Katie considered her father's question quite seriously for a few seconds. "Yes, Daddy, I would."

Sara and Joe couldn't help laughing.

"Well, finish your breakfast," Joe said. "We're going to have a long day today because we're going to see a play. You get to stay up until midnight!"

Katie scooted back in under the covers and pulled the plate of food back over to her lap.

Dressed and ready by noon, the threesome left the hotel room just as the maid was about to knock on the door to clean. Outside, the air was cold and damp, a gray fog hanging thickly over the city, obscuring the tops of the buildings. They walked through Union Square first to look at the giant Christmas tree again. Then they walked down the hill to

Nordstrom's. The department store was enormous, the interior like the Tower of Babylon, open in the center going up ten or twelve floors, Joe guessed.

They rode the escalators up and up, walking around the circular balconies and stopping from time to time to peer over the railings to see how high up they were. After they reached the top, they stepped inside one of the stores and asked a sales clerk where Santa Claus was.

The young clerk, who looked like one of Joe's students, glanced down at Katie and said, "Santa's down in the basement." Joe and Sara looked at each other and laughed out loud, realizing they'd have to go all the way down again.

They found the long line of parents with their toddlers waiting for Santa.

Katie tapped Joe's arm, and Joe bent down to listen to her.

"This is just like the movie we watched last night," she whispered. "Except it's in color."

Joe laughed and relayed Katie's observation to Sara, who struggled to laugh.

"I hope Santa shows soon, or I might faint. It's so hot," Sara said.

A few minutes later, the children in the front of the line began to cheer and applaud. Accompanied by two attractive young women, who looked like college cheerleaders in short green elf costumes, a large fat man dressed in a Santa suit strode toward the throne, which was perched atop a high stage so that all the children in line could watch what was going on. The Christmas decorations around the stage were elaborate but appealing. The rest of the children laughed and clapped, and the line started to move.

"Thank God!" Sara said. She had already removed Katie's coat and was holding it along with her own in her arms.

"Let me hold the coats, and you walk around for a while," Joe told Sara.

"Are you sure?"

"Sure," Joe said. "Go outside and get some fresh air."

Katie was straining to see Santa.

"Okay," Sara said. "I'll be back in thirty minutes."

Joe watched as Sara headed straight for the elevator. He knew she would go outside immediately to cool off. He suspected she might have a cigarette too. As the line inched along, Katie started losing interest in Santa.

"How much longer, Daddy?"

"Well, at this pace, I'd say it's going to be almost an hour."

"An hour!" Katie said. She started to cry.

"Hey hey hey," said Joe, kneeling down. "You'd better not cry, you'd better not pout," Joe whispered, trying to sing into Katie's little ear.

"Where's Mommy?" Katie said, trying not to cry.

"She just went to look around the store a little. Maybe she went to buy you a toy."

This possibility calmed Katie down, and it helped that the line advanced a little. Joe stood up again and looked around. The basement of Nordstrom's was packed with people, so it was hard to see anything. The line for Santa had been roped off, but now it had curled back on itself. There must have been a hundred people.

The line inched forward, and after about twenty minutes, Sara returned smiling.

"I feel much better," she said to Joe. He could smell that she'd been smoking. "Why don't you take a break now?"

"I think I will," said Joe.

He looked down at Katie, who seemed lost in thought, so he decided not to upset her by saying goodbye. Joe pushed through the people in line and made his way toward a less-crowded aisle. He decided he would go to the toy department and buy some little toy that might occupy Katie's time while she waited in line.

The toy department was more crowded than the area he had just left, but he braved it anyway. He found a red-and-white teddy bear that played different Christmas songs when he pushed its belly.

Back at the line, Sara and Katie were just three people away from seeing Santa. Joe decided to hold on to the teddy bear and give it to her another time, maybe in the morning for the drive home.

"They want twenty-five dollars for a photo," Sara told him, pointing to the sign that stood atop a pole.

"We should've bought a disposable camera," Joe said.

Sara's expression registered deep disappointment. "I want a picture, Joe," she said. "I want Katie to be able to remember this weekend in case the worst happens."

Joe was shaken back to the reality of his situation. In a few weeks, he would go on trial for murder, just like Scott Peterson had after Laci Peterson's body was found just across the Bay near the remains of their unborn child.

"Yeah, of course," he said. "Let's get the damn photograph."

By that point, it was finally time for Katie to climb the ramp up to Santa's throne. Holding both parents' hands, she bravely walked toward the giant red figure. The attractive elves guided them into position and helped Katie up on the big man's lap.

Up close, Santa looked like an actor in heavy makeup. His beard and moustache looked real enough, but his lips and cheeks were too red and his eyebrows looked plastic. Katie stared at him either in awe or disbelief, Joe couldn't tell which. He asked her if she had been a good girl.

"I've been exceptionally good this year," she said.

The Santa laughed and held his belly, playing the part.

"You are a very precocious young lady!" Santa laughed.

"I know."

One of the elves leaned toward Sara.

"Parents," she said, "we need to have you get on either side of Santa and lean in."

Sara and Joe had watched dozens of couples get into place for the photo, so they knew what to do. Once they were in place, the strobe light flashed.

"What special toy do you want Santa to bring you on Christmas Eve?" Santa asked after the flash.

"Well, I can always use more Lego sets, Santa," she said. "And I guess I'd like a doll because Aunt Suzy showed me the ones you brought her when she was a little girl, and they're real nice. But what I really want the most is for Mommy and Daddy to live together again."

Santa looked up at Joe and Sara, his blue eyes gazing at them curiously from behind empty gold eyeglass frames that rested on his overly reddened nose.

"Well," Santa told Katie, "that's up to your Mommy and Daddy, but I'll sure see what I can do to help."

"Thank you, Santa," Katie said.

"Anything else?"

"Yes," she said. "I don't want a pony like Linda does. She's a girl at my new babysitter place. But I do want my own Erector Set, like the one Bobby Wong plays with at day care. He won't share with girls."

"Oh, he won't?" said Santa. "Well, I'll just have to speak to Bobby Wong's parents about that, won't I, dear?"

"Yes, Santa," Katie said, "you really should."

Sara and Joe watched as Katie happily climbed off the big man's lap and followed one of the elves over to a barrel filled with candy canes.

Once they made their way off the platform, they followed a roped path that led behind Santa's stage and, after a long walk down a narrow hallway, deposited them back in the middle of the toy department, which was packed with people. Joe pushed through the people who were blocking the aisle like cattle waiting for slaughter. Every once in a while, he turned back to see if

Sara and Katie were keeping up. He had almost made it to the escalator when he heard Sara calling him.

"Joe!" Sara called. "Katie's gone!"

Joe looked all around Sara, but he couldn't see the top of Katie's head anywhere. He pushed back through the crowd and joined Sara, whose face had gone white with panic.

"She was holding my hand, and she let go for a second. And when I turned around, I couldn't see her!"

"Katie!" Joe yelled. "Katie! Where are you?"

"Katie! Katie!" Sara screamed.

Joe pushed back in the direction where they had come from, searching frantically for Katie. There were lots of little girls, but not one was Katie. He kept pushing through the people. When he turned back toward Sara, she was several feet away, apparently trapped by the crowd and crying.

"Go get help, Sara!" Joe yelled to her. "Get store security. Get the police, Sara. I'll keep looking."

Sara nodded, but she was almost hysterical. She turned but didn't know where to go.

"Just tell the clerk, Sara," Joe yelled, pointing toward a crowded counter.

Sara burst into tears and forced herself in front of a couple at a cash register and started yelling at the store clerk. Joe saw the clerk pick up a phone, so he turned back around and pushed toward the path that had led them away from Santa's throne. He looked up at the ceiling, searching for one of the darkened glass domes that covered a security camera. When he spotted one, he waved at it and mouthed the words, "I lost my daughter!" He hoped someone could read lips.

He reached the narrow hallway as another family was walking their toddler away from the back of Santa's stage. The couple gave him a strange look as if he might be waiting at the end of the hall to molest their child. At the mouth of the hall, Joe stood in the open space and surveyed the crowded aisles as best he could. There was no sign of Katie.

Had she been kidnapped?

Katie might have been kidnapped! He felt certain of it.

And then his knees went weak.

The person who had taken Katie was probably the murderer, Joe realized.

"Katie!" he yelled again. "Katie, where are you?"

Joe was sure that the murderer who had killed Autumn Smith had been following him. The monster who had raped and murdered Patricia Miller had taken his daughter! Why in God's name had he targeted Joe's family?

With tears streaming down her cheeks, Sara suddenly pushed through the crowd with two security guards behind her. Joe grabbed her arms.

"What if the killer has her, Sara?"

Sara went limp in Joe's arms, and Joe had to hold her up.

"I was just thinking the same thing. Oh my god!" she yelled. "He's going to kill her, Joe."

Joe turned to the older of the two security guards. He pointed up at the ceiling.

"Have they seen anything?" he asked the guard.

"We don't know yet," the guard replied. "Do you have a photograph of her?"

Joe and Sara looked at each other.

"Yes!" Sara said. "We just had a picture taken with Santa!"

"We forgot to get it," added Joe.

"Well, that would be a good place to start," said the guard calmly.

The guard led them back through the exit hallway toward the store Santa.

"Joe, if she's been taken by that monster, I won't be able to live."

"Don't say that, Sara. We'll find her."

"Oh god, Joe. What if he tries to rape her?"

Sara almost collapsed again. She could barely walk.

The image of some man trying to rape Katie sickened Joe. He felt an intense rage growing inside him, and he knew he would kill whoever had stolen his daughter if only he could find him.

Another happy couple with two young children walked toward them down the narrow hallway. When the couple saw Sara crying and the security guards, they clutched their own children more tightly, and Joe was intensely jealous that they still had their children.

Behind the couple walked one of Santa's young elves, and with her was Katie, smiling.

"Did you lose someone?" the elf asked.

"Katie!" Sara screamed. She ran up to Katie and held her tightly in her arms.

Joe rushed over and bent down, hugging both Katie and Sara tightly in his arms.

"Why are you crying, Mommy?" Katie asked.

"Because I thought we had lost you, baby," Sara said through her tears.

"Where were you, Katie?" Joe asked.

"I went back to talk to Santa, but they wouldn't let me."

The elf explained, "Lots of children are waiting to see Santa, honey."

"That's right, Katie," Joe said, trying to smile through his tears. "We've got to give the other children a chance too."

"All right, Daddy," Katie said.

After pushing their way through the store, clutching Katie's hands tightly, Joe and Sara hurried back up the hill to the hotel.

Once Katie climbed back onto her rollaway bed and began watching television, she drifted off to sleep and napped through the afternoon. Sara and Joe lay side by side on their bed, holding hands with each other, watching their daughter sleep.

"I thought we'd lost her, Joe," Sara said. Then she rolled over and buried her face in Joe's shoulder, sobbing.

"So did I."

Chapter Thirty

That night, Joe and Sara debated whether to take Katie out again to see the play. They all dressed up anyway as if to go, but Joe said they'd make a final decision after dinner. In the hotel restaurant, they ate quietly.

Their meals were excellent. Joe had a petite cut of prime rib with a creamy horseradish sauce while Sara had a thick lamb chop with mint jelly. Katie had breast of duck with orange glaze, and she ate heartily. Joe and Sara picked at their food, enjoying their glasses of wine more.

"We can't lock her away from the world forever, I guess," Joe whispered to Sara over his wineglass.

"I'd like to," said Sara. "But I guess if we're careful and hold on to her tightly enough, she won't get lost again."

Katie perked up, hearing their conversation. "I wasn't lost before," she explained. "You only thought I was lost, but I wasn't. I knew right where I was."

Sara smiled at Katie and pretended to take her nose between her fingers.

"We can go to the play, Katie," Joe told her. "As long as you promise to hold hands with one of us."

"I promise."

"And you mustn't go off on your own again, Katie," Sara warned her. "There are awful, terrible people out there who might take you away from us for good."

Katie looked up into Sara's face seriously and said, "I promise. I won't let the terrible people take me away. I'll only go with the nice people, like Santa's elf."

Sara turned to Joe as if to ask, "How do we make her understand?"

"Katie," Joe said. "Sometimes, you can't tell the good people from the terrible people. In fact, sometimes, the terrible people dress up like nice people just to trick you."

Katie looked up at her parents and nodded.

"Let's change the subject," Sara pleaded.

"I agree," said Joe, checking his watch. "Actually, it's time we pay the bill and walk down to the theater. The play starts in about twenty minutes!"

"We don't want to be late, do we, Daddy?"

"No, honey, we don't."

The production of Charles Dickens's *A Christmas Carol* lacked the excitement of the film versions. The sets were not very elaborate, and there were few effects, save for a little fake snow and offstage sounds. The actor who played Scrooge delivered his lines with enthusiasm and an exaggerated British accent, but the other actors seemed to be walking through their parts as if being filmed for Masterpiece Theater. It was a dreary, disappointing production; and Katie fell asleep by intermission, so they decided to go back to the hotel room early.

Joe picked Katie up in his arms and carried her out of the magnificent old theater that had been restored since the 1989 earthquake. He was not alone. Several other fathers were carrying sleepy children out of the theater.

After getting Katie tucked safely into bed, Joe and Sara undressed sadly as if realizing that the holiday weekend, which had started with so much promise, was now ending. Never before had either one of them lost track of Katie, so never before had the reality of losing her seemed real.

From the bathroom, Sara called out to Joe, who had already slipped under the covers. "I want a cigarette, Joe. Can I smoke in bed, or do you want me to stay in here?"

The truth was, he didn't like either option.

"Come to bed," he called. "Your smoking won't bother me."

Dressed in the same revealing light pink nightgown she had worn the night before, Sara came out of the bathroom with a lit cigarette between her fingers. After climbing into bed, she inhaled deeply and held the smoke deep inside her lungs before exhaling.

"Who do *you* think the killer is, Joe?"

"I honestly don't know," he said. "I only know that it's not me."

"But it must be someone who knows you."

"Why do you say that?"

She exhaled again, saying, "Because of Autumn Smith's murder. That doesn't seem random. It seems as if the killer chose her because he was trying to frame you."

"That's why I've always thought it was either Gary Grimes or Marty Miller."

"Maybe Gary Grimes, based on what you've told me. But why would Marty Miller kill his own sister?"

"I don't know. Maybe she was going to report him to the police for molesting her when she was younger?"

"Maybe," Sara said, sucking her cigarette again. "But then why kill Autumn if he was screwing her?"

"Jesus, Sara. Do you really want to play Sherlock Holmes right now?"

"Yes," she said, blowing out a stream of smoke. "I do."

Joe repositioned himself in the bed, sitting up straighter and propping his back up against the headboard.

"Okay," he said. "Let's suppose that Marty Miller has always been molesting his sister and maybe other girls too. All his life."

"Okay. Let's say that."

"He's gotten away with it for years because his sister, Patricia, was into it. She liked it. Then Autumn came along, and for a while, they were a happy threesome."

"Like *Three's Company?*"

"Right," said Joe. "He was Jack Tripper or, actually, Jack the Ripper."

"Or Marty the Raper."

"Right. Then things go wrong. Patty gets jealous, maybe, and threatens to tell the police that her brother molested her when she was a little girl."

"So that might explain why he killed his sister."

"Yes. And after Patricia's murder, Autumn gets frightened, and now *she* threatens to go to the police."

"But didn't Marty have an alibi for the day of Autumn's disappearance?"

"According to the police, he was at work. Dunn and Marino told me his alibi checked out, but I told them to check it again."

"Did they?"

"I don't know," Joe admitted. "He's still my top suspect, though."

"That's only because he punched you in the face," said Sara. She looked at her cigarette, which was half gone. "Who else do you suspect."

"I told you. Gary Grimes."

Sara laughed, flicking her ash into the ashtray on the nightstand. "He also hit you in the face. Do you suspect everybody who's ever hit you?"

"He's creepy. I'm sure he's a Peeping Tom."

"If this were a mystery novel," Sara said, "we'd have to rule out the most obvious suspects and examine the least likely suspects. Who else could it be?"

"But this isn't a novel, Sara. This is real. In real life, usually the most obvious suspects *are* guilty."

"Indulge me for a minute, Joe. After all, you're the literary professor, not me."

"Okay, who is the least obvious suspect, and why should we be suspicious of him?" Joe asked sarcastically.

"Or her," Sara said. "What makes you think it could only be a man?"

"C'mon, Sara."

"Play along, Joe. If this were some twisted murder mystery, who would we least suspect?"

Joe put his index finger alongside his mouth and wrinkled his brow, pretending to concentrate deeply. "I guess I'd least suspect *you*," he said.

Sara laughed while taking a drag on her cigarette. With it clenched between her teeth, she reached over and pretended to strangle Joe.

"You've discovered my secret life!" she said. "I'm really a lesbian murderess!"

"Don't," said Joe. "Now you're creeping me out."

Just then, Katie moaned a little and rolled over.

In a lower voice, Joe said, "Well, I suppose if this were a twisted novel, I'd suspect my poet friend, Cass Johnson. She *did* sort of point me in the direction of Autumn Smith when she shared that poem with me. And the murders did start around the same time she moved up here from LA to take the teaching job."

"Wait a minute," Sara said. "Haven't the police confirmed that the first victim was a college student from Los Angeles?"

"Yes," Joe said. "The earliest victim was a college student travelling from LA to Oregon during the late summer to return to college."

"Could your friend Cassandra and this student have driven up from LA together?"

Joe thought about it for a minute.

"I suppose so, but I just can't see Cassandra Johnson as a murderer. Besides, the police said that the women were raped."

Sara started laughing but caught herself and muffled her voice. "Maybe this is like that Jim Carrey movie *Ace Ventura*. Maybe Cass is actually a guy in drag!"

Joe laughed out loud. "If she is, she's one beautiful guy!"

Hating the way the room now smelled of cigarette smoke, he watched as Sara crushed out her cigarette. The ugly gray smoke hung in the darkened room.

"I just don't think Cass is the murderer," Joe said.

"Well, who else? What about Craig Richmond? You've never gotten along with him."

"I've considered him a couple of times," Joe admitted. "But there's nothing about him that makes him look guilty."

"Except that he knows you, and he knows your schedule well enough to know when your whereabouts might be hard to pin down, in case he wanted to pin something on you."

"That's true, I suppose."

"And like you, he's a teacher at CLU, so he knows some of the same students you know."

"Like Autumn Smith."

"Was she a student in one of his classes too?"

"Yes, I think so," Joe said. "He does seem like the kind of guy who would have an affair with one of his students."

"Did he have Patricia Miller in one of his classes too?"

"I'm not sure. Maybe."

"Did he teach in LA before coming to CLU?"

"Maybe, Sara. I think he taught at UCLA right after he left Rutgers," Joe said, getting annoyed. "I really don't know. I'm not the lead investigator on the case. All I know is that he seems egotistical enough to have had an affair with some of his students."

"But then, so do you," Sara said.

"Well, so does Dr. Thorne, according to Joan Ngo."

"Dr. Thorne is having an affair with one of his students?" Sara asked incredulously.

"Not now," Joe said. "At least, not that I know of. But when Joan Ngo was interviewing me on campus, she remembered Thorne from when she was a student at CLU. She said that Thorne used to lust after the young coeds."

"Horny Thorny?" joked Sara.

"That's my department chair you're mocking. He's the one who hired me, remember?"

"Yeah, but mainly because he's chums with your old mentor at LSU."

Joe thought of Professor Jack Claire, his aging mentor from LSU, and wondered how he and his wife were doing.

"You've met Dr. Thorne," Joe said to Sara. "What's your impression of him? Could he be a rapist and a strangler?"

"Well, physically, even at his age, I suppose he could be. He is in pretty good shape for a man his age. Remember that sixty-seven-year-old man back east who was keeping sex slaves locked up in his cellar?"

"Yeah, vaguely," Joe said. "But Thorne just doesn't seem like he's capable of murder."

"I agree," said Sara. "He's too genteel. Of course, that could all be an act. I mean, how *do* murderers act when they're out in public? Dr. Hannibal Lecter was pretty genteel too."

"Thorne was creeping around outside my office last week," Joe said. "I didn't tell you about this, but my office was vandalized."

"How?" Sara asked.

"Someone spray-painted the word 'killer' on my office door and broke the window."

"Why didn't you tell me, Joe?"

"It would have been just one more bad thing, and I'm tired of bad things happening all around me. I didn't want to depress you any more than you already are."

"And Dr. Thorne was there?"

"Yeah. He seemed to show up right after I got to my office, almost like he'd been waiting to see my reaction."

"That's weird," Sara said, more seriously.

"Of course, someone could have told him about the damage, and he could have shown up at the same time I did purely by coincidence."

"True," said Sara, "but there seem to be a lot of strange coincidences in this whole nightmare."

Joe's eyes suddenly widened.

"Another weird coincidence that day was one of the campus police officers who showed up when I reported the vandalism."

"What about him?"

"He said he knew Autumn Smith."

Sara looked seriously at Joe. "Did you get a strange feeling from him?"

"Yeah," Joe laughed. "He was angry at me! As if he wanted to punch me in the face!"

"See!" Sara said. "You only suspect the guys who want to punch you!"

"Still," Joe said seriously. "I should get that guy's name and give it to Bill Morgan or Detective Dunn."

"Hey," Sara said. "We haven't ruled out those two, have we?"

"As far as I can tell, we haven't ruled anyone out yet!" Joe scoffed. "In fact, we've added some names to the list of usual suspects who weren't on my list before."

"Like who?"

"Like you for one," Joe laughed. "And Cass for another."

"And Dr. Thorne for a third. Anyone else?"

"Well, two of my students seem to have a connection to Patricia Miller. Nicholas Adams and Marco Hernandez. I think Bill Morgan said one of them used to work with her at the restaurant."

"Tell me about them, Joe."

Joe couldn't help himself. He yawned mightily, and then so did Sara.

"I'm getting too tired to play this game anymore," Joe admitted. "I need to get some sleep."

"But we haven't really solved anything yet," Sara said.

"Did you think we actually would, Sara?" Joe asked, turning off the light next to the bed. "This isn't an Agatha Christie novel, Sara. This is my life. And I've seen what the inside of prison looks like now."

He rolled over, away from Sara.

"I know," Sara replied quietly.

"And I know what's going to happen if they find me guilty. I'm going to lose you and Katie and spend the rest of my life in prison for crimes I didn't commit."

"I realize that," Sara said, rubbing Joe's shoulder.

"I wish all this *were* a fucking novel," Joe said in disgust.

"What would you do? Read the last page to find out what happens?"

"No," said Joe. "I'd burn it."

It was clear to Sara that Joe was exhausted. She reached over and turned out the lamp on her bedside table, and then she lay awake in the darkness, listening to the sound of her daughter's breathing. A few minutes later, Joe was snoring.

Quietly, Sara got out of bed and went into the bathroom, closing the door ever so gently behind her. She took another cigarette out of the pack in her purse, lit it, drew in a deep breath, held it as long as she could, and then exhaled into the brightly lit room. She sat down on the edge of the bathtub and inhaled again.

Before she could control herself, her face twisted, and she began to cry.

CHAPTER THIRTY-ONE

After a late breakfast in the hotel restaurant where Joe gave Katie the teddy bear he had bought at Nordstrom's, they packed up the car and drove north on Highway 101 so Katie could see the Golden Gate Bridge. But the weather was cold and foggy, and the upper towers of the bridge were shrouded in a thick fog that was being blown in fiercely from the Pacific Ocean. Even though Joe stayed in the slow lane, Katie could not see Alcatraz Island because the Bay was obscured by the heavy fog. She perked up when they drove into the tunnel, but they came out on the other end so quickly that she was disappointed.

She had not been impressed with Joe's gift at first, but in the car, she played with the little bear in the backseat. By the time they had turned off Highway 101 to take Highway 37 over to Vallejo, Katie was asleep, her arms around the little stuffed bear.

The rest of the drive back to Sacramento was solemn. Joe and Sara didn't speak for the first forty minutes of the drive, and the fog was heavy until they reached Fairfield where it lifted, only to reveal a gray overcast sky.

"Do you want to come home with me?" Joe asked Sara, who appeared to be daydreaming out the window.

"Do you mean to Davis?"

"Yes," Joe said. "To our home."

"No, Joe. That wouldn't be a good idea. I've got all my stuff at Susan's, and Katie's all checked in at the new day care center."

At Susan's apartment building, Joe carried Sara's and Katie's bags while Sara roused Katie and forced her to walk. When they walked into the apartment, Susan greeted them tentatively.

"Well?" she asked. "Did you have an enjoyable weekend?"

"Don't ask," Sara replied.

"Why? What happened?"

"We nearly lost Katie inside Nordstrom's after waiting in line for almost two hours to see Santa Claus, and the play was so boring that we left at intermission."

Joe set the bags down in the living room, hurt by Sara's response. He looked at Susan's garish Christmas tree, white with pink lights and red ornaments.

"That's too bad," said Susan.

Joe knew she was dying to say, "I told you so."

The three adults stood on the plush off-white carpet of Suzy's condo, looking at each other uncomfortably. Katie had plopped down on the light blue sofa and fallen back to sleep. Joe was hoping he'd be invited to stay for dinner, but it was obvious they wanted him to leave.

"Well, I guess I should head back to Davis," he said finally.

"Okay," Sara said. She started walking him toward the door. "That's probably a good idea. I've still got some papers to grade."

Joe stopped suddenly, and Sara almost bumped into him.

"I want to say goodbye to Katie."

"Don't wake her up, Joe," Sara told him.

He looked into Sara's eyes until she turned away. Then he walked over to where Katie was sleeping and bent down to kiss her on the cheek. Her eyes fluttered open.

"Bye-bye, Daddy," her sleepy voice said.

"Bye, Katie," he told her. He knelt down and hugged her tightly, and her little arms finally came up around his neck.

At the door, Sara touched Joe's arm.

"Remember, Joe," she said. "We're flying to New Orleans late Tuesday night on the red-eye. I don't think I'll see you before we leave, but I'll see you at my parents' place for Christmas."

"Assuming the district attorney will let me leave the state," Joe said.

Susan, who had been listening from a distance, walked toward them.

"I've spoken to Bill about that, Joe," she said quietly. "He's going to petition the DA's office, but he says you shouldn't plan on it."

"What?" Sara said.

"Better to plan on being disappointed," said Susan. "That way, if you can leave the state while out on bail, it will seem like a gift."

"What are my chances?" Joe asked his sister-in-law.

"Frankly, not very good," she said.

Sara turned around and looked up into Joe's eyes.

"I'm sorry, Joe. I figured you'd still be able to join us in Baton Rouge."

"I guess I'll have Christmas alone," Joe said, trying not to cry. He looked at Suzy.

"Unless you'd like company?"

"I'm going back home too, Joe."

With that, Joe turned and walked down the hallway toward the elevator.

"Joe!" Sara called. "Joe, come back, and say goodbye to me."

He pushed the button, and the doors of the elevator parted immediately. He had hoped that he'd have a few minutes for Sara to run down the hall and grab him, but as soon as the doors opened, he stepped in and turned around. Sara was still standing in the hallway just outside the door to Susan's condo as if tethered there. The elevator doors closed slowly, and Joe's hand went up to cover his face.

On Monday morning, which was as cold and gray as Sunday had been, Joe put the phone back on the wall and answered it the first five times it rang. Reporters were calling to set up interviews, but he simply said "No comment" and "On the advice of my attorney, I am not speaking to reporters any longer."

After the tenth ring in an hour, he took the phone off the wall again. He spent the day preparing topics for the final exam, writing them out by hand on a yellow legal pad before typing them on the computer. Later, he went downtown to Kinko's and made copies for his students.

When he returned home, a news van was parked in front. He pulled into the driveway and ignored the reporter, someone he didn't recognize, and the cameraman who trotted down the driveway toward him. He went in through the back door and ignored the knocks at the front door and the redundant rings of the doorbell. After a while, the van left.

By four that afternoon, Joe Conrad was finished with all the work he would have to do for the fall semester until his students had written their finals. He had even averaged the grades in his roll book up to the final exam.

As dusk fell, he put on his jogging sweats and went running. He jogged through the park behind the Veteran's Memorial Center to the greenbelt that provided open space for some of the newer neighborhoods, and when he was too tired to continue, he turned around and headed back. The lights along the greenbelt slowly came to life, and Joe jogged along slowly, passing a few people now and then. Sometimes, a runner jogged toward him, often with a dog on a leash; and they would exchange glances and nod at each other. Occasionally, a few would turn and look back, recognizing Joe's face from the news.

That night after dinner, though he was not a serious fan, he watched Monday night football. It was too good to miss. The New Orleans Saints were playing the San Francisco 49ers, and Joe was torn. When he had grown up in Louisiana, the Saints had been a losing team; so he had shifted his loyalties to the 49ers, impressed by Joe Montana and Steve Young. But in recent years, there had been a reversal of fortunes, and the Saints often looked better than the 49ers.

The game served its purpose. It took his mind off Katie and Sara and helped get him through the night. He slept fitfully, waking up several times to rid himself of the beer he had consumed during the game. His bladder was not accustomed to six bottles of Coors.

He finally slept until after eight Tuesday morning, missing his opportunity to call Sara and Katie before they left for school. With no reason to rush, Joe stayed in bed, dozing on and off until almost noon.

Before leaving for Stockton, Joe called Suzy's condo again and left a message.

"Sara, I just wanted to say goodbye to you and Katie before you leave for New Orleans. Katie, honey," he said, his voice beginning to crack, "I'm going to try my best to see you at Christmas, but I might not be able to. I love you very much, Katie, so you have a wonderful Christmas even if Daddy isn't there. I'll call you every day. Suzy, please push Bill Morgan to petition the DA's office in time for me to fly back there—"

Abruptly, the message machine beeped, and the phone went dead.

When he reached campus, he found it quiet and dark. Many students had left for the holidays since many tenured professors did not require finals. Under his office door, with plywood substituting for the glass window, Joe found a large red envelope with his name written in white ink, in large looping cursive as if by a professional calligrapher: *Joseph L. Conrad.* He set his briefcase down on the desk and opened the envelope and read the Christmas card reluctantly.

> *Joe, I'm leaving for L.A., so won't see you until spring semester. I hope you have a joyful Christmas despite the unwarranted difficulties. Love, Cass.*

A "joyful" Christmas? He closed the door to his office and sat with his head in his hands, choking back tears at the prospect of being alone for the rest of December, spending Christmas away from his wife and daughter, with no friends or family surrounding him.

By the time his class was ready to begin, Joe had freshened up in the restroom and put on his professional face. His students did not need to be concerned about their teacher, only about their final exam.

The students filed into the classroom that last Tuesday night subdued by the task ahead and apprehensive about the topic. Once all of the students had arrived—even a serious-looking Nick Adams—Joe closed the door to the room and distributed the final exam topics. He read the directions aloud, and the students settled into the work of writing their papers. They would have two hours.

Joe worked at the desk in the front of the classroom, revising his syllabus and course schedule as if planning for the spring semester despite the knowledge that he probably wouldn't be teaching.

In fact, he'd probably spend most of the spring being tried for murder.

Several times, he fought the temptation to go to his office and call Sara again, but he knew that she would have called him if she had wanted to say goodbye.

At a few minutes before eight, there was a knock on the door of the classroom. It startled Joe and several of the students sitting in the front. Joe was reminded of the previous visits to his classroom, one by Gary Grimes and the other by the police.

Both had ended badly.

He surveyed the class. Acutely aware of recent events, every student had stopped writing and was watching to see what he would do. Wary, Joe walked over and opened the door cautiously while every student watched. Looking disheveled and wet, Sara stood in the poorly lit hallway.

"Sara!" Joe said, surprised. "What are you doing here?"

"I need to speak to you, Joe," she said, almost crying.

"Where's Katie?"

"Suzy's watching her."

"Shouldn't you be at the airport?" Joe said.

"We're not leaving tonight after all," Sara said, looking past Joe at the students who were staring at them. "Can we talk out here?"

"Of course," Joe said. He looked at the students, who went back to writing.

After shutting the door, they walked down the hall toward his office.

"How did you get here?" Joe asked her.

"I took the Mustang."

"I'm happy to see you," Joe said. "But what are you doing here, Sara?

"I need to tell you something. It can't wait."

Joe unlocked the door to his office and turned on the lamp. They sat down facing each other.

"What is it?" Joe said softly.

Tears fell from Sara's eyes, and she searched the carpet for a way to say what she had to tell him.

"I couldn't leave without telling you something face-to-face, Joe," she said, still looking down.

Joe reached over and gently lifted her face so that she was looking at him. He expected her to tell him how much she loved him, so he was smiling at her, ready to hug and kiss her.

"Joe, you're not going to like it."

Joe's heart thumped inside his chest. Had she decided that she was definitely going to divorce him?

"I'm pregnant, Joe!"

Prepared for bad news, he shook his head, a little confused.

"Why would you say I'm not going to like that news? I'm delighted."

"Joe," she said firmly, "I'm not going to keep it."

At first, he thought that she meant that she would give the baby up for adoption.

"What do you mean?"

"I'm getting an abortion, Joe. I can't bring this baby into the world knowing that you're probably going to jail for the rest of your life."

Joe stared at her, unable to grasp what she had just told him.

"I'm sorry, Joe," she said, crying even harder.

His first impulse was to slap her for even thinking about aborting their baby. He was angry and confused.

"How far along are you?" he managed to ask.

Sara wiped her eyes with her hands. "At least two months," she said, her voice faltering. "Maybe three."

Joe looked at her silently, uncertain what to say or do next.

"I think it was Halloween night," she said. "Remember?"

Of course he remembered. Until recently, Halloween night had been the last time they had made love in months.

Joe checked his watch. It was just after eight o'clock.

"Look, Sara. I've got to finish this final exam. The students only have thirty minutes left. Can you just wait here until they finish, and then we can talk this out?"

She shook her head from side to side. "I should get back to Katie."

"Just wait here for me, Sara. That's the least you can do."

As soon as he saw her fierce reaction, he knew he shouldn't have said it that way. She stood immediately.

"You can't order me around, Joe!"

"I know, I know," he said, standing. He tried to grab her by the shoulders, but she backed away.

"This is my decision, Joe. It's hard enough as it is."

"But it's our baby, Sara. At least give me time to talk to you about it."

Her face was twisted with pain and anger. To Joe, she seemed irrational, like a cornered animal that was trying to decide whether to fight or flee.

"We don't leave until Thursday," she told him. "We can talk about this tomorrow."

With that, she turned her back on Joe and opened the door to his office to leave. Joe reached out and grabbed her wrist to stop her, but she jerked her wrist away.

"When would you have the abortion, Sara? It's hard to do in Louisiana, so are you going to wait until after Christmas?"

She spun back around and leaned toward him.

"Tomorrow morning, Joe," she blurted. "I've scheduled it for tomorrow morning. That's why I drove all the way down here in the rain to see you."

Her voice was loud enough that the students might be able to hear her. Joe tried to calm her down.

"Just come back inside, and wait here for me, Sara. Please. Just for a few more minutes."

He could see that she was indecisive at first, but then the door to the classroom opened, and one of the students appeared in the hallway. Evidently, Nicholas Adams was already finished with the final. He walked down the hall, looking at Joe and Sara.

"I'm finished, Professor Conrad," he said guardedly. "Is it okay to leave?"

"Yes," Joe said. "Of course."

The student averted his eyes from the troubled scene and started down the stairs, disappearing out of sight.

"See," said Joe. "It won't be much longer. Just wait."

"No, Joe," said Sara. "I've made up my mind."

With that, she spun around and walked toward the stairs. Joe watched her, unsure what to do. Should he forget about his students and go after her?

He decided to go back into the classroom and hurry his students along. Then he would follow Sara back to Suzy's apartment, and they could talk all night if they had to.

At least she had not gotten onto that airplane with Katie. That was a good sign.

Another student was carrying his blue book up to the desk when Joe came back in. A few students looked up, but most continued to write feverishly. The world could be in turmoil, but students still wanted their grades.

At eight-thirty, two students were still writing. All the rest had turned in their exam booklets and left. A few had quietly thanked Joe and shaken his hand.

"I'm afraid time's up," Joe told the students.

An Hispanic woman in her midthirties closed her booklet and gathered her belongings, but the other woman continued to write.

"There really is a time limit," Joe told the woman. She ignored him and continued writing anyway.

After the Hispanic woman left, Joe walked down the row between the desks and pinched the pages of the test booklet between his thumb and index finger.

"I'm sorry, but I have to take this now."

The woman looked up angrily.

"But I'm not finished yet," she said sternly. She went back to writing.

"Tell you what," Joe said, gritting his teeth. "Slip it under my door when you *are* finished."

Joe gathered up his books and papers and hurried back to his office for his briefcase. He locked the office door and bounded down the stairs two at a time.

"Professor Conrad!" the student called after him. "I'm finished!"

He left her at the top of the stairs waving her blue book and calling his name.

As he ran through the campus, the pounding rain suddenly stopped. Before climbing into his car, Joe looked up to see the edge of the clouds and the starry night sky. A full moon hung low in the west. It was going to be a beautiful winter's night. Looking back from where he had come, he saw a dark figure rushing toward him. Was it the student still chasing him?

As the dark figure jogged closer, it did not look like the outline of the woman. It looked like a large man in a long heavy coat. Whoever it was, the man was definitely trying to catch up to him.

Joe started the engine and sped out of the parking lot. He raced through traffic on Hammer Lane, pushing the little Ford to its limits. Sara had only a twenty-minute head start, so if he hurried, he might be able to catch her before she made it back to Sacramento. They could go somewhere and speak in private, without Sara's sister butting in.

Speeding north on Interstate 5, Joe weaved in and out of traffic. By the Highway 12 exit, the traffic had thinned considerably, but fog was beginning to form.

Ten minutes later, Joe sped by a car that was pulled over on the shoulder, its emergency lights flashing. The car's hood was up. He recognized the long hood.

It was a Mustang. It was *his* Mustang.

Joe slammed on his brakes and swerved over into the slow lane, right in front of another car, which immediately swerved over into the fast lane to avoid hitting him. Joe slowed the Escort down and pulled off the freeway onto the shoulder, gravel kicking up and hitting the underside of the car. He was about a mile beyond the Mustang.

He put the Escort in reverse and backed up on the shoulder as quickly as he could, hearing the whine of the engine and fearing that he might blow a head gasket.

When he reached the Mustang, he waited for a big rig to pass, and then he threw open his car door and walked back to talk to Sara.

The Mustang was empty.

Joe looked around in the darkness. A few cars were headed toward him. He looked ahead. The overpass where he had waited in the news van with the cameraman for the killer to approach Joan Ngo was up ahead.

He realized he was at Lost Slough.

Looking down over the embankment, he saw a car in the distance, driving slowly on the frontage road. Beams of light from the car's headlights bounced along the bumpy road as the car headed toward the spot where Joe had gone once to look for the crime scene tape. Somehow, he knew it was the killer's car.

Somehow, he knew the killer had Sara.

His heart pounding against his chest, Joe ran back to Sara's little Escort and jumped in, starting the engine again and flooring the gas pedal to reach the freeway exit as quickly as he could. Joe was determined to follow the car he had seen, whether or not it was the killer's.

But in his heart, Joe knew the worst was happening.

As fog began to build, Joe found the turnoff to the frontage road. He drove by the same decrepit gate he had driven by days earlier. Nearly skidding off the muddy road a few times, Joe slowed down just enough to stay on the bumpy road. He followed the curves of the road through the high bushes until, without warning, he almost slammed into the back of a small sports car, a Triumph Stag. This spot came well before the little cul-de-sac where Joe had parked before.

Without thinking, Joe jumped out of his car and ran up to the passenger's door of the sports car. The car was empty and locked.

Joe stood silently in the darkness, listening. His eyes adjusted to the dim light. He looked up. Although obscured by a thin cloud, the full moon in the western sky shone down brightly.

He could barely make out a narrow path in the brush, and as he listened in that direction, he heard the muffled sounds of someone moaning.

Joe ran into the brush and tried to follow the sounds.

"C'mon, you bitch," someone growled from up ahead. "Walk a little, damn it!"

The path started to wend its way up the embankment of the levee on the north side of Lost Slough. Joe estimated that they were about half a mile from the freeway, hidden by the tall reeds and bushes.

The moaning voice he heard next was unmistakably Sara's.

From the bottom of the embankment, Joe saw the large figure dragging a woman by her arms. Her hands seemed to be tied together. The man appeared on the top of the levee and then disappeared on the other side, dragging the kicking woman with him.

Joe scurried up the hillside, but the grass was wet and slippery.

Finally, reaching the top of the levee, Joe looked around. The figures had not gone directly over the side here as it had seemed from down below. Joe walked along the top of the levee for a few yards, trying again to pick up the sounds. The freeway was ahead of him, and more bare trees were behind him. Joe could see his car and the other, smaller car reflected in the moonlight on the frontage road in the distance.

Another set of headlights was making its way through the rising fog toward the spot where Joe had parked. Was this an accomplice? Maybe there were two killers!

He kept looking forward and behind, trying to find the figures he had been chasing.

Suddenly, he heard a muffled scream from behind, and he spun around and ran.

Down the embankment near the water, about forty yards from him was a flat grassy spot. Joe could see it from the top of the levee. A man was hunched over the body of a woman, and the woman wasn't moving.

In the darkness, even with the bright moonlight, it was impossible to see if the woman was Sara or not—but it had to be. Joe was certain it was.

What difference did it make? Someone needed help!

Looking around for a weapon, Joe saw a rock about the size of a grapefruit on the edge of the levee. He picked up the rock and quietly went down the embankment behind the man.

Sneaking up on this guy wouldn't be easy. What was he doing?

The woman, whomever she was, lay perfectly still. The man, wearing black gloves, was using a knife to cut duct tape off of her ankles. For a moment, too far away to do anything yet, Joe just watched the man work. Once the tape was off, the man reached up and started unbuttoning the woman's jeans.

The woman stirred and moaned, regaining consciousness.

Joe knew he had to make his move.

As the man reached back as if to hit the woman again, Joe rushed up behind him and struck the back of his head as hard as he could with the rock.

The man shook his head and turned around to look at Joe. Joe was stunned to see a face he recognized. The man seemed equally shocked, especially when Joe struck him again in the left temple with the rock.

The man collapsed on top of Sara, who was only just beginning to awaken.

Joe pushed the man off of his wife and reached down to grab Sara by the arms, which were still taped together. Joe pulled her to her feet, and her eyes fluttered open.

"Come on, Sara," Joe yelled. "Wake up! We've got to get out of here!"

Sara was still half unconscious. Joe ripped the tape off her mouth.

"Ouch!" yelled Sara, sounding drunk.

"Come on, Sara! We've got to get out of here!"

Joe half carried her up the side of the embankment to the top of the levee. From there, Joe could see another figure getting out of a car that was parked behind his own. Their only chance was to make it back to the freeway and flag down someone who might help them.

But Joe would not be able to flag down CHP Officer Rick Harris because Harris was lying in the grass behind him, knocked unconscious by a blow to the temple. It was Officer Harris Joe had recognized hunched over Sara, the CHP cop who had stopped that first day when Joe had found the body of Patricia Miller. Officer Harris, who had shown up at Patricia Miller's funeral. It was Harris who had stopped when Joan Ngo was serving herself up as bait.

But who was the other man? Who was the man parked behind Joe's car, who had evidently followed him from campus? Was it Harris's accomplice?

Sara seemed to be okay. She was walking better though she stumbled every so often. Joe was hurrying her along the top of the levee toward the freeway. Somehow, they had to make it there before Harris woke up and before his accomplice found them.

A gunshot exploded behind them. Joe looked back. Harris was standing on top of the levee now, about sixty yards behind them, and he was taking aim.

Something slapped Joe's right kidney just as he heard the second gunshot. It felt as if Sara had slapped his side very hard with her hand, but both of her hands were around his neck.

"What happened?" Sara asked, still sounding drunk.

Joe looked at her face. Maybe her jaw was broken. Blood seemed to be coming from her mouth.

But the sudden burning pain in Joe's side forced him to realize that he had been shot.

"Let's go, Sara!" he screamed.

Together, they ran toward the freeway. A third shot rang out—Joe felt it blow by his left ear. They had reached the point where the levee went under the freeway. Joe had not counted on the fence. He could barely keep Sara on her feet, let alone lift her over the fence that was meant to keep animals off the interstate. They had no choice but to go underneath the freeway.

The occasional roar of truck tires above them startled Joe. Sara was slowly becoming more alert. In the darkness under the overpass, Joe looked back and saw Harris walking toward them rapidly. The gun was hanging in his right hand down at his side, and his left hand was holding his temple. Joe imagined that it was bleeding profusely.

The top of the levee narrowed dramatically underneath the freeway. Joe realized that he was now exactly across from the spot where it had all started, where he had discovered Patricia Miller's body. Once they reached the other side, they should be able to climb the embankment to the freeway, just as Joe had done that Monday morning after Thanksgiving.

"Where are we, Joe?" Sara mumbled.

"We're under Interstate 5," Joe said. "We're at Lost Slough."

"Why are we running?"

"Don't you remember, Sara? The killer kidnapped you?"

Sara started to push away from Joe as if he were the killer.

"No no no!" Sara said.

They had come out from underneath the freeway. Below them to the left were tall stiff reeds and the cold water of the slough. Above them to the right was the embankment that went up to the freeway. The only problem was that a fence again kept them from climbing up to the pavement.

"Sara, can you climb this fence?"

"What?"

"Sara!" Joe yelled. "He's behind us! He's coming! We've got to get away."

A gunshot exploded on the other side of the overpass, the loud bang ringing against the concrete and the bright flash briefly illuminating the blackness.

Harris was forty yards away, and he just kept coming.

Sara pulled free of Joe's grip and instinctively ran away. Joe's plan to get to the freeway had fallen apart. He followed Sara, who was now running west on the top of the levee, toward the setting full moon. She was too easy to see. Joe knew he had to get her down off the top of the levee into the brush where they might have a chance. He dared not look back, afraid that Harris was right behind him.

"Come back here!" yelled Harris in a strange deep voice that Joe had never heard. Harris's voice was amplified by the concrete over his head.

Joe finally managed to catch up with Sara. She looked at him, her eyes wide open. She was fully alert now, clearly terrified.

"He's going to kill us both, Joe," she said, sobbing as they ran. "One of us has to get away for Katie's sake."

Instantly, Joe realized that he would have to sacrifice himself in order to save Sara and the baby she was carrying. It was an easy call.

Just ahead was a large valley oak, its branches silhouetted against the bright night sky. Joe pulled Sara off the top of the levee, and they stumbled down the embankment on the far side of the tree. Thick brush surrounding the base of the tree provided cover.

"You're bleeding!" Sara said. She had grabbed Joe's waist as they half fell down the embankment.

"It's not that bad," Joe lied.

"Ollie, ollie, ox in free!" Harris yelled from above them.

"Sara," Joe whispered. "Hide in these reeds, and I'll draw him across the water to the other side."

In the moonlight, Sara peered into Joe's eyes. She was crying fiercely but was trying to stay quiet. She lurched toward him and kissed him hard on the mouth as if for the last time, and then she pushed her way into the reeds. In seconds, she had all but disappeared.

Joe stepped down into the stream, removing his jacket as he entered the water. He put the jacket over his right arm as if still pulling Sara along.

The dark water was freezing. Joe waded into it up to his waist, and with another step, he sunk down to his chest. The hell with the jacket. He started swimming to the other side, and with a few weak strokes, he was across.

When Joe looked back, he saw Harris at the top of the levee, aiming the gun at him. Joe lurched left just as the gunshot exploded, and the bullet pierced the water next to his right side.

Harris pulled the trigger again, but Joe heard the click of an empty gun.

"You're a lucky son of a bitch, Conrad!" Harris growled. "Where's that lovely wife of yours? Did she go on ahead and leave you behind?"

Joe waited on the far side of the slough while Harris carefully made his way down the embankment to the water. Harris pushed through the reeds at the same clearing Joe had used, going right by Sara, who was still hiding in the tall reeds.

Now Joe had to lead him as far away as possible, but before he turned around to climb out of the water, he saw another figure at the top of the levee. Was this an accomplice?

Joe didn't have time to think. He pushed his way up out of the water into a field of reeds. The water now came up to his knees, making it difficult to run or walk, but Joe knew that Harris would have an equally difficult time.

The moon was as bright as Joe had ever seen it in his life. It hung low in the sky over the swampy marshlands, almost ready to sink behind the bare branches of the oaks. Joe knew where he wanted to take Harris. If he could lead him into the wooded area between Lost Slough and Middle Slough, he'd have a hundred places to hide on dry land, and he could eventually circle back toward the freeway and get help.

Beyond the reeds as he ascended out of the water, finally, he pushed into thorny bushes that tore at his face and grabbed his clothing. In the middle of the bushes, he tried to change directions, hoping to throw Harris off his trail if only a little.

"I'm going to cut your head off, Conrad," Harris said in a strangely deep voice. "And then I'm going to make your wife hold it while I rape her."

The thought of Harris raping Sara so outraged Joe that he suddenly stopped and looked for a piece of wood to use as a club. If Harris was out of ammo, then Joe might stand a fighting chance.

But when Joe stopped, he suddenly felt light-headed. He reached down and gingerly touched the wound. It was sticky and painful, and Joe realized that he was going to vomit.

He dropped to his knees and vomited as quietly as he could, but he could hear Harris pushing through the brush nearby.

It's almost over, Joe told himself.

On his knees still, Joe turned his head slightly in time to see Harris push past, the moonlight behind him. Harris had walked right by Joe without seeing him. Joe had another chance!

He suddenly felt a little better. Holding on to a tree, Joe hoisted himself up and peered into the brush. Harris was heading east, turning back toward the freeway. That meant Joe would have to go west, toward the flashing radio towers.

But Joe had forgotten that someone else was pursuing them both. As Joe pushed through the brush to work his way west, he heard someone coming up close behind.

Joe broke through the brush into a clearing. He was on solid land now, and he could run. His side on fire with pain, he ran as fast as he could. Fog was beginning to rise right out of the soil itself, like steam vented from city sewers.

"There you are!" Harris growled. "I was afraid I'd lost you."

Joe didn't look back, but it sounded as if Harris was only twenty yards away. Up ahead were more bushes. He headed into the brush, hoping to get away.

When Joe was through some of the brush, he turned south abruptly, hoping to throw Harris off again. He was able to run around some tall bushes, but then he slipped and fell into muddy water. He had landed in a large muddy pond of algae-filled water; and the more he tried to wade through it, the more it pulled him down, the heavy mud and algae clinging to his clothes.

Even with the fog rising eerily up from the water, Joe could see Harris gaining on him. Harris seemed steadier on his feet, wading into the water smoothly, fog swirling around him as he approached Joe.

Exhausted, Joe gave up. He sat in the thick muddy water, facing Harris, who marched toward him relentlessly. Half of Harris's face was covered in blood. It looked black in the moonlight, but the whites of his eyes seemed to glow.

"You must be close to bleeding out by now, Conrad," Harris said. "You were stronger than I ever expected you to be."

Harris was standing over Joe now, and Joe was losing consciousness. He hoped Sara had gotten back to the freeway and found help. At least she was probably safe. Maybe he could keep Harris here long enough to give Sara more time.

"I think you might lose your badge for this, Officer Harris," said Joe, barely able to stay conscious.

"Maybe," Harris said in his weird low voice. "But who's going to tell?" Harris was smiling, his white teeth almost glowing in the darkness. "You?"

Joe saw the moonlight on the blade of the knife as Harris bent down.

"I think not," said Harris. "Your lovely wife? No. I'll find her shortly. Just like I tracked down your little friend Autumn. She was quite something. I think I enjoyed her best."

Harris grabbed Joe's hair with his left hand and reached back with the knife in his right hand.

Suddenly, a bird screeched, a great white egret; and it rose from the brush, flapping its long white wings noisily beside the swampy pond and took flight.

Startled, both men watched the bird as it rose into the foggy night.

Harris laughed. Turning his attention back to Joe, he said, "That bird scared the hell out of me, Professor."

Joe knew he was about to die, but he managed to say, "Some people think birds are the eyes of God. Did you know that, Officer Harris?"

Joe watched as the dark figure shook his head from side to side.

"No, I did not, Professor," Harris said, almost laughing, the knife ready to slash Joe's throat. "You learn something new every—"

Harris couldn't finish because something hit the back of his head hard. Joe heard the sound, like a watermelon breaking open. Harris fell forward on top of Joe, and Joe had to work hard to get out from under the heavy body, his mouth filling with the slimy water.

Another man was standing in the moonlight where Harris had been.

"You okay, Professor Conrad?" the dark figure asked.

Joe recognized the voice immediately.

"Hell no!" he screamed. "Get this asshole off me, Dunn!"

Detective Dunn reached down and helped Joe to his feet. Harris was blowing bubbles in the swampy water.

"Excuse me a minute," Dunn said. He reached down and slapped handcuffs on to Harris's wrists, and only then did he pull Harris up out of the water, rolling him onto his back on the ground. Harris was still out cold.

"You've been following me, haven't you, Dunn?" Joe said, feeling dizzy.

"Yes, I have," Dunn said.

"That's police harassment," Joe said, but he was fading fast. He stumbled through the water back onto solid ground where he spun around and dropped onto his back. He could barely see the moon now. It was setting behind the bare trees, and the fog was thickening. Dunn knelt down next to him and pulled Joe's sweater and shirt up.

"You've lost a lot of blood, Joe," Dunn said.

Joe detected concern in Dunn's voice. But Joe couldn't hold his head up any longer. He lay on the wet ground and stared up at the stars through layers of rising mist. From the distance came a sound like that of a child crying, and for a moment, Joe wondered if Katie was nearby. The approaching sirens grew more distinctive.

"You know," Joe said. "This is really a very lovely place."

And then Joe slipped into a cold darkness he had only known in dreams.

CHAPTER THIRTY-TWO

His head still bandaged, Eric Harris lay on his cot in the Sacramento County Jail, pleased with himself, grinning, while remembering his first victim. He did not consider his daughters victims because he had not killed them, and his desire for them was different from the feeling of absolute power he derived from his games with strangers.

The first was the most thrilling. He had never known joy and excitement like that before. She was young, probably in her early twenties, like most of the others. He never checked her identification, so he didn't know her name. Names didn't matter. That's one thing he had learned. When you set yourself free, as he had, very little really matters. Even being locked up wouldn't matter. But she was delightful. Eric closed his eyes and tried to remember all of it exactly as it had happened.

It was early, about eight-thirty one evening in the middle of the week. Not even dark yet because it was late spring. He was off duty. His wife had left him, taking his daughters the year before, and he was antsy. Their divorce had just become final. Long-distance divorce. He didn't even know where in Texas they were living.

That was one of the requirements for her not to file charges against him for molesting their daughters. She had arranged it through her attorney.

Who was playing God then?

It didn't matter. One day, his girls would seek him out. He knew they wanted him, secretly. He could wait.

That first night, he decided to drive up to Sacramento and visit the juice bars where young women danced nude. The one on Highway 50 was his favorite. No one recognized him there.

On his way, just north of Stockton, he had encountered her. She was off to the side of the southbound lanes, so he had had to drive across the median strip to get to her. But he had done that a thousand times in his patrol car. Now he was in his Triumph Stag.

He didn't even recognize her as his first victim. Not at first. She was merely a young lady whose car had broken down. As an off-duty highway patrolman, he felt obliged to stop. She was frightened of him in the beginning, even when he showed her his badge and CHP identification. Her fear of him was annoying. He was trying to help her, but she resisted.

He finally convinced her that he was trustworthy. She got into his car, wary at first; but as he drove her toward Stockton, she loosened up.

Too much.

She was stupid. She didn't even know about the emergency phones along the freeway. When he pointed one out to her and asked her why she hadn't called for help, she shook her head and said, "Didn't know what that was. Thought it was for you cops and firemen." He asked her where she was from. "Wisconsin," she said with an accent as thick as butter: "Wiz-*can*-sin."

In his jail cell, Eric laughed out loud, remembering her ridiculous accent.

"What're you doing in California?" he asked her. But he knew by her heavy makeup and the way she was dressed—tight-fitting hot pink shorts, a pink cotton sleeveless shirt about three sizes too small, and red high-heeled sandals—that she was on her way to LA.

"I'm going to Hollywood!" she said, smiling broadly for the first time. She didn't even realize how ridiculous she looked and sounded.

"Oh?" he had replied nonchalantly as if he encountered women going to Hollywood every day. "Going to be in the movies?"

"Hopin' to, yeah," she said. "Won a beauty contest in my hometown and then won again at the county fair. Didn't get to go to the state competition 'cause I couldn't find a sponsor. But the girl that won looked a lot like me, so I figure I could've won, had I gone and all."

"Yep," he had said. "Sounds like it."

"Met a guy at the county fair who told me he was talent scout out of Hollywood. Gave me his card and everything. Told me to look him up if I was ever in Hollywood. So I figure, what the hay, might as well, right?"

He grinned. "Right," he agreed. "What do your parents think about you driving all this way alone?"

Her answer changed his life.

"Oh," she said, "my parents are no longer living. Dad died of lung cancer about five years ago, and Mom died of brain cancer about three years ago. I didn't even know there was such a thing as cancer of the brain. Did you?"

"I guess it's pretty rare," he said. But he started thinking.

"Yeah, I'll say. Both of 'em smoked like haystacks, you know."

"You mean smokestacks, don't you?"

"Yeah, them too. But if you've ever seen a haystack on fire, you'd know what I mean," she said in her little condescending, ignorant voice.

That was the straw that broke the camel's back, Harris mused.

"Do you have any brothers or sisters?"

"No," she said wistfully. "No, it's only me. My dad had a brother, but he was killed in Vietnam. So that was the end of my family, when my ma died, I mean."

"I'm sorry to hear that," he said, but he was already thinking about it.

On his cot, recalling those moments, Eric's heart started racing, just as it had that night; and he felt almost light-headed as if he might faint. But it was thrilling.

"Yeah. I'm footloose and fancy-free, so to speak, so's I can go anywheres and do just about anything."

In his car, Eric had turned slowly and looked over at her. *Completely free? Yes. What a wonderful feeling. Completely liberated from all that binds us.*

He was already getting an erection.

"Do you mean to say," he asked carefully, his voice deepening with anticipation, "that you have no family?"

"Nope!" she answered as carefree as a child. "Broke up with my boyfriend after about six years of goin' steady if you can believe it. Caught him cheatin' on me with one of my best girlfriends if you can believe that! I mean, look at me, and then look at her!"

"That's just awful," Harris said. It was such a cliché, he nearly burst out laughing. Her existence seemed puny. "Surely, someone must know where you're headed."

"Oh, sure," she said. "I told 'em at the place where I work that I was headed for Hollywood. They all laughed at me, but I'm going to show 'em."

"I'm sure you will," he said, grinning. "You are a very sexy young woman."

She had looked over and flashed her wide smile at him, saying, "Well, thank you. Thank you very much."

Then realizing there were no boundaries, he had offered this to her, "You know, my wife was in a few movies when she was younger."

"Really?" the girl from Wisconsin asked.

"Yes, but it was before I met her. She was just an extra, but she was in about a dozen movies."

"Wow! Any I might remember?"

Eric smiled. "Well, let me think."

She was looking at him now with great anticipation, her face so close he could smell her cheap, heavy perfume and feel the air from her nostrils against his cheek, which aroused him even more.

He didn't really have a plan at first, but he took the next exit. It was finally getting dark. Up ahead, he could see the flashing lights of the radio towers standing against the deep orange remains of the sunset.

"Is there a gas station on this road?" she asked, her voice sounding fearful now.

"Oh, yes," he said. "See those towers? That's where we're headed. It's a little place called Paradise," he lied. His heart was racing with anticipation.

Then he noticed that she was reaching down to undo her seat belt, and that infuriated him.

So he hit her.

With his right hand, he hit her as hard as he could on the side of her head, and her head bounced off the window. The shocked and surprised look on her face reminded him of the look he had seen on his wife's face when she caught him with their daughter. He hit her two more times, and she slumped forward. Hitting her so hard hurt his hand. *Next time, I should wear gloves.*

At the first dirt road, he pulled in and drove as far as he could. He was on the edge of a vineyard. His little car bounced along the dirt road. He drove around to the back of the vineyard near the embankment of a levee where heavy brush hid the car from view.

Obviously dazed and weak, the girl from Wisconsin struggled to undo her seat belt, which she managed to do. Then she fumbled for the door handle, but he struck her again—this time in the back of head, which hurt his hand even more.

"Damn it!" he had yelled as if his injury was her fault.

Her forehead had slammed against the door window, and he was worried that her head would break the glass. It was time to get her out of the car.

Turning off the lights and engine, he climbed out and walked around his car, reaching the door at about the same time she flung it open and tried to climb out. He watched her, amused. She didn't look like a beauty queen now. And finally, she wasn't talking anymore, with that irritating little voice of hers.

When she staggered away from the car, he followed her, laughing. She reminded him of a buck he had wounded while hunting with other cops up north. They had followed it into a copse of trees where it stood, gasping for air, its legs trembling. He had taken the kill shot, putting a bullet in the back of its head.

But he didn't want to shoot her. That would ruin her. He wanted her alive but weak. One of her sandals had come off, so she was limping. He followed her for a while and finally caught up to her between two rows of thick grapevines. He grabbed her hair, jerking her head back. She fell down at his feet and started to cry.

"Please," she said weakly. "Please don't kill me," she sobbed, but her voice was frail as if she was losing consciousness.

Her pleas thrilled him, though. He had the ultimate power.

He straddled her, dropped to his knees on top of her, and she struggled to free herself for the last time. He struck her across the face one final time, which knocked her cold. Her shorts were hard to pull off at first, but her top was easy to push up, and she wasn't wearing a bra. Even in this dim light, he could see her magnificently firm breasts.

My, but she was nice!

Lying on his cot, eyes closed tight, Eric smiled and remembered how delightful she had felt underneath him. He finished that first time so quickly that it was almost disappointing. He hadn't been with a woman for over a year.

When he was zipped up, he stared down at her sleeping body. Quiet and naked, she looked very good. Delicious. He wanted to keep her, but he knew that would be impossible.

What to do?

Eric had never strangled anyone before that night late in May. It was much easier than he thought it would be. He pressed his thumbs against her windpipe, which collapsed like a soft garden hose under his grip. She struggled spasmodically at the very end, but it was easy to control her. And after a few minutes, she went completely limp.

Eric had been startled by the rush of air that escaped from her mouth as soon as he released his hands from her throat, and for a moment, he thought that she had been holding her breath and faking her death. But he watched her in the dim light of the clear night, and she didn't move at all.

At first, he wanted to bury her, but he didn't have a shovel. He decided to carry her over the embankment and leave her under the brush. He knew the animals would take care of her over the next few weeks. But when he was climbing down the other side, he slipped and dropped her body, which rolled down into the water of the slough.

Why not?

Eric knew that the water would dissolve his semen and wash away any trace evidence he had left. Her body would float slowly through the delta toward the ocean. It might be found tomorrow or next month—hard to know.

He hurried back to the spot where he had raped her and gathered up her panties, shorts, and sandals. The panties he held close to his face for several minutes. He desired to keep them, but he knew that many killers had been convicted because of just such souvenirs. He carried all her clothing up over the levee. These pieces of rubbish too, he tossed into the stream. The clothing floated on top of the black water. Then it disappeared in the darkness. He could no longer see the girl's body or the clothing.

Then he started getting nervous.

Had someone seen him when he had stopped to help the girl? What about the girl's car? Should he try to move it?

No. He would do nothing. If the car was still there in the morning when he started his patrol, he would pull over, run the plates, and report it as abandoned by the owner, just as he had done legitimately a dozen times before. By doing his own job, he would help to remove the evidence. The car would be towed to a storage facility and held for sixty days. Tickets would be mailed to the registered owner. If no one claimed it, it would be sold at a police auction or to the junkyard. Routine.

That night, he drove back home instead of going on to Sacramento. He watched television until midnight then took sleeping pills, as he did almost every night, and slept until morning.

During his patrol the next day, he found that the car had been stripped during the night. Wheels, seats, stereo, dashboard, even half of the engine parts—all taken. Even the license plates had been stolen. He reported it and stayed to watch the tow truck driver use a cable to drag the shell of the car up on the titled flatbed of the car carrier. No one ever asked him about the Wisconsin car again.

During those days immediately after his first "wicked game," as he had come to think of it, listening repeatedly to the Chris Isaak song, he thought about it over and over again. What had he done wrong? He hadn't worn gloves, so he dug out a new pair of leather driving gloves, still in their box, that his wife had gotten for him years earlier for his birthday. He had just finished restoring his Triumph. It was a thoughtful gift, but in those days, he had disliked wearing gloves. Now he became aroused whenever he pulled those gloves over his long fingers. And under the driver's seat, he always carried duct tape and condoms.

He had to wait almost two months before another lovely young woman presented herself to him. That second time, he had come prepared.

On the bunk in his jail cell, waiting to be interviewed again by that know-nothing prick, Dunn, Eric opened his eyes and smiled. He could play this new game too. He would bide his time. Prison couldn't hold him forever. An opportunity would present itself, he knew.

CHAPTER THIRTY-THREE

The next week was hard on Sara. The thought of leaving Joe, of divorcing him, had been bad enough. But the thought of losing him forever had deeply saddened her. She hated the idea of Katie growing up unable to see her father ever again. Losing her father at age four and a half would mean that Katie would barely remember anything about him. Sara didn't want that for Katie.

In the reeds, when it was clear that Joe had led both men away from her, she resolved to keep Joe's memory alive for Katie. She would keep pictures of Joe around the house always, and she would freely tell the story of the night her husband bravely gave his life to save hers.

Shivering in the reeds that night, she had also resolved to keep Joe's second child. She would not go through with the abortion even though she had decided to do so when she had left Joe at his office.

That cold December night had been a turning point for her. When she had first been picked up by the I-5 Strangler and realized he was going to kill her, she had resolved to live life to its fullest if she were to escape. Unable to remember most of the attack, she did remember the first time Harris hit her in the head, his fist as hard as a shovel. She vaguely recalled being pulled through the wet grass out by Lost Slough, the place Joe had spoken of so often.

And she remembered Joe leading her away from her attacker, taking her to safety, ready to give his own life to save hers. She still shivered when she remembered crouching down in the reeds, covering her mouth with her hands as she watched the killer stomp through the water chasing Joe. She had almost stood up when another man rushed down the embankment and crossed the slough at the same spot a few minutes later.

She had not crossed the dark water to learn the fate of her husband, too terrified that there were two killers pursuing him. Instead, she had gone back up the embankment and made her way to the freeway. She had climbed up to Interstate 5 just as the first police cars screeched to a stop. An ambulance arrived ten minutes later; and after a long wait, she watched as men struggled to bring Joe, wrapped in a blanket, up the side of the embankment on a stretcher. He looked dead, even as the men worked on him. They had called for the Life Flight helicopter, which had landed on the freeway and taken Joe to the UC Medcenter in Sacramento.

Now standing over him as he lay asleep in the hospital bed, Sara stroked Joe's hair. His eyes opened slowly.

"Hi," he said. He had been sleeping on and off for the last few days since the operation that removed what was left of his right kidney. The gunshot had damaged it beyond repair.

"Hi," Sara answered softly. She leaned down and kissed him lightly on the cheek.

"When is Detective Dunn stopping by?" Joe asked.

"Right after lunch," said Sara. "Are you sure you're up to it?"

"Yeah, but I want my lawyer present."

Sara smiled. "Suzy's making sure of that. She and Bill Morgan should be here soon."

With Sara sitting in the room, Joe dozed on and off until lunch—bland lukewarm chicken soup, sliced peaches and pears, and yogurt. He was off salt and starch and caffeine.

As promised, Suzy arrived with Bill Morgan at about one o'clock; and Detective Ryan Dunn squeezed into the small private room shortly after, his light blue shirt the color of his eyes.

"Now what, Detective?" Joe asked. "More questions?"

Dunn laughed a little. "No," he said. "I've got the answers this time."

"And some good news, Joe," Bill Morgan said. "The DA is going to drop the murder charges against you tomorrow."

"Thank God!" Joe said, his voice weak.

"We've got DNA evidence linking Officer Harris to the body of Lilly Nguyen," Dunn explained. He opened his notepad. "And we have a witness at Autumn Smith's apartment complex who recognized a picture of the Triumph Stag that Harris owned. The witness remembers seeing it there the day Autumn Smith disappeared."

"That's great news," said Sara, patting Joe's hand.

"How did Harris pick Autumn?" Joe asked weakly.

"Harris was diabolical," Dunn explained. "He says he noticed Autumn at Patricia Miller's funeral."

"I'm sure he did!" Joe remembered how she was dressed.

"Harris noticed how she reacted to you, Joe. It didn't take much for him to learn there was a connection between you two, and he knew that if something happened to another student of yours, you'd become our prime suspect."

"He was right about that," Suzy added. "But I don't understand something, Ryan. Weren't most of the victims taken at night, like Patricia and Lilly? Why the sudden change to daytime?"

"That's simple," Dunn laughed. "Harris usually worked the day shift. Once the pattern of killings became apparent, the CHP switched him to night patrols so he would be on the lookout for the killer. Little did they know he *was* the killer. That's how he was able to kidnap Autumn in the afternoon. By pure coincidence, Joe didn't have much of an alibi for that day. That's when I really began to suspect you, Joe."

Dunn peered into Joe's eyes, and Joe couldn't help but squirm, which forced a grin to tug at the detective's lips.

"Besides the physical evidence," continued Dunn, "Harris himself is telling all. He's told us where to find two more bodies."

Sara gasped. "You mean there are even more victims?"

"Harris started picking up stranded females shortly after his wife left him. She's living in Texas now with her two daughters. Turns out Harris had been molesting his oldest daughter since she was about five, and he had started on the younger girl. That's when the older one finally told Mom what was happening. She didn't believe it at first until she caught him in the act."

"Why didn't she report him to the police?" Sara demanded.

Dunn lowered his glasses to look at Sara seriously. "He was the police, remember? Besides, she was terrified of him, Mrs. Conrad. According to her, this other brutal personality came out when Harris was off duty. It seems that while he was on duty, he was CHP Officer 'Ricky' Harris—very professional and very well liked. But off duty, after a few shots of vodka, he turned into 'Eric.' And Eric was a monster. Harris's wife, Julie, had seen this other side emerge slowly over the years. But she didn't realize he was hurting their daughters."

"So it really was a case of Jekyll and Hyde," Joe said.

"Yeah," Dunn answered. "The docs will have a field day with him. I'm sure they'll find out he hated his mother. Who knows? From what I've learned, Harris was a good cop while he was on the job. There was only one complaint about him from a woman he stopped about five years ago."

"His first victim?" asked Suzy.

"Not exactly," Dunn responded. "She said in her complaint that Officer Harris pulled her over for no reason and tried to seduce her. He tried to get her to follow him to a place where they could be alone. She got angry and told him to shove it, and he allowed her to leave. She drove straight to the CHP headquarters in Woodland and reported the incident. Her father is a retired CHP officer himself, so she knew people."

"Nothing was done to Harris back then?" Suzy asked.

"Oh, he was reprimanded. But he hadn't really done anything, and there never was another complaint, so the whole matter was dropped."

"And Officer Harris was allowed to rape and murder half a dozen other women," Sara said. "Not to mention the trauma he caused his own daughters."

"There just wasn't any reason to look at Harris before," Dunn tried to explain. "No evidence he was the killer until he left a hair behind. Lilly Nguyen fought back pretty good. She hit him on the side of the head hard enough to get one of his hairs stuck in her ring."

"I managed to hit him pretty hard too," Joe said.

"Yes, you did," Dunn agreed. "He required three stitches in his temple, thanks to you."

"Now I suppose you're going to arrest me for striking an officer," Joe joked.

Dunn managed a tiny grin. "I'll let it go this time, Professor. After all, I hit him pretty hard too. I fractured his skull."

"You saved my life, Detective," Joe said, his voice cracking. "When I think about what he was going to do to Sara that night, I get sick to my stomach."

"Well then, don't think about it," said Dunn. "That's the trouble with you intellectuals, you think too much."

Joe reached out his hand, the one without an IV tube, and Dunn shook it gently.

"Thank you, sir," Joe said, tears filling his eyes.

Sara found the gifts Joe had purchased in the trunk of his car. On Christmas Day, she brought Katie to the hospital, and they opened packages together in Joe's room. Between Christmas and New Year's Eve, Joe granted another interview to Joan Ngo, the one reporter who had believed him. She interviewed him while he was doing physical therapy in the hospital. Sara and Katie visited Joe in the hospital every day until he was released.

In mid-January, Joe received a call from the president of Central Lutheran University congratulating him on his heroism. He had been impressed by the favorable publicity. Joan Ngo had interviewed Sara as well, and she had told the story of Joe rescuing her from Eric Harris, the I-5 Strangler. The president told Joe he could come back to teach in the spring if he was well enough. The school would renew his contract for three more years.

In April, wild mustard bloomed between rows of grapes in the vineyards on both sides of the freeway. Joe commuted from Davis three days a week, just as he had done in the fall. Sara's belly swelled. Sometimes, the baby kicked. Katie giggled whenever she felt her brother's foot move inside her mother's tummy.

One bright, chilly morning, Joe saw a large white egret perched on the branch of a valley oak, preening itself majestically above diaphanous layers of fog. It had the wings of an angel.

The End

CPSIA information can be obtained at www.ICGtesting.com
Printed in the USA
BVOW08s1242230516

449185BV00001B/1/P